LIBRARY OF NEW TESTAMENT STUDIES

628

Formerly the Journal for the Study of the New Testament Supplement Series

Editor
Chris Keith

Editorial Board
Dale C. Allison, John M. G. Barclay, Lynn H. Cohick, R. Alan Culpepper,
Craig A. Evans, Robert Fowler, Simon J. Gathercole, Juan Hernández Jr., John
S. Kloppenborg, Michael Labahn, Matthew V. Novenson, Love L. Sechrest, Robert
Wall, Catrin H. Williams, Brittany E. Wilson

Paul and Matthew among Jews and Gentiles

Essays in Honor of Terence L. Donaldson

Edited by
Ronald Charles

LONDON • NEW YORK • OXFORD • NEW DELHI • SYDNEY

T&T CLARK
Bloomsbury Publishing Plc
50 Bedford Square, London, WC1B 3DP, UK
1385 Broadway, New York, NY 10018, USA
29 Earlsfort Terrace, Dublin 2, Ireland

BLOOMSBURY, T&T CLARK and the T&T Clark logo are trademarks of
Bloomsbury Publishing Plc

First published in Great Britain 2021
This paperback edition published in 2022

Copyright © Ronald Charles and contributors, 2021

Ronald Charles has asserted his right under the Copyright, Designs and Patents
Act, 1988, to be identified as Author of this work.

All rights reserved. No part of this publication may be reproduced or
transmitted in any form or by any means, electronic or mechanical,
including photocopying, recording, or any information storage or retrieval
system, without prior permission in writing from the publishers.

Bloomsbury Publishing Plc does not have any control over, or responsibility for, any
third-party websites referred to or in this book. All internet addresses given in this
book were correct at the time of going to press. The author and publisher regret any
inconvenience caused if addresses have changed or sites have ceased to exist, but can
accept no responsibility for any such changes.

A catalogue record for this book is available from the British Library.

A catalog record for this book is available from the Library of Congress.

ISBN: HB: 978-0-5676-9408-9
PB: 978-0-5676-9819-3
ePDF: 978-0-5676-9409-6
ePUB: 978-0-5676-9411-9

Series: Library of New Testament Studies, ISSN 2513–8790, volume 628

Typeset by Newgen KnowledgeWorks Pvt. Ltd., Chennai, India

To find out more about our authors and books visit www.bloomsbury.com
and sign up for our newsletters.

Contents

CV of Terence L. Donaldson — vii

Introduction *Tabula Gratulatoria* — 1

Part 1 Paul — 7

1. Paul without Judaism: Historical Method over Perspective *Steve Mason* — 9
2. A Displaced Jew: The Specific Nature of Paul's Earthly Identity *Leif Vaage* — 41
3. The New Creation Motif in Romans 8:18–27 in Light of the Book of Jubilees *Ronald Charles* — 59
4. Did Paul Think in Terms of Two-Age Dualism? *L. Ann Jervis* — 75
5. Remapping Paul within Jewish Ideologies of Inclusion *Matthew Thiessen* — 87

Part 2 Matthew — 97

6. Beyond Universalism and Particularism: Rethinking Paul and Matthew on Gentile Inclusion *Anders Runesson* — 99
7. Matthew's Trojan Horse: The Construction of Christian Identity in the Sermon on the Mount through a Stereotype of the Scribes and Pharisees *Stephen Black* — 113
8. From Tamar and Mary to Perpetua: Women and the Word in Matthew *Catherine Sider Hamilton* — 131
9. The "Parting of the Ways" and the Criterion of Plausibility *Adele Reinhartz* — 147
10. Mark 14:51–52: A Socio-Rhetorical Reading of the Text and Conclusions Drawn from the History of Its Interpretation *L. Gregory Bloomquist and Michael A. G. Haykin* — 157

List of Contributors — 181
Index — 183

Curriculum Vitae

Terence L. Donaldson

I. Biographical Information

1. Personal

Address	*College*		*Home*
	Wycliffe College		10 Yonge Street
	5 Hoskin Avenue		Unit 3013
	Toronto, ON		Toronto, ON
	M5S 1H7		M5E 1R4
Telephone			416-319-7245 (mobile)
E-mail			terry.donaldson@utoronto.ca
Citizenship			Canadian

2. Education

Doctor of Theology (Th.D.)

    1978–82; degree conferred May 1982
    Wycliffe College and the University of Toronto
    Thesis title: "Jesus on the Mountain: A Study in Matthean Theology"
    Supervisor: Richard N. Longenecker

Master of Theology (Th.M.)

    1977–8; degree conferred May 1979
    Wycliffe College and the University of Toronto
    Thesis title: "Moses Typology in the Proclamation and Polemic of the Early Church: A Study in the Rhetoric of Church–Synagogue Separation"
    Supervisor: Richard N. Longenecker

Master of Religion (M.Rel.)

> 1976–7; degree conferred May 1977 (advanced standing granted on basis of work done at Regent College)
> Wycliffe College
> *Thesis title*: "The Salvation of the Gentiles in Early Jewish Christianity"
> *Supervisor*: Leslie Hunt

(Master of Christian Studies)

> 1974–6 (requirements completed, but degree waived in lieu of credit at Wycliffe College)
> Regent College, Vancouver
> *Thesis title*: "The Theme of Rejection in Matthew's Gospel"
> *Supervisor*: Larry Hurtado

Bachelor of Science (B.Sc.)

> 1966–70; degree granted June 1970
> University of Toronto

3. Professional Appointments

Current

University unit of primary appointment: TST
TST college of appointment: Wycliffe
Present appointment:

> Lord and Lady Coggan Professor Emeritus of New Testament Studies
> Rank at retirement: Full Professor
> 2016–

Date of appointment to full membership in the Advanced Degree faculty: 1999
Status-only appointment:

> Full Member (continuing)
> Department for the Study of Religion and School of Graduate Studies
> University of Toronto
> 2001–

Previous

Lord and Lady Coggan Professor of New Testament Studies
Wycliffe College, Toronto

1999–2016
Director of Advanced Degree Studies, Toronto School of Theology
(60% secondment from Wycliffe College)
2006–11
Professor of New Testament and Biblical Languages
College of Emmanuel & St. Chad, Saskatoon
1982–99
Associate Member, Department of Religious Studies,
University of Saskatchewan, Saskatoon
1982–99
Member, College of Graduate Studies & Research
University of Saskatchewan, Saskatoon
1990–9
Visiting Instructor in Biblical Studies
Institute for Christian Studies, Toronto
1982 (winter semester)

4. Honors

Visiting Fellowships, Clare Hall and the Faculty of Divinity, University of Cambridge, 2011–12
Francis W. Beare prize, for *Judaism and the Gentiles*; awarded by the Canadian Society of Biblical Studies, 2009
President, Canadian Society of Biblical Studies, 2008–9
Honorary degree, Doctor of Canon Law, awarded by the University of Emmanuel College, Saskatoon, 2001
Francis W. Beare prize, for *Paul and the Gentiles*; awarded by the Canadian Society of Biblical Studies, 1998
Student Essay Prize, Canadian Society of Biblical Studies, 1979

5. Professional Affiliations and Activities

Memberships

Canadian Society of Biblical Studies (since 1979)
Society of Biblical Literature (since 1981)
Studiorum Novi Testamenti Societas (since 1993)
Anglican Association of Biblical Scholars

Offices and Roles

Editor, *Studies in Christianity and Judaism/Études sur le christianisme et le judaïsme*, 2009–19
Member, Steering Committee, Pauline Epistles Section, Society of Biblical Literature, 2007–13

President, Canadian Society of Biblical Studies, 2008–9
Vice-President, Canadian Society of Biblical Studies, 2007–8
Editorial Board, *New Testament Studies*, 2005–8
Editorial Board, *Journal of Biblical Literature*, 2002–8
Book Review Editor, *Toronto Journal of Theology*, 2000–7
Editorial Advisory Board, *Studies in Religion/Sciences Religieuses*, 1998–2001
Council Member, Society of Biblical Literature, 1997–9
Treasurer and Membership Secretary, Canadian Society of Biblical Studies, 1990–5

6. Language Proficiency

Reading proficiency in French, German, Hellenistic Greek, Biblical Hebrew, Aramaic, Latin.

II. Scholarly and Professional Work

1. Research Endeavors

Areas of Specialization and Research

Second Temple Judaism; Jewish "patterns of universalism"; Gospel of Matthew; Paul; New Testament and anti-Judaism; Gentilization of early Christianity; Church–synagogue relations in the ante-Nicene period

Current Research Project

Ethnicity, identity, and the development of "Gentile Christianity" in its Jewish and Roman imperial contexts, from its beginnings through to the end of the second century (though with some attention to the conversion of Constantine and the Christianization of the empire).

2. Research Awards

Research Grant, Social Sciences and Humanities Research Council of Canada: "Gentile Christian Self-Definition, the Parting of the Ways and the Christianization of the Roman Empire," 2015–18 ($44,832)
Research Grant, Social Sciences and Humanities Research Council of Canada: "Identity, Ethnicity and the Emergence of Gentile Christianity," 2009–12 ($35,050)
Research Grant, Social Sciences and Humanities Research Council of Canada: "Gentilization in Judaism and Early Christianity," 2001–4 ($29,100)
University of Saskatchewan, Publication Fund Award for *Religious Rivalries and the Struggle for Success in Caesarea Maritima*, 1999 ($2000)

Research Grant, Social Sciences and Humanities Research Council of Canada: "The Gentilization of Early Christianity and the Struggle for Success," 1998–2000 ($8050)

Sabbatical Grant, Continuing Education Program, Anglican Church of Canada, 1995 ($1600)

Research Grant, Social Sciences and Humanities Research Council of Canada: "The Gentilization of Early Christianity, From Jesus to Justin," 1992–5 ($21,000)

Doctoral Fellowship, Social Sciences and Humanities Research Council of Canada, 1978–81

3. Publications

Books

Gentile Christian Identity from Cornelius to Constantine: The Nations, the Parting of the Ways, and Roman Imperial Ideology (Grand Rapids, MI: Eerdmans, forthcoming), 600 pp. (estimated).

Jews and Anti-Judaism in the New Testament: Decision Points and Divergent Interpretations (London: SPCK; Waco, TX: Baylor University Press, 2010), 176 pp.

Judaism and the Gentiles: Jewish Patterns of Universalism (to 135 CE) (Waco, TX: Baylor University Press, 2007), 563 pp.

Paul and the Gentiles: Remapping the Apostle's Convictional World (Minneapolis, MN: Fortress Press, 1997), 409 pp.

Jesus on the Mountain: A Study in Matthean Theology (JSNT Suppl. 8; Sheffield: JSOT Press, 1985), 326 pp.

Edited Book

Religious Rivalries and the Struggle for Success in Caesarea Maritima (Studies in Christianity and Judaism 8; Waterloo, ON: Wilfrid Laurier University Press, 2000), 398 pp.

Articles in Academic Journals

"Supersessionism and Early Christian Self-definition," *Journal of the Jesus Movement in its Jewish Setting* 3 (2016): 1–32. (**R**)

"'Gentile Christianity' as a Category in the Study of Christian Origins," *Harvard Theological Review* 106 (2013): 433–58. (**R**)

"'We Gentiles': Ethnicity and Identity in Justin's *Dialogue*," *Early Christianity* 4 (2013): 216–41. (**R**)

"Royal Sympathizers in Jewish Narrative," *Journal for the Study of the Pseudepigrapha* 16 (2006): 41–59. (**R**)

"Jewish Christianity, Israel's Stumbling and the *Sonderweg* Reading of Paul," *Journal for the Study of the New Testament* 29 (2006): 27–54. (**R**)

"What I Learned Teaching NT 101," *Toronto Journal of Theology* 16 (2000): 251–65. (**R**)

"'For Herod Had Arrested John' (Matt 14:3): Making Sense of an Unresolved Flashback," *Studies in Religion/Sciences Religieuses* 28 (1999), 35–48. (**R**)

"Nicodemus: A Figure of Ambiguity in a Gospel of Certainty," *Consensus: A Canadian Lutheran Journal of Theology* 24 (1998): 121–4.

"The Law That Hangs (Matt 22:40): Rabbinic Formulation and Matthean Social World," *Catholic Biblical Quarterly* 57 (1995): 689–709. (**R**)

"'Riches for the Gentiles' (Rom 11:12): Israel's 'Rejection' and Paul's Gentile Mission," *Journal of Biblical Literature* 112 (1993): 81–98. (**R**)

"Proselytes or 'Righteous Gentiles'? The Status of Gentiles in Eschatological Pilgrimage Patterns of Thought," *Journal for the Study of the Pseudepigrapha* 7 (1990): 3–27. (**R**)

"The Mockers and the Son of God (Matt 27:37–44): Two Characters in Matthew's Story of Jesus," *Journal for the Study of the New Testament* 41 (1991): 3–18. (**R**)

"Rural Bandits, City Mobs and the Zealots," *Journal for the Study of Judaism* 21 (1990): 19–40. (**R**)

"Zealot and Convert: The Origin of Paul's Christ-Torah Antithesis," *Catholic Biblical Quarterly* 51 (1989): 655–82. (**R**)

"The 'Curse of the Law' and the Inclusion of the Gentiles: Galatians 3.13–14," *New Testament Studies* 32 (1986): 94–112. (**R**)

"Parallels: Use, Misuse and Limitations," *Evangelical Quarterly* 55 (1983): 193–210.

"Levitical Messianology in Late Judaism: Origins, Development and Decline," *Journal of the Evangelical Theological Society* 24 (1981): 193–207. (**R**)

"Moses Typology and the Sectarian Nature of Early Christian Anti-Judaism: A Study in Acts 7," *Journal for the Study of the New Testament* 12 (1981): 27–52. (**R**)

"The New Testament and Anti-Semitism: Three Important Books," *TSF Bulletin* 4 (1981): 12–14.

"Israel and the Church: A Middle Position," *Crux* 15 (1979): 11–13.

Chapters in Multi-Authored Volumes (All Invited)

"Gentiles." In *Oxford Bibliographies in Biblical Studies*. Ed. Christopher Matthews. New York, NY: Oxford University Press, 2018 (15,000 words). (**R**)

"'Nations,' 'Non-Jewish Nations' or 'Non-Jewish Individuals': Matt 28:19 Revisited." In *Matthew Within Judaism: Israel and the Nations in the First Gospel*. Ed. Anders Runesson and Daniel M. Gurtner (Atlanta, GA: SBL, forthcoming). (**R**)

"Paul, Abraham's Gentile 'Offspring' and the Torah." In *Torah Ethics and Early Christian Identity*. Ed. David M. Miller and Susan Wendel (Grand Rapids, MI: Eerdmans, 2016), 135–50.

"Paul within Judaism: A Critical Evaluation from a 'New Perspective' Perspective." In *Paul within Judaism: Restoring the First-Century Context to the Apostle*. Ed. Mark D. Nanos and Magnus Zetterholm (Minneapolis, MN: Fortress Press, 2015), 277–301.

"The 'Plain Meaning' of Rom 3:28, 4:5 and the Place of Paul's Juridical Language: A Response to Carsten Claussen." In *Modern Interpretations of Romans: Tracking Their Hermeneutical/Theological Trajectory*. Ed. Daniel Patte and Cristina Grenholm (London: Bloomsbury T&T Clark, 2013), 109–19.

"What Can We Know of Jesus?" In *Guide for the Christian Perplexed*. Ed. Thomas P. Power (Eugene, OR: Pickwick, 2012), 1–24.

"Supersessionism in Early Christianity." *CSBS Bulletin* 69 (2009–10): 1–27.

"The Juridical, the Participatory and the 'New Perspective' on Paul." In *Reading Paul in Context: Explorations in Identity Formation*. Ed. Kathy Ehrensperger and J. Brian Tucker (Library of New Testament Studies; London: T&T Clark, 2010), 229–41.

"Introduction to the Pauline Corpus." In *The Oxford Bible Commentary: The Pauline Epistles*. Ed. John Barton and John Muddiman (Oxford: Oxford University Press, 2010), 27–56. (**R**)

"Son of God." In *New Interpreters Dictionary of the Bible*, Vol. 5 (Nashville, TN: Abingdon, 2009), 335–41. (**R**)

"Nations." In *New Interpreters Dictionary of the Bible*, Vol. 4 (Nashville, TN: Abingdon, 2009), 231–8. (**R**)

"The Field God Has Assigned: Geography and Mission in Paul." In *Religious Rivalries in the Early Roman Empire and the Rise of Christianity*. Ed. Leif Vaage (ESCJ 18; Waterloo, ON: Wilfrid Laurier University Press, 2006), 109–37.

"Apostle." In *New Interpreters Dictionary of the Bible*, Vol. 1 (Nashville, TN: Abingdon, 2006), 205–7. (**R**)

"The Vindicated Son: A Narrative Approach to Matthean Christology." In *Contours of Christology in the New Testament*. Ed. Richard N. Longenecker (Grand Rapids, MI: Eerdmans, 2005), 100–21.

"Introduction to the Pauline Corpus." In *The Oxford Bible Commentary*. Ed. John Barton and John Muddiman (Oxford: Oxford University Press, 2001), 1062–83. (**R**)

"Introduction." and "Concluding Reflections." In *Religious Rivalries and the Struggle for Success in Caesarea Maritima* (Studies in Christianity and Judaism 8; Waterloo, ON: Wilfrid Laurier University Press, 2000), 1–8, 331–9.

"Jerusalem Ossuary Inscriptions and the Status of Jewish Proselytes." In *Text and Artifact in the Religions of Mediterranean Antiquity: Essays in Honour of Peter Richardson*. Ed. Stephen G. Wilson and Michel Desjardins. (ESCJ 9; Waterloo, ON: Wilfrid Laurier University Press, 2000), 372–85.

"In Search of a Paul Neither Lutheran nor Idiosyncratic: James D. G. Dunn's *The Theology of Paul the Apostle*." *Critical Review of Books in Religion* (1998): 35–55.

"Israelite, Convert, Apostle to the Gentiles: The Origin of Paul's Gentile Mission." In *The Road From Damascus: The Impact of Paul's Conversion on His Life, Thought and Ministry*. Ed. Richard N. Longenecker (Grand Rapids, MI: Eerdmans, 1997), 62–84.

"Guiding Readers—Making Disciples: Discipleship in Matthew's Narrative Strategy." In *Discipleship in the New Testament*. Ed. Richard N. Longenecker (Grand Rapids, MI: Eerdmans, 1996), 22–41.

"Moses Typology and the Sectarian Nature of Early Christian Anti-Judaism: A Study in Acts 7." In *New Testament Backgrounds: A Sheffield Reader*. Ed. Craig A. Evans and Stanley E. Porter (Sheffield: Sheffield Academic Press, 1997), 230–52.

"Jesus and the Dead Sea Scrolls: Context." In *Whose Historical Jesus?* Ed. William E. Arnal and Michel Desjardins (ESCJ 7; Waterloo, ON: Wilfrid Laurier University Press, 1997), 188–9.

"'The Gospel That I Proclaim among the Gentiles' (Gal 2:2): Universalistic or Israel-Centred?" In *Gospel in Paul: Studies on Corinthians, Galatians and Romans for Richard N. Longenecker*. Ed. Ann Jervis and Peter Richardson (Sheffield: Sheffield Academic Press, 1994), 166–93.

"Jewish/Christian Relations." In *The Early Church: An Annotated Bibliography of Literature in English*. Ed. Thomas A. Robinson (ATLA Bibliography Series 33; Metuchen, NJ: Scarecrow Press, 1993), 229–46.

"Thomas Kuhn, Convictional Worlds, and Paul." In *Origins and Method: Towards a New Understanding of Judaism and Christianity. Essays in Honour of John C. Hurd*. Ed. Bradley H. McLean (JSNTS 86; Sheffield: Sheffield Academic Press, 1993), 190–8.

"Triumph," "Virtue," "Zealot," *International Standard Bible Encyclopedia*, Vol. 4 (Grand Rapids, MI: Eerdmans, 1988), 922, 993, 1175–9.

"Nicolaitans," "Principles," *International Standard Bible Encyclopedia*, Vol. 3 (Grand Rapids, MI: Eerdmans, 1986), 533–4, 973.

"Thessalonica." In *Major Cities of the Biblical World*. Ed. R. K. Harrison (Nashville, TN: Thomas Nelson, 1985), 258–65.

Conference Proceedings

"The Law that 'Hangs' (Matt 22:40): Rabbinic Formulation and Matthean Social World," *SBL Seminar Papers* (Atlanta: Scholars Press, 1990), 14–33.

Book Reviews

Amy-Jill Levine and Marc Zvi Brettler (eds.). *The Jewish Annotated New Testament* (Oxford: Oxford University Press, 2011). In *Studies in Christian–Jewish Relations*, http://ejournals.bc.edu/ojs/index.php/scjr/.

Matthew Thiessen. *Contesting Conversion: Genealogy, Circumcision, and Identity in Ancient Judaism and Christianity*. Oxford: Oxford University Press, 2011. In *Touchstone: Heritage and Theology in a New Age*, forthcoming.

Giorgio Jossa. *Jews or Christians? The Followers of Jesus in Search of Their Own Identity* (WUNT I/202; Tübingen: Mohr Siebeck, 2007). In *Toronto Journal of Theology* 26 (2010): 230–2.

Lloyd Kim. *Polemic in the Book of Hebrews: Anti-Judaism, Anti-Semitism, Supersessionism?* (Eugene, OR: Wipf and Stock, 2006). In *Toronto Journal of Theology* 24 (2008): 260–2.

Simon J. Gathercole. *The Preexistent Son: Recovering the Christologies of Matthew, Mark, and Luke* (Grand Rapids, MI: Eerdmans, 2006). In *Toronto Journal of Theology* 23 (2008): 190–2.

D. A. Carson, Peter T. O'Brien, and Mark A. Seifrid, eds. *Justification and Variegated Nomism: Vol. 2. The Paradoxes of Paul* (Tübingen: Mohr Siebeck; Grand Rapids, MI: Baker Academic, 2004). In *Biblical Theology Bulletin* 36 (2006): 86–7.

Michele Murray. *Playing a Jewish Game: Gentile Christian Judaizing in the First and Second Centuries CE* (Wilfrid Laurier University Press, 2004). In *University of Toronto Quarterly* 75 (2006): 229–30.

Seyoon Kim. *Paul and the New Perspective: Second Thoughts on the Origin of Paul's Gospel* (Grand Rapids, MI: Wm. B. Eerdmans, 2002). In *Toronto Journal of Theology* 19 (2003): 82–3.

Donald Harman Akenson. *Saint Saul: A Skeleton Key to the Historical Jesus* (Montreal: McGill-Queen's University Press, 2000). In *McMaster Journal of Theology and Ministry*, (2001): 4, http://www.mcmaster.ca/mjtm/.

Karl P. Donfried and Peter Richardson (eds.). *Judaism and Christianity in First-Century Rome* (Grand Rapids, MI: Eerdmans, 1998). In *Toronto Journal of Theology* 17 (2001): 285–7.

Lauri Thurén. *Derhetorizing Paul: A Dynamic Perspective on Pauline Theology and the Law* (WUNT 124. Tübingen: Mohr Siebeck, 2000). In *Biblical Interpretation* 9 (2001): 230–2.

John L. White. *The Apostle of God: Paul and the Promise of Abraham* (Peabody, MA: Hendrickson, 1999). In *Toronto Journal of Theology* 16 (2000): 281–2.

Martin Hengel and Anna Maria Schwemer. *Paul between Damascus and Antioch: The Unknown Years* (Louisville, KY: Westminster John Knox Press, 1997). In *Review of Biblical Literature* (1998), http://www.sbl-site.org/SBL/Reviews/reviews.html/, and *Journal of Biblical Literature* 117 (1998): 752–4.

Jeffrey A. D. Weima. *Neglected Endings: The Significance of the Pauline Letter Closings* (JSNTSup 101; Sheffield: Sheffield Academic Press, 1994). In *Studies in Religion/Sciences Religieuses* 27 (1998): 80–1.

Wolfgang Kraus. *Das Volk Gottes: Zur Grundlegung der Ekklesiologie bei Paulus* (WUNT 85; Tübingen: Mohr-Siebeck, 1995). In *Journal of Biblical Literature* 117 (1998): 368–9.

Bruce Chilton and Jacob Neusner. *Judaism in the New Testament: Practices and Beliefs* (London/New York: Routledge, 1995). In *Canadian Catholic Review* 15 (July/August 1997): 31.

Rainer Riesner. *Die Frühzeit des Apostels Paulus: Studien zur Chronologie, Missionsstrategie und Theologie* (WUNT 71; Tübingen: J.C.B. Mohr [Paul Siebeck], 1994). In *Toronto Journal of Theology* 13 (1997): 115–16.

Scott J. Hafemann. *Paul, Moses, and the History of Israel: The Letter/Spirit Contrast and the Argument from Scripture in 2 Corinthians 3* (Peabody, MA: Hendrickson, 1996). In *Toronto Journal of Theology* 13 (1997): 275–6.

Eckhard Rau. *Von Jesus zu Paulus: Entwicklung und Rezeption der antiochenischen Theologie im Urchristentum* (Stuttgart/Berlin/Köln: Kohlhammer, 1994). In *Journal of Biblical Literature* 115 (1996): 548–50.

C. K. Barrett. *Paul: An Introduction to His Thought* (Louisville, KY: Westminster/John Knox, 1994). In *Consensus: A Canadian Lutheran Journal of Theology* 22 (1966): 114–15.

Raymond E. Brown. *The Birth of the Messiah* (upd. ed.; New York, NY: Doubleday, 1993). In *Religious Studies and Theology* 13–14 (1995): 120–1.

Michael Knowles. *Jeremiah in Matthew's Gospel: The Rejected-Prophet Motif in Matthean Redaction* (JSNTSup 68; Sheffield: Sheffield Academic Press, 1993). In *Studies in Religion/Sciences Religieuses* 24 (1995): 124.

Raymond E. Brown. *The Death of the Messiah* (New York, NY: Doubleday, 1994). In *Anglican Journal* (Sept. 1994): 15.

N. Thomas Wright. *The Climax of the Covenant: Christ and Law in Pauline Theology* (Minneapolis, MN: Fortress, 1992). In *Toronto Journal of Theology* 10 (1994): 131–2.

Larry P. Hogan. *Healing in the Second Temple Period* (NTOA 21; Freiburg: Universitätsverlag/Göttingen: Vandenhoeck & Ruprecht, 1992). In *Critical Review of Books in Religion* 6 (1993): 122–4.

Austin Farrer. *The Essential Sermons* (ed. Leslie Houlden; London: SPCK, 1991). In *Canadian Catholic Review* 11 (Feb. 1993): 31.

Craig C. Hill, *Hellenists and Hebrews: Reappraising Division within the Earliest Church* (Minneapolis, MN: Fortress, 1991). In *Toronto Journal of Theology* 9 (1993): 127–9.

J. Andrew Overman. *Matthew's Gospel and Formative Judaism: The Social World of the Matthean Community* (Minneapolis, MN: Fortress, 1990). In the IOUDAIOS electronic discussion network, Vol. 2.021 (Oct. 1992).

James H. Charlesworth. *Jesus within Judaism: New Light from Exciting Archaeological Discoveries* (Anchor Bible Reference Library; New York, NY: Doubleday, 1988). In *Religious Studies and Theology* 10 (1990): 96–8.

Amy-Jill Levine. *The Social and Ethnic Dimension of Matthean Salvation History* (Lewiston/Queenston/Lampeter: Edwin Mellen, 1988): In *Journal of Biblical Literature* 109 (1990): 723–5.

The New Revised Standard Version. In *Anglican Journal* 116 (Sept. 1990): 14.

C. M. Tuckett. *Reading the New Testament: Methods of Interpretation* (Philadelphia, PA: Fortress, 1987). In *Religious Studies Review* 15 (1989): 66.

Eugene B. Borowitz. *Contemporary Christologies: A Jewish Response* (New York, NY and Toronto: Paulist Press, 1980). In *TSF Bulletin* 6 (1982–3): 29.

J. Jocz. *The Jewish People and Jesus Christ after Auschwitz* (Grand Rapids, MI: Baker, 1981). In *TSF Bulletin* 6 (1982–3): 27.

Bernard T. Smyth. *Paul: Mystic and Missionary* (Maryknoll, NY: Orbis Books, 1980). In *TSF Bulletin* 4 (1981): 19.

Koenig, John. *Jews and Christians in Dialogue: New Testament Foundations* (Philadelphia, PA: Westminster Press, 1979). In *Crux* 16 (1980): 31–2.

M. Wilcox. *I Saw Heaven Opened: The Message of Revelation* (Downer's Grove, IL: Inter-Varsity Press, 1975). In *Journal of the Evangelical Theological Society* 19 (1976): 260–1.

4. Presentations

Invited Lectures in External Academic Contexts

"*Omnes gentes*: Gentile–Christian Identity Construction, the Parting of the Ways, and "the Nations" in Roman Imperial Ideology," Baylor University, January 2016.

"*Omnes gentes*: 'The Nations' in Jewish and Roman Context and the Formation of Gentile Christian Identity," McMaster University, March 2013.

"'Gentile Christianity' as a Category in the Study of Christian Origins," New Testament Seminar, University of Cambridge, January 2012.

"'We Gentiles': Ethnicity and Identity in Justin's *Dialogue*," Hebrew, Jewish and Early Christian Studies Seminar, University of Cambridge, November 2011.

"Supersessionism in Early Christianity," Colloquium in Honor of Alan F. Segal, Barnard College, December 2010.

"Supersessionism in Early Christianity," Presidential Lecture, Canadian Society of Biblical Studies, in Ottawa, May 2009.

"The Juridical, the Participatory and the 'New Perspective' on Paul," Department of Religious Studies, McMaster University, February 2002.

"The Vindicated Son: A Narrative Approach to Matthean Christology," H. H. Bingham Colloquium in New Testament, at McMaster Divinity College, June 2001.

"What I Learned Teaching NT 101," Inaugural Lecture, Lord and Lady Coggan Chair in New Testament Studies, February 9, 2000.

"Israelite, Convert, Apostle to the Gentiles: The Origin of Paul's Gentile Mission," presented at the H. H. Bingham Colloquium in New Testament, at McMaster Divinity College, June 1996.

"Guiding Readers—Making Disciples: Discipleship in Matthew's Narrative Strategy," presented at the H. H. Bingham Colloquium in New Testament, at McMaster Divinity College, June 1995.

"The Law That Hangs (Matt 22:40): Rabbinic Formulation and Matthean Social World," Winnipeg Biblical Studies Colloquium, May 1990.

Papers Presented at Scholarly Meetings and Symposia

"*Ethnē* ('Gentiles') as an Ascribed Identity: What Did Non-Jewish Christ-Believers Make of It?" presented at the meetings of the Studiorum Novi Testamenti Societas, in Athens (August 2018).

"James Parkes and the 'Parting of the Ways,'" presented at the meetings of the Canadian Society of Biblical Studies in Regina, Saskatchewan (May 2018), and at the TST Biblical Department Seminar (November 2016).

"'Nations,' 'Non-Jewish Nations,' or 'Non-Jewish Individuals': Matt 28:19 Revisited," presented at the Society of Biblical Literature meeting in San Antonio, Texas, November 2016.

"Abraham's Seed, Natural Law in a Pessimistic Tenor, and Paul's *ethnē*-in-Christ," presented at the meetings of the Studiorum Novi Testamenti Societas (SNTS) in Montreal, August 2016.

"'I Am Speaking to You Gentiles': What Did Paul's Converts Think of This Ascribed Identity?" presented at the Society of Biblical Literature meeting in Baltimore, November 2013.

"*Omnes gentes*: 'The Nations' in Jewish and Roman Context and the Formation of Gentile Christian Identity," presented at the Seminar for Culture and Religion in Antiquity, University of Toronto, January 2013.

"*Adversus Judaeos/pro gentibus:* The Place of the Gentiles in Early Christian Anti-Judaic Exegesis," presented at the Society of Biblical Literature meeting in Chicago, November 2012.

"*Goyim, ethnē, gentilis,* Gentiles: The Invention of a Category," presented at the Canadian Society of Biblical Studies meeting in Waterloo in May 2012.

"'We Gentiles': Ethnicity and Identity in Justin's *Dialogue,*" presented at the Canadian Society of Biblical Studies meeting in Fredericton in May 2011.

"Priests to the Nations, Light to the World, Guides in Life for all Mortals," presented at the Society of Biblical Literature meeting in New Orleans in November 2009.

"Supersessionism in Early Christianity," presented at the International Meeting of the Society of Biblical Literature, Rome, August 2009 and at a Colloquium in Honor of Alan Franklin Segal, Barnard College, December 2010.

"The 'Plain Meaning' of Rom 3:28, 4:5 and the Place of Paul's Juridical Language: A Response to Carsten Claussen," presented at the meetings of the Society of Biblical Literature in San Diego in November 2007.

"Royal Sympathizers in Jewish Narrative," presented at the Society of Biblical Literature meeting in San Antonio in November 2004.

"Ethical Monotheism and the Gentiles in the *Letter of Aristeas*," presented at the Canadian Society of Biblical Studies meeting in Winnipeg in May 2004.

Special Session: "Religious Rivalries and the Struggle for Success," organized for the Society of Biblical Literature meeting in Toronto in November 2002.

"Jewish Christianity, Israel's Stumbling and the *Sonderweg* Reading of Paul," presented at the meetings of the Studiorum Novi Testamenti Societas in Durham, England, August 2002.

"The Absence from Paul's Letters of Any Injunctions to Evangelize," presented at the Society of Biblical Literature meeting in November 2000.

"The Field God Has Assigned: Geography and Mission in Paul," presented at the Canadian Society of Biblical Studies meeting in St. Catherines in May 1996.

"'For Herod had arrested John' (Matt 14:3): Making Sense of an Unresolved Flashback," presented at the Society of Biblical Literature meeting in San Francisco in November 1997.

"A Visit to Caesarea Maritima," a slide-illustrated introduction to the city and its remains presented at the Canadian Society of Biblical Studies meeting in Montreal in May 1995.

"'The Gospel That I Proclaim among the Gentiles' (Gal 2:2): Universalistic or Israel-Centred?" presented at the Society of Biblical Literature meeting in Washington DC in November 1993.

"Abraham's Gentile Offspring: Contratextuality and Conviction in Romans 4," presented at the Society of Biblical Literature meeting in San Francisco in November 1992, and the Canadian Society of Biblical Studies meeting in Ottawa in June 1993.

"'Riches for the Gentiles' (Rom 11:12): Israel's 'Rejection' and Paul's Gentile Mission," presented at the Society of Biblical Literature meeting in Kansas City in 1991.

"Why Paul's Mission to the Gentiles?" presented at the Canadian Society of Biblical Studies meeting in Victoria in 1990.

"The Law That Hangs (Matt 22:40): Rabbinic Formulation and Matthean Social World," presented at the Society of Biblical Literature meeting in New Orleans in 1990.

"Preaching Circumcision: Gal. 5:11 and the Origin of Paul's Gentile Mission," presented at the Society of Biblical Literature Meeting in Chicago in 1989.

"The Mockers and the Son of God (Matt 27:37–44): Two Characters in Matthew's Story of Jesus," presented at the Society of Biblical Literature meeting at Anaheim in 1988.

"Zealot and Convert: The Origin of Paul's Christ-Torah Antithesis," presented at the Canadian Society of Biblical Studies meeting in Windsor in 1988.

"Proselytes or 'Righteous Gentiles'? The Status of Gentiles in Eschatological Pilgrimage Patterns of Thought," presented at the Canadian Society of Biblical Studies meeting in Winnipeg in 1986.

"The 'Curse of the Law' and the Inclusion of the Gentiles: Galatians 3.13–14," presented at the Canadian Society of Biblical Studies meeting in Guelph in 1984.

"The Mountain as an Eschatological Site/Symbol in Second Temple Judaism," presented at the Canadian Society of Biblical Studies meeting in Halifax in 1981.

"Moses Typology and the Sectarian Nature of Early Christian Anti-Judaism: A Study in Acts 7," presented at the Canadian Society of Biblical Studies meeting in Montreal in 1980.

"Parallels: Use, Misuse and Limitations," presented at the Canadian Society of Biblical Studies meeting in Saskatoon in 1979; CSBS Student Prize Essay.

Other Presentations

"Coups, Conspiracies and Cover-ups: Decoding the Popular Fascination with Jesus and Christian Origins," presented as the T.W. Smyth Memorial Lecture, St. John's Church, Elora, Ontario, October 2006.

"The NT and Sexual Orientation": Oral Presentations in the Diocese of Qu'Appelle (clergy conference, Sept. 1992; diocesan synod, Oct. 1993; Christ Church, Edmonton, 2004); video presentation in "Hearing Diverse Voices—Seeking Common Ground: A Program of Study on Homosexuality and Homosexual Relations" (Anglican Church of Canada, 1994).

III. Teaching and Supervisory Activity

Basic Degree Courses Taught (preceding seven years)

WYB 3714 HS: Salvation as Liberation in Paul, Winter 2015
WYB 1501 HF: From the Gospel to the Gospels, Fall 2014
WYB 3641 HF: Matthew's Story of Jesus, Fall 2014
WYB 2501 HS: Interpreting the New Testament, Winter 2014
WYB 1501 HF: From the Gospel to the Gospels, Fall 2013
WYB 3424 HF: From the Maccabees to Masada, Fall 2013
WYB 3714 HF: Salvation as Liberation in Paul, Fall 2012
WYB 1501 HF: From the Gospel to the Gospels, Fall 2012

Basic Degree Theses Supervised (preceding seven years)

Master of Divinity, Aidan Armstrong, 2016
Master of Theological Studies, Karen Friesen, 2016
Master of Theological Studies, Matt Groenveld, 2014

Graduate/Advanced Degree Courses Taught (preceding seven years)

WYB 5032 HS: Early Christian Self-Definition, Winter 2018
WYB 5032 HS: Early Christian Self-Definition, Winter 2016
WYB 6714 HS: Salvation as Liberation in Paul, Winter 2015
WYB 5981/RLG 3655 HS: Readings in Jewish Literature, Winter 2015
WYB 6641 HF: Matthew's Story of Jesus, Fall 2014
WYB 5032 HS: Early Christian Self-Definition, Winter 2014
WYB 5981/RLG 3655 HS: Readings in Jewish Literature, Winter 2013
WYB 3424 HF: From the Maccabees to Masada, Fall 2013
WYB 6714 HF: Salvation as Liberation in Paul, Fall 2012

Advanced Degree/Graduate Theses Supervised

Masters Students

Master of Theology, University of St. Michael's College, Robert Edwards, "Clement of Alexandria's Gnostic Interpretation of the Old Testament," 2014.
Master of Theology, University of St. Michael's College, Catherine Jones, "An Apologetic Interpretation of Flavius Josephus Based on His Portrayal of the *lēstēs* in *The Jewish War*," 2006.
Master of Theology, Wycliffe College and the University of Toronto, Bart Eriksson, "Martin Luther and the New Perspective on Paul," 2004.
Master of Sacred Theology, College of Emmanuel & St. Chad, Saskatoon, Graham Knox, "Plight and Solution in Early Buddhist and Pauline Christian Perspective," 2001.

Master of Sacred Theology, Lutheran Theological Seminary, Saskatoon, David Waldner, "The Politics of Paul: A Rhetorical-Critical Examination of Philippians 3:1b-4:1," 2000.

Doctoral Students

Doctor of Philosophy in Theology, University of St. Michael's College, Ho Jin Nam, "Attitude Towards the Torah and Gentiles in Matthew 28:18–20; The End-Time Proselytes, Righteous Gentiles or New People?" 2017.

Doctor of Philosophy in Theology, University of St. Michael's College, Luke Amoussou, "Acts as a Hidden Transcript of Political Resistance: The Lukan Narrative of Infrapolitics," 2014.

Doctor of Philosophy, University of Toronto, Ronald Charles, "Paul: A Diasporic Migrant Worker among the Nations," 2014 (codirector with John Marshall). Published as *Paul and the Politics of Diaspora* (Minneapolis, MN: Fortress Press, 2014).

Doctor of Philosophy in Theology, University of St. Michael's College, Catherine Sider Hamilton, "Innocent Blood Traditions in Early Judaism and the Death of Jesus in Matthew," 2013. Published as *The Death of Jesus in Matthew: Innocent Blood and the End of Exile* (SNTSMS; Cambridge: Cambridge University Press, 2017).

Doctor of Philosophy in Theology, University of St. Michael's College, Stephen Black, "John, Elijah or One of the Prophets: How the Markan Reader Understands Jesus through John/Elijah," 2012.

Doctor of Philosophy in Theology, University of St. Michael's College, Murray Baker, "Founding Pauline Small Groups: An Examination of Material in the Pauline Letters Using a Small Group Founding Model," 2012.

Doctor of Philosophy in Theology, University of St. Michael's College, Joan Campbell, "Divided Family and Fictive Family: An Investigation of Kinship Relations in the Fourth Gospel," 2005. Published as *Kinship Relations in the Gospel of John* (Washington, DC: Catholic Biblical Association, 2007).

Doctor of Philosophy in Theology, University of St. Michael's College, John Bertone, "The Law of the Spirit: Experience of the Spirit and Displacement of the Law in Romans 8:1–16," 2004. Published under the same title (New York, NY: Peter Lang, 2005).

Doctor of Philosophy in Theology, University of St. Michael's College, Stephen Chambers, "Paul, His Converts and Mission in 1 Corinthians," 2004.

Post-Doctoral Fellows

Matthew Thiessen, "Ethnic Difference and Community Formation in the Letters of Paul," SSHRC Post-Doctoral award, Department for the Study of Religion, University of Toronto, 2011–12.

IV. Service

Within TST or the University of Toronto

Academic Dean, Wycliffe College, 2013–16
Lead designer and writer, proposal for a new conjoint Ph.D. program (Ph.D. in Theological Studies) (2012–13)
Director of Advanced Degree Programs, Toronto School of Theology, 2006–11
Chair, Advanced Degree Council, Toronto School of Theology, 2004–6
Advanced Degree Director, Wycliffe College, 1999–2006
(multiple additional tasks and committees)

Outside TST and the University of Toronto

Assessment of Research Grant Proposals for the Social Sciences and Humanities Research Council of Canada (2002, 2005, 2007, 2008, 2010)
External assessor, promotion and tenure review, Prof. Joan Campbell, Atlantic School of Theology (2009)
Assessment of manuscript, Aid to Scholarly Publication, Canadian Federation for the Humanities and Social Sciences (2008)
External assessor, promotion review, Prof. Mary Ann Beavis, University of Saskatchewan (2006)
Assessment of research grant proposal submitted to the Katholieke Universiteit Leuven, Belgium (2006)
Assessment Committee, Postsecondary Education Quality Assessment Board of Ontario (2005)
External assessor, promotion review, Prof. Stephen Westerholm, McMaster University (2004)
Adjudication Committee, Aid to Research and Transfer Journals, Social Sciences and Humanities Research Council (2004)
External assessor, promotion and tenure review, Prof. Michael Brown, Candler School of Theology, Emory University (2004)
Adjudication Committee, Aid to Research and Transfer Journals, Social Sciences and Humanities Research Council (2001)
External assessor, SPARC Review of the Department of Religion, Bishop's University, Lennoxville, Quebec (fall 2000)
Seminar cochair, "Religious Rivalries and the Struggle for Success: Jews, Christians and other Religious Groups in Local Settings in the First Two Centuries," Canadian Society of Biblical Studies, 1995–2000
Director, Graduate Studies Program, Saskatoon Theological Union, 1995–9
(See also "Professional Affiliations and Activities" above)

Introduction

This Festschrift celebrates the work of Terence L. Donaldson. As a former student of Professor Donaldson, I consider it an honor and a privilege to have worked as the editor of this volume. I first shared the idea of a Festschrift with Catherine Sider Hamilton, a former student of the honoree, who immediately thought it was an excellent idea. She encouraged me to pursue the project, and if it were not for the overwhelming demands on her schedule as a parish priest and as an extremely busy scholar, she would have been more than willing to be at my side as a coeditor. I thank her for her encouragement and ongoing support. Indeed, I have to thank all the contributors who have responded with eager enthusiasm to participate in this Festschrift. Other scholars, whose works are not included here, were also very willing to contribute but had to send their regrets because of several other pressing commitments or even because of illness. A *Tabula* of the names of all scholars who wished to honor Professor Donaldson is added at the end of this introduction. Donaldson's scholarly achievements and the respect he has gained among peers have made my task as an editor a real pleasure. The positive responses from high-caliber scholars and the rigor of their analyses offered throughout the chapters in this volume testify to the high esteem that scholars of various generations and of different genders, social-locations, historical and theological positions have for Professor Donaldson, an extraordinary and very unassuming New Testament (NT) scholar.

I have known Terry—as he is usually known—since 2005. I went to his office at Wycliffe College, University of Toronto, with a newly purchased copy of his *Paul and the Gentiles*.[1] I wanted to do my graduate studies under his supervision at the Toronto School of Theology. With his usual calm demeanor, he assured me he would be glad to be my thesis supervisor but that although I already had a 3-year M.Div. degree and I had done quite a bit of reading in the field prior to meeting with him, I needed to complete an M.T.S. at Wycliffe to broaden my theological horizon. I registered as a student and went to the mandatory weekend retreat for new students. There, in a beautiful setting outside of the bustling city of Toronto, I discovered a joyous human being and a fun professor. Terry invited me to play Scrabble with him and others. But it was not English Scrabble. It was in Hebrew! Also, to my delight as a violinist, I discovered he

---

[1] Terence L. Donaldson, *Paul and the Gentiles: Remapping the Apostle's Convictional World* (Minneapolis, MN: Fortress, 1997).

was a very decent banjo player. For a night of songs and games, we just played and played together while others were singing. I knew right then that there was something fascinating about this person. Later on, I learned that his undergraduate degree from the University of Toronto was in Mathematics. One can see traces of that training in his work as a biblical scholar. There is always in his work a search for precision and for beauty, for balance and for nuance, for logical development and for capturing vast amounts of information in ways that help one see patterns without ever imposing rigid or formulaic propositions on the materials under study. One may, for example, refer especially to Terry's *Judaism and the Gentiles* for this kind of careful approach.[2] In that magisterial work Donaldson summarizes the ways in which Jews envisaged Gentile relation to the covenantal Jewish God in four distinct ways: sympathizing with Judaism, being ethical monotheists, participating in eschatological salvation, or converting to Judaism.

When I finished my M.T.S. and was accepted to do my Ph.D. with the Religious Studies Department at the University of Toronto, I was very glad to have Terry as the cosupervisor of my doctoral dissertation, alongside Professor John W. Marshall. I could not have asked for a better team to guide and help me in my scholarly journey. Throughout my years of research and development as a young scholar, Terry has always been a firm, gentle, and quiet mentor. His notes on what I needed to do in my work were always clear. The distance between professor and student was appropriately maintained. I was lucky to be an apprentice learning how the craft was done from two great masters. After I successfully defended my dissertation on February 7, 2014, Terry invited me to have lunch with him. I was surprised and glad. I thanked him for being there for me and also for being such a great model of a scholar, mentor, husband, and genuine and caring human being.

It is only after I finished my dissertation and started to work as a professor myself that I realized the pressure one is under as an academic. When I submitted my drafts as a doctoral candidate, I had thought I would receive feedback right away. Terry would usually say to me that my chapter was next on his pile to occupy his close attention, and indeed he would get back to me in a reasonable and timely manner. It never really occurred to me to consider the almost insurmountable task and pressure that a university professor working in a large research institution might face. Terry was busy as a professor, active researcher (he always had one day totally devoted to his research projects), administrator, and the myriad other roles one is assigned in a university context. As a student, I lived in a different world. I realize today that my students occupy a different universe. I thought I was busy until I started my own career. It is remarkable that in the busyness of his life Terry has been able to pursue a number of extremely important scholarly questions for more than thirty years. Donaldson's scholarship in the field of NT broadly conceived is very important, especially as he has pushed scholars to pay closer attention to the complex relations between early Christ-followers—who were mostly non-Jews—and the Jewish matrix from which the narrative of the Christian proclamation comes. In four clearly articulated monographs,

---

[2] Terence L. Davidson, *Judaism and the Gentiles: Jewish Patterns of Universalism (to 135 CE)* (Waco, TX: Baylor University Press, 2007).

Donaldson presents a research trajectory that is both solid and informative.³ At the writing of this edited volume he also has a forthcoming monograph on *Gentile Christian Identity from Cornelius to Constantine*.⁴ This edited volume is important for the development of scholarship in the ways in which some prominent NT scholars engage Donaldson's contributions to sharpen some of his conclusions and to honor him for his work and friendship. These essays are located at the intersections of three bodies of literature— Paul, Matthew, and Second Temple Jewish Literature—as well as with themes and questions that have been central to Donaldson's work: Christian Judaism and the parting of the ways, Gentiles in Judaism and early Christianity, and anti-Judaism in early Christianity.

Donaldson's scholarly achievement, as well as his dedication to his students and commitment to scholarly pursuits across the academic divide, has made it a pleasure for me to be in conversation with a variety of scholars. The essays included in this Festschrift testify to the wide array of colleagues eager to engage with Donaldson's work and to push the scholarly conversations in further and fruitful directions.

Overview of the Volume

Chapter 1 is from Steve Mason. Mason is very interested in probing historical questions. He challenges some of the categories now taken for granted, such as Judaism, to study Paul. The question that guides his analysis is a simple, yet profound one: "How did Paul present himself to the groups of Christ-followers he established, in relation to Judean law, custom, and culture?" To Mason, there was not a lexical category of "Judaism" known to Paul and his contemporaries. His important contribution pushes us to be more attentive to history and to historical figures like Paul in their particular historical and linguistic milieu.

Chapter 2 is by Leif Vaage. His style of writing and of thinking is provocative and inimitable. He moves from modern anthropology, to ancient history, and to biblical studies to push the reader to reassess his/her understanding of Paul's earthly identity. What comes to us from Vaage's analysis is the presentation of an ancient figure who appears stranger and, perhaps, much more interesting than simply understanding Paul as being "this" (by nature a Jewish self) or "that" (an identity framed by Christ and understanding himself as a citizen of heaven).

My contribution in Chapter 3 explores the theme of the new creation in *Jubilees* and Romans. I have shown some similarities between human sin and the decay of creation in *Jubilees* and Romans, but the two texts could hardly be more dissimilar in some respects, for example, in the place the two accord to Israel and the law, although in this area there are important agreements. I also maintain, alongside Donaldson and

---

³ *Jesus on the Mountain: A Study in Matthean Theology* (Sheffield: JSOT Press, 1985); *Paul and the Gentiles*; *Judaism and the Gentiles*(Jews and Anti-Judaism in the New Testament; Waco, TX: Baylor University Press, 2010).
⁴ Terence L. Davidson, *Gentile Christian Identity from Cornelius to Constantine* (Grand Rapids, MI: Eerdmans, forthcoming).

other scholars, that for Paul the believer lives in two ages, as the new has dawned and broken into the old.

Ann L. Jervis' essay (Chapter 4) is placed right after my analysis, because in a brilliant piece of writing, she challenges most of what I advanced. For her Paul was not thinking in terms of two-age dualism. Rather, she understands Paul to conceive the risen Christ as actively present in the lives of his followers, in anticipation of his return. Ann's chapter and mine may be read as fruitful conversations in order to understand Paul's language better.

I have placed Matthew Thiessen's essay at the end of Part 1, the section on Paul, because his reflections on remapping Paul within Jewish ideologies of inclusion echo some of the language present in the previous chapters, namely, how modern categories are sometimes imposed on the ancient world and how theological preoccupations may sometimes be favored in lieu of clear historical investigation. Thiessen's essay is about mapping Pauline studies historically, but also helping the modern reader understand what exactly Paul was thinking in his time with regard to how God had mapped out Gentiles.

Part 2 is on Matthew. Anders Runesson's essay, Chapter 6, provides an excellent link between the two parts. In this chapter Runesson argues that while Matthew would agree with Paul on the continuing validity of the law for the Jewish people, the two come to conflicting conclusions about what this would mean for the nations as they try to solve the Gentile problem.

Chapter 7 is by Stephen Black. Black argues that the Sermon on the Mount is in large part constructed upon a negative stereotype of the Scribes and Pharisees. By making the Scribes and Pharisees a necessary negative foil by which Jesus' higher righteousness can be understood, Matthew makes them constitutive of any "Christian" identity that is built upon this higher righteousness.

Catherine Sider Hamilton focuses on women and the word in Matthew in Chapter 8. Hamilton begins with a close analysis of the place and significance of the women in the Matthean genealogy; she brings to bear on this analysis the treatment of women in Second Temple Jewish texts such as *Jubilees* and Pseudo-Philo—with thanks to Donaldson, whose interest in and thorough knowledge of Second Temple Judaism sparked her own. She then shows how Matthew's interest in women as speakers of the word and bearers of God's purpose is well developed.

Adele Reinhartz writes the penultimate chapter of the volume, which focuses on an issue that has been at the core of Donaldson's research: the "Parting of the Ways" between Judaism and Christianity. Chapter 9 addresses the different ways in which the criterion of plausibility has been employed in the discourse on this issue, and draws on examples from scholarship on Pauline literature, the Gospel of John, Josephus, Justin Martyr, and rabbinic literature.

Chapter 10, written by L. Gregory Bloomquist and Michael Haykin, may be much more difficult for a reader to situate in a volume on Matthew and Paul among Jews and Gentiles. As we now know so well from postcolonial and feminist studies, sometimes what is not said is as important as what is said. They probe a somewhat puzzling incident as narrated in Mark 14:51–52 to consider why a passage like this was left out of an otherwise equally graphic portrayal of the passion in Matthew, as well as in other gospel accounts. Their proposal is both intriguing and theologically promising.

In the spirit of friendship and respect for a great scholar and a genuine caring human being, I, alongside other colleagues and friends, present this Festschrift to Professor Terry Donaldson with respect and admiration. I also want to thank his wife, Lois, and his adult children Graeme, Meredith, and David.

Tabula Gratulatoria

Robert Derrenbacker
Stephen Chambers
John Kampen
John W. Marshall
Richard S. Ascough
Mark Nanos
Edith Humphrey
Paula Fredriksen
Margaret Y. MacDonald
John S. Kloppenborg
Philip A. Harland
Harry O. Maier
Colleen Shantz
Cecilia Wassen
Peter Richardson
Bradley H. McLean
Bruce W. Longenecker
Richard N. Longenecker
Michael Knowles
Don Garlington
Catherine Jones
Ho Jin Nam
Murray Baker
Joan Campbell
John Bertone
Luke Amoussou
Robert Jewett
Steve Notley
N. T. Wright

Part One

Paul

1

Paul without Judaism: Historical Method over Perspective

Steve Mason

Looking back on Pauline research in the last decades there is one trend which is generally accepted in international scholarship, namely that Paul is a Jew, and that he must be understood on the background of Judaism and the O.T.

Johannes Munck[1]

A nomenclature which is thrust upon the past will always end by distorting it, whether by design or simply as a consequence of equating its categories with our own, raised, for the moment, to the level of the eternal. There is no reasonable attitude toward such labels except to eliminate them.

Marc Bloch[2]

When I left a chair in ancient history to take up a New Testament (NT) post (2011), my world changed in many ways. What struck me most about the graduate-student cadre in the new setting was their fascination with "the new perspective on Paul" (hereafter NP). This impressed me, first, because the "new" perspective was older than most of them. Second, it seemed a tiny boat, lashed to the already small ship of Paul's corpus, for so many researchers. Third, most seemed at least as concerned about alignment with a Paul-guru or theological tradition as with the open-ended project of understanding the historical Paul. This last impression was strengthened during research for an SBL panel on part of N. T. Wright's *Paul and the Faithfulness of God* (2013).[3] I found the internet heaving with debates about whether Wright's Paul fit the NP and, more earnestly, whether Wright was *sound* in relation to a theological standard. Any distinction between Wright's own theology and that of Wright's Paul was hard to detect. I could not help thinking: "Some of you say I belong to Sanders,

---

[1] Johannes Munck, "Pauline Research since Schweitzer," in *The Bible in Modern Scholarship* (ed. J. Philip Hyatt; Nashville, TN: Abingdon, 1965), 166–77 (174).
[2] March Bloch, *The Historian's Craft* (trans. P. Putnam; New York, NY: Vintage, 1953 [manuscript ca. 1943]).
[3] N. T. Wright, *Paul and the Faithfulness of God* (London: SPCK, 2013).

some to Dunn, some to Wright, some to Campbell (Douglas or William). What about *me*, Paul?"

The NP was inaugurated by James Dunn's 1982 T.W. Manson Memorial Lecture.[4] Challenging E. P. Sanders' then-recent *Paul and Palestinian Judaism* (1977), Dunn argued that Paul's turn to Christ had to be more intelligible from Jewish-biblical sources than Sanders had suggested (concluding section). The NP has endured in part because understanding Paul as a scriptural exegete, more or less "within Judaism," catalyzed the long-developing, widespread, and multifaceted evolution of scholarship captured by the epigraph from Munck.[5] Once Paul is housed securely within Judaism, the classical assumption that he laid the foundation of a distinctive "Christian" theology crumbles, and a new question about when Christianity and Judaism "parted ways" opens for bids.[6] Although studying Paul as a Jewish exegete has been the prevailing direction of scholarship for more than a generation, some scholars have found the NP and its ilk still too encrusted with vestigial church language, in continuing to speak of pre-1970s "Christianity," "Christians," "churches," "missionaries," "faith/belief," and the like. They have called for a more "radical"' perspective, which begins from the assumption—and happily ends with the conclusion—that Paul lived wholly "within Judaism." They want a new vocabulary that does not traffic in distinctively Christian language, which they view as anachronistic.[7]

In what follows, I do not mean to suggest that while everyone has been searching for Paul, I have found him: "Relax everyone: He is over here!" Rather, I propose that the normal sense of what it means to study a figure *historically* seems almost impossible with Paul because the theological stakes are so deeply internalized. E. P. Sanders, my first Paul teacher, was genuinely concerned to understand the historical figure, irrespective of theological consequences. But Jacob Neusner challenged his portrait of Palestinian Judaism for being far too theological,[8] whereas Dunn, who thought Sanders' Judaism about right, found his Paul unhistorical (in the section that follows).

---

[4] James D. G. Dunn, "The New Perspective on Paul," *BJRL* 65 (1983): 95–122.
[5] E.g., Richard B. Hays, *Echoes of Scripture in the Letters of Paul* (New Haven, CT: Yale University Press, 1993); Terence L. Donaldson, *Paul and the Gentiles: Remapping the Apostle's Convictional World* (Minneapolis,MN: Fortress, 1997); N. T. Wright, *Paul and the Faithfulness of God* (2 vols.; Minneapolis, MN: Fortress, 2013).
[6] E.g., Lloyd Gaston, *Paul and the Torah* (Vancouver: University of British Columbia Press, 1987); Alan F. Segal, *Paul the Convert: The Apostolate and Apostasy of Saul the Pharisee* (New Haven, CT: Yale University Press, 1990); Gabriele Boccaccini, *Middle Judaism: Jewish Thought 300 BCE to 200 CE* (Minneapolis, MN: Fortress, 1991); James Dunn, *Jews and Christians: The Parting of the Ways, A.D. 70 to 135* (Tübingen: Mohr, 1992); Daniel Boyarin, *A Radical Jew: Paul and the Politics of Identity* (Berkeley, CA: University of California Press, 1994); Boyarin, *Border Lines: The Partition of Judaeo-Christianity* (Philadelphia, PA: University of Pennsylvania Press, 2004); Pamela Eisenbaum, *Paul Was Not a Christian: The Original Message of a Misunderstood Apostle* (San Francisco, CA: HarperOne, 2009).
[7] Magnus Zetterholm, "Paul within Judaism: The State of the Questions," in *Paul within Judaism: Restoring the First-Century Context to the Apostle* (ed. Mark D. Nanos and Magnus Zetterholm; Minneapolis, MN: Fortress, 2015), 34: "proponents of … Paul within Judaism perspectives … share *the assumption* that the traditional perspectives … need to be replaced by a *historically more accurate view*. … I am quite confident that Christianity will survive a *completely Jewish Paul*."
[8] Jacob Neusner, "Review of *Paul and Palestinian Judaism*," *HR* 18 (1978): 177–91.

Now the "Paul within Judaism" (PWJ) group finds the NP theological, imagining its own work to be, in the end, historical: restoring Paul at long last to his proper first-century Jewish setting.[9] Notice that "historical" here means *accurate* in relation to a particular understanding of how things really were.

It is easy for scholars of all backgrounds and persuasions to say sincerely that they seek the real Paul, meaning the historical figure. It is more difficult to accept what historical research—into all events, conditions, and personalities—requires. Since Herodotus "fathered" *historiē*, and again after its revival in the Humboldtian research university, history has meant the open-ended, methodical investigation of problems of the human past.[10] Responsible inquiry is its only requirement—*not* accuracy in relation to preconceived images. If we knew the past in advance, after all, we would not need to investigate it. Whatever prestige history has comes from its relentlessly truth-seeking, ever-questioning nature. If we give that up and descend into camps, we forsake history's aegis. One can only investigate responsibly if one is not invested in conclusions, which must change with new information and insight. As the ancient physician Galen stressed (*De sectis*), a medical research group committed to its propositions in advance is only a dogmatic *hairesis*.

Likewise with the human past, a program that exists to elaborate what it already believes about the past cannot do history. Since no one today knows much about the Paul who lived in the first century, the criterion for a "historical Paul" cannot be correspondence with a known image. The historical Paul is the assemblage of low-resolution, tentative images that reside in the minds of historians willing to study him in his ancient contexts, constantly moving between testing interpretations and imagining explanations.[11] The long and painful conflict between historical and theological research was obvious before our times. The two sides had a rough time getting along in the long nineteenth century because of the then-clear difference between open-ended questioning and belief.[12] These issues were real and divisive. They tend to be blurred today, when *perspectives*, arising from presuppositions deemed equally legitimate, minimize conflict in the public academic square.

---

[9] Mark D. Nanos, "Introduction," in Nanos and Zetterholm, *Paul within Judaism*, 8-9: "the prevailing constructions of the apostle have not begun from the most probable historical hypotheses; they have not been approached from the most historiographically grounded sensibilities; they have not been developed around the most historically likely choices." The scholars in this volume share a "commitment to the quest to understand the historical Paul … letting the theological chips fall where they may." But see the works in nn. 3-4 among dozens of others.

[10] E.g., R. G. Collingwood, *The Idea of History* (ed. Jan van der Dussen; Oxford: Oxford University Press, 1994), 7-10, 19-20; Bloch, *Historian's Craft*, 20, 71, 87; Frederick C. Beiser, *The German Historicist Tradition* (Oxford: Oxford University Press, 2011), 1-25.

[11] Terence L. Donaldson, *Jews and Anti-Judaism in the New Testament* (Waco, TX: Baylor University Press, 2010), is a model of careful method.

[12] Of countless examples, the relatively tame British standoff between Benjamin Jowett's circle and their opponents around 1860 gets at the central issues. Cf. Benjamin Jowett et al., *Essays and Reviews* (London: Longman, Green, Longman, and Roberts, 1861) with William E. Jelf et al., *Faith and Peace* (London: Saunders, Oatley, 1862).

A Lutheran, Catholic, or Jewish Paul must be sound. That is the price of being an icon. But the evidence of Paul's letters (Phil 3; 2 Cor 10–13; Galatians) and early legacy (James 2:14; Acts 21:20–28; 2 Pet 3:15–16; Marcion, Ebionites, pseudo-Clementines) show that many of his contemporaries did not find him *simpatico*.[13] Paul reciprocated their disdain (later in this chapter). Where did such conflicts come from, if he was clearly devoted to Judaean ancestral customs? Why were similar accusations not made of Peter or James? Did the author of Acts invent the hostile impressions of Paul that he attributes to Judaeans, Christian believers or not, in chapter 21? Did Irenaeus fabricate the Ebionites, who

> reject the apostle Paul, maintaining that he was an apostate from the law … [and who] practise circumcision, persevere in the observance of those customs that are enjoined by the law, and are so Judaean in their style of life that they even adore Jerusalem as though it were the house of God? (*C. Haer.* 1.26.2)[14]

Paul's fans and detractors alike, from Marcion via the Popes, Luther, and NT scholar B. F. Westcott through most of the twentieth century, understood him to have declared the end of Moses' law.[15] Before the last generation, Jewish academics with serious knowledge of early Christian texts tended, reciprocally, to follow Voltaire and Thomas Paine in distinguishing Jesus, a recognizably Jewish teacher, from Paul, a figure rather alien to Judaism. Kaufmann Kohler's entry in the *Jewish Encyclopedia* (1906), for example, spoke of Paul's pathology and "unparalleled animosity and hostility to Judaism."[16] Although the Third Reich did not emerge organically from Christian anti-Judaism, this long tradition of divorcing Pauline Christianity from Judaism was crucial to the "German Christian" movement and undoubtedly played a role in the European churches' co-optation, causing deep soul-searching after the war—as we see in the final version of *nostra aetate* (1965) or Rosemary Radford Ruether's *Faith and Fratricide* (1974).[17] One need not doubt that the swing to a profoundly Jewish Paul, with the implicit claim that a colossal misreading underlies traditional interpretation, comes with all sincerity and moral justification. History upsets holisms, however, with its interest in particulars, contexts, and change. That is why history and tradition are at odds.

---

[13] See Gerd Lüdemann, *Opposition to Paul in Early Christianity* (trans. M. E. Boring; Minneapolis, MN: Fortress, 1989); Patrick Gray, *Paul as a Problem in History and in Culture: The Apostle and His Critics through the Centuries* (Grand Rapids, MI: Baker, 2016). Wayne Meeks, ed., *The Writings of Paul* (New York, NY: W.W. Norton, 1972), 176–84, 288–301, excerpts from ancient and modern detractors.

[14] Cf. Origen, *C. Cels.* 2.1; 5.61, 65.

[15] E.g., Kenneth Stow, *Popes, Church, and Jews in the Middle Ages: Confrontation and Response* (London: Routledge, 2007); B. F. Westcott (as Dunelm) in William Knight, *The Arch of Titus and the Spoils of the Temple* (London: Religious Tract Society, 1896), 9–11.

[16] Kohler at http://www.jewishencyclopedia.com/articles/13232-saul-of-tarsus. Cf. Joseph Klausner, *Jesus of Nazareth: His Life, Times, and Teaching* (New York, NY: Macmillan, 1926), 64; Hyam Maccoby, *The Myth-Maker: Paul and the Invention of Christianity* (New York, NY: HarperSanFrancisco, 1987); Geza Vermes, *Jesus in His Jewish Context* (Minneapolis, MN: Fortress, 2003), 40–52.

[17] *Faith and Fratricide, The Theological Roots of Anti-Semitism* (New York, NY: The Seabury Press, 1974).

Asking historical questions does not mean claiming a chimerical *objectivity*. Objectivity does not enter into it, even as an aspiration unmet. Hypothetical reconstruction can never acquire the status of fact (a *factum*, done and dusted); it lives on a different cognitive plane. Especially when we feel confident in speculating about the lost realities behind the scant survivals from antiquity, we must doubt because there is so much we cannot know. There are, however, *evidential facts* in the data of our meager survivals. These—such as the presence or absence of terms—are the same for everyone who cares to look. In what follows, I shall focus on these facts.

Delighted to share in honoring Terry Donaldson, whom I have considered a model of scholarly probity since our graduate-student days, I offer this essay in a constructive historical vein. In a recent volume representing the PWJ approach, Donaldson wrote a typically circumspect review, which highlighted several problems with this perspective. I shall take one of his positive reflections on the volume, however, as my departure point:

> I also appreciate the attention that is given to terminological matters. Many of the terms and categories used in critical reconstructions of the past are *laden with meanings and connotations* that have accumulated through centuries of subsequent use, which readily leads to *anachronisms, distortions, and false assumptions*.[18]

This is a basic principle of ancient history. Alas, when it comes to terms and categories we all find it easier to strain out the gnats in others' work while we swallow whole the camels we find more congenial.[19] I shall push farther in this direction, hoping to be radical enough to get at some ignored ancient roots.

---

[18] Donaldson, "Paul within Judaism: A Critical Evaluation from a 'New Perspective' Perspective," in Nanos and Zetterholm, *Paul within Judaism*, 283 (emphasis added).

[19] As much of my research has been devoted to "the rectification of names," I am sympathetic; cf. Mason and Tom Robinson, *Early Christian Reader* (Peabody, MA: Hendrickson, 2004), 7–10. PWJ scholars place weight on framing categories, however—diaspora, gospel, Judaism—that had no currency, while their concern for shades of meaning in *pistis* is difficult to follow. Cf. Anders Runesson, "The Questions of Terminology: The Architecture of Contemporary Discussions in Paul," in Nanos and Zetterholm, *Paul within Judaism*, 59–68: "Christians" is not emic language in Paul; etic definitions would be hazardous; and even if Acts 11:26 were trusted concerning early use, *Christianoi* might be better rendered "messianics." But we normally transliterate (rather than translate) place and group names. Although Christ-followers preferred in-house terms—brothers and sisters, slaves of Christ, in Christ—all known outside observers thought that *Christiani* had been around for decades before 100 CE (Josephus, *Ant.* 18.64 in the most likely authentic part, 93 CE referring to the 30s; Pliny, *Ep.* 10.96, on former Christians who *left* 25 years earlier; Tacitus, *Ann.* 15.44.2 and Suetonius, *Ner.* 16.2 on Christians in Nero's Rome). Cf. John Barclay, "'Jews' and 'Christians' in the Eyes of Roman Authors c. 100 CE" in *Jews and Christians in the First and Second Centuries: How to Write Their Histories* (ed. Peter J. Tomson and Joshua Schwartz; Leiden: Brill, 2013), 313–26; Birgit van der Lans and Jan N. Bremmer, "Tacitus and the Persecution of the Christians: An Invention of Tacitus?" *Eirene: Studia Graeca et Latina* 53 (2017): 301–33. Although the apparently Latin *-ianus* might suggest an origin with the authorities (but "Herodians"), 1 Pet 4:16 and Acts 11:26; 26:18 assume that the name did not trouble Christ-followers. Ignatius' delight in *christianismos* (below) assumes long familiarity with "Christian." We do not know whether Paul knew the term, as we have only some of his letters to fellow believers.

I would formulate the historical problem of this essay this way: How did Paul *present himself* in relation to Judaean law and custom in his letters to his converts (not: What did Paul *think* or why)? My reasons for not formulating the problem in terms of "Judaism" will become clear presently. I do not seek to defend a particular Paul, but rather invite readers to reflect with me on the parameters for pursuing this important figure historically.[20] How would Paul look if we put aside ingrained modern categories to think in terms that were available to him and his contemporaries in the eastern Mediterranean under Rome (in the first two sections)? In the third section, I offer a sketch of what seem to me the beginnings of a plausible direction. In honor of our subject, I postpone elaborating the "problem" until the concluding section, after this embryonic "solution."

Paul Did Not Know about Judaism

In case my title should suggest that whereas other scholars place "Paul within Judaism," I would place him *outside* it, I hasten to explain that my argument is more basic. Paul, Peter, Philo, Josephus, and their contemporaries were *all* without Judaism, because the category was not available to them. This is not a matter of mere semantics. Coming to terms with ancient discourse and its categories, leaving our comfort zones for that foreign territory, just as we would if we were studying ancient India or China, and as we routinely do in studying other aspects of the Roman empire, seems to me the beginning of historical understanding.

On the threshold of Christianity's transformation from persecuted nuisance to most-favored status, in the early 300s, the man who would soon write a panegyric of the transformative emperor Constantine was still preoccupied with justifying the Christian faith. In his *Preparation of the Gospel*, Eusebius boldly addresses the central criticism of this faith over the past three centuries. Whereas Pindar's motto "*Nomos* is king" had echoed through centuries as the axiomatic foundation of social order (Herodotus 3.38.4; Origen, *C. Cels.* 5.40), many Christians were following Paul's lead in declaring themselves *not* to be under law (ὑπὸ νόμον) at all.[21] For Paul, the most salient *nomos* had been that of Moses, which defined life for Judaean communities throughout the Mediterranean, including his own before he followed Christ.[22] The *nomoi* of his non-Judaean converts were the customs and traditions of their respective *poleis*. The Christians' opponents cared little about what these people believed, but insisted that they show loyalty to their *nomoi*. They must return to the *cosmos* and embrace the calendar, festivals, sacrifices, and civic institutions of one *polis* or another,

---

[20] Cf. Dunn, "New Perspective": "to see Paul properly within his own context, to hear Paul in terms of his own time" (100); Nanos and Zetterholm, *Paul within Judaism*, 9: "committed to proposing ... pre-Christian ... questions about Paul's concerns and those of his audiences and contemporaries ... a historical portrait of Paul."

[21] E.g., 1 Cor 9:20; Gal 3:23; 4:4, 32; 5:18; Rom 6.14–15.

[22] Cf. Josephus, *Antiquities* 1–11 and *Against Apion*; Diodorus Siculus 34/35.1.1–4; Strabo 16.2.34–37; Tacitus, *Hist.* 5.3–5.

not pretend to float above it all with their claims to esoteric truth or the bizarre hope of evacuation into the sky.[23] By the early fourth century, from a position of rapidly growing confidence, Eusebius turns the tables and debuts the game-changing Christian lexical palette: "*Christianismos* breaks with both *Hellēnismos* and *Ioudaismos*, yes. Deal with it!" (1.5.5).

Back at the beginning, Paul had parried the same accusation of defection from civic loyalty without benefit of Eusebius' capsule lexicon. Rejecting demands from others for this-worldly affiliation, he declared: "our political community (ἡμῶν ... τὸ πολίτευμα) exists in heaven, from where we also await a saviour-lord, Jesus Christ" (Phil 3:21). By about 200 CE, increasingly learned Christian writers felt strong enough to confront the "champions and avengers of laws and ancestral institutions" (Tertullian, *Apol.* 5–6). Thus Tertullian, for example:

> This is what our project is against: it is against the arrangements made by the ancestors, authoritative opinions [or models] passively received, the laws of those in power, and the reasonings of the wise; it is against antiquity, custom, coercion; it is against precedents, marvels, and wonders—all of which conspired to create your corrupt view of the Deity. (*Ad nat.* 2.1.7)

Claiming a pristine revealed truth in Christ, Christ-followers often viewed variegated local traditions as moldy and corrupting, not as the beautifully varied gardens of the *oikoumenē*, which gave security and substance to human life. Although Tertullian, like Paul, has the customs of all *gentes* and *nationes* in view, as for Paul the Judaeans are his most germane example because they were the precursors of Christians. God had once chosen that *gens*, but abandoned them and transferred his favor to more faithful followers from *all nations* (*ex omni iam gente et populo et loco cultores sibi adlegeret deus multo fideliores in quos gratiam transferret*, *Apol.* 21.4–6), in a community no longer defined by local tradition.[24] *Ethnos-* or *gens*-identity, identified with ancestral customs and laws, has lost its relevance. Clement's *Exhortation to the Greeks* weaponizes the same points, contrasting customs "handed down from fathers" with revealed truth: "Let us then steer clear of custom! Let us steer clear of it like a dangerous headland. .... Custom is a snare, a trap, a pit, an evil treat" (*Protr.* 10, 12.1). At least fictively from the Roman side, the character Caecilius in Minucius Felix's *Octavius* mocks Christ-followers' claim to stand above nations and tribes (*gentes nationesque*), in their arrogant expectation that the universe will burn while these naïfs alone are saved (11.1). The philosopher Celsus assails the same view (Origen, *C. Cels.* 5.14–16). Inured to such criticism, however, Tertullian is still confidently awaiting the coming conflagration, in which the world with its ancient ways and origin-claims (*cum tanta saeculi vetustas et tot eius nativitates uno igni haurientur*), magistrates, philosophers, poets, and other scoffers, will be consumed (*Spect.* 30). Although each of these authors

---

[23] Celsus in Origen, *C. Cels.* 5.25–26, 33; Porphyry (or similar) in Macarius Magnes, *Apocr.* 3.30, in R. Joseph Hoffmann, *Porphyry's against the Christians: The Literary Remains* (Amherst, MA: Prometheus, 1994), 59; Julian, *C. Gal.* [Loeb] 39a–43a, 141c–141b, 238d, 314c, 343c–356e.

[24] All translations are mine.

writes with distinctive turns of phrase in a particular context, and their larger views differ, they all see themselves as cleaving to central Christian positions established most clearly by Paul.

It was this conflict between conformity to *nomos* and cold rejection of it that Eusebius reframed in his table-turning lexicon: "*One might fittingly* use the label ἰουδαϊσμός for the constitution arranged according to the law of Moses, connected with the one God over all, and ἑλληνισμός to express *in nuce* the superstitious belief in many gods, as in the ancestral customs of all the *ethnē*."[25] His optative-mood creativity would make no sense if everyone had always known that ἰουδαϊσμός or ἑλληνισμός had such meanings. Outside of Christian usage, no one knew this vocabulary.

Outsiders had indeed seen Christians as halfway between Hellas and Judaea—taking the worst elements from each while committing themselves to neither. Eusebius agreed about the in-between position but rejected the inference that "Christianism" was derivative. It may only have "recently been made the *nomos* for all humanity of the inhabited earth" (νεωστὶ πᾶσιν ἀνθρώποις τοῖς καθ' ὅλης τῆς οἰκουμένης νενομοθετημένη), with Christ's arrival, but Christian faith was in fact, for him, "the oldest community of piety and most ancient philosophy" (τὸ μεταξὺ τούτων παλαιότατον εὐσεβείας πολίτευμα, καὶ ἀρχαιοτάτη μέν τις φιλοσοφία), antedating both Moses and polytheism—which is to say, "Judaism" and "Hellenism" (*Dem. ev.* 1.2.9). Recalling Paul in Gal 3.6-29, Eusebius used the new words to claim that Moses' system, encapsulated in his curse of Israelites who failed to fulfil *every bit* of the law (sharing Paul's odd reading of Deut 27:26), was a late change to the simple faith of the patriarchs, which had effectively been *Christianism before Christ*.

The main incubators of this Christian lexicon before Eusebius, as far as we can see, were Tertullian in Latin and Origen in Greek. Tertullian pairs every use of *Christianismus* with *Iudaismus*, as a way of contrasting gospel with Law or "legal servitude" (*Marc.* 4.6, 33; 5.4, 6). He also frequently uses *Iudaismus* on its own—some twenty times. Origen anticipates Eusebius most directly, using ἰουδαϊσμός some thirty-three times to mean the belief system based in Moses' law. Most telling, his eight-volume refutation of Celsus has ἰουδαϊσμός nine times and reinterprets Celsus to speak of "Judaism" (1.2.2), though Celsus does not use the word in his own voice. This matches the evidence that Porphyry and Julian, who knew a great deal about Christians and Judaeans, never thought to use ἰουδαϊσμός.[26] The Christian lexicon of reductive -isms reached its full flowering with Epiphanius, decades after Eusebius. He created a flowchart of falsehood by calling out five "mothers," or wombs, of deviance, which he called Barbarism, Scythism, Hellenism, Judaism, and Samaritism (*Anc.* 12.8; *Pan.* 1.2 [Holl] 1.157-197).

Using -ism language for belief systems was thus a Christian innovation. No non-Christian would have thought, upon seeing such words, that they intended *systems of thought or belief*. A barbarism (βαρβαρισμός) was a turn of speech (cf. Strabo 14.2.28),

---

[25] *Dem. ev.* 1.2.2: Τὸν μὲν ἰουδαϊσμὸν εὐλόγως ἄν τις ὀνομάσειε τὴν κατὰ τὸν Μωσέως νόμον διατεταγμένην πολιτείαν, ἑνὸς ἐξημμένην τοῦ ἐπὶ πάντων θεοῦ, τὸν δὲ ἑλληνισμόν, ὡς ἐν κεφαλαίῳ φάναι, τὴν κατὰ τὰ πάτρια τῶν ἐθνῶν ἁπάντων εἰς πλείονας θεοὺς δεισιδαιμονίαν.

[26] Cyril has it at *Proph. min.* 1.659; *Comm. Joann.* 2.108; *Comm. Luc.* 72.864, not when citing Julian.

akin to a solecism (σολοικισμός) at sentence level and contrastable with Hellenism (ἑλληνισμός), which meant adopting or affecting pure Greek (Aristotle, *Poet.* 1458a). Compare our use of "Americanism" ("Can I get fries with that, going forward?") and Britishism ("I'm peckish"). As we can still see in their English descendants— baptism, ostracism, Laconism, Medism, Atticism—Greek -ισμός nouns referred to actions: baptizing, ostracizing, Medizing, and so on. Χριστιανισμός began its life the same way. It meant Christian*izing* over against ἰουδαϊσμός, or Judaizing (below). As both terms lost their dynamic sense, apparently through being freeze-dried in Latin, they gradually came to form a Christian luggage-set for contending *belief systems*, or "religions."

That is why Ἰουδαϊσμός and the others are found almost exclusively in Christian authors. Any reader can confirm the following facts. First, of the 393 occurrences of ἰουδαϊσμός in the database of the Thesaurus Linguae Graecae, 388 are Christian. The other five come from a single Judaean text (*2 Maccabees*) and one that borrows from it (*4 Maccabees*). Second, all known occurrences of Latin *Iudaismus* are Christian. Third, in spite of its title, Menachem Stern's indispensable three-volume compendium, *Greek and Latin Authors on Jews and Judaism*, contains no instance of "Judaism," either ἰουδαϊσμός or *Iudaismus*, from the pen of an outside observer. Fourth, in the extensive corpora of the Hebrew Bible/LXX, Philo, Josephus, *1 Maccabees*, the pseudepigrapha, Qumran Scrolls, and the NT (outside Gal 1.13–14), no ἰουδαϊσμός or Hebrew equivalent such as *yahadut* appears. Given that scholars *do* rely on "Judaism" when discussing these texts—try to imagine an academic discussion of Galatians, Romans, or Matthew without "Judaism"—is it not worth asking why ancient authors felt no such need? Are we missing something that was obvious to them?

For readers wondering why I seem to ignore ἰουδαϊσμός in *2 Maccabees* and perhaps Gal 1.13–14 (if considered Judaean), I should explain.[27] The author of *2 Maccabees*—if not Jason of Cyrene, whose work he abridges—was partial to -ισμός action-nouns. His apparent innovations include "arming with a breastplate" (θωρακισμός) and "eating entrails" (σπλαγχνισμός; 6.7, 21; 7.42), which more or less vanish from later literature.[28] He also introduces three cultural -ισμός words: ἀλλοφυλισμός, "foreignizing" (4.13; 6.24), ἑλληνισμός, "hellenizing" (4.13), and ἰουδαϊσμός, "judaizing" (2.21; 8.1; 14.38 [twice]). Since his programmatic statement at 4.13 speaks of a "peak of ἑλληνισμός" and an "advance in ἀλλοφυλισμός." These two terms must refer to the *actions* of hellenizing and foreignizing, as one would expect from the form. No extant later author finds a use for "foreignizing" in a life-and-death cultural struggle. Given this context, it is easiest also to understand the neologism ἰουδαϊσμός in the same way, as the proper counter-movement of Judaeans to the rampant foreignizing or hellenizing of their ancestral customs. These need, ironically, to be judaized in order to be restored to their proper place. Thus we read that ἰουδαϊσμός was what armed Judaean groups were *doing*, at the risk to their lives (8.1; 14.38), for which they could well be punished—not for *being* Judaeans, something they could not change, but for persisting in certain actions.

---

[27] Mason, "Jews, Judaeans"; *Orientation*, 175–220.
[28] Other words of this class have extremely slender attestation prior to his eager use of them: ἐμφανισμός (3.9), ὑπομνηματισμός (2.13; 4.23), and καθαρισμός (1.18, 36; 2.16, 19; 10.5).

Another way the author describes that persistence is with the noun ἀναστροφή: a constant striving, turning and returning, or commitment to Judaean ways, instead of "capitulating to foreignizing." The author praises old Eleazar for precisely this determination (6.23-24).

Any Greek speaker could have deduced from morphology and context what ἀλλοφυλισμός, ἑλληνισμός, and ἰουδαϊσμός mean in this extraordinary work, even though the words themselves were not otherwise used this way. The conflict described by this author, which summoned his literary creativity with this form of word, left hardly any occasions for their later use, once that famous but unique crisis had passed. Ἰουδαϊσμός might have disappeared with the others if the Judaean Paul had not found the occasion to recall *2 Maccabees* with a new ironic twist. When some of his Gentile recruits for Christ in Asia Minor, influenced by other teachers, decided they should judaize, after coming to suspect that Paul had corrupted the apostles' teaching by ignoring its Judaean content (Gal 1:6; 2:14; 3:1-3; 4:21; 5:2-12), he revived this language to convey the energy he had *formerly* devoted to Judaean customs, to convince them that he was by no means overlooking Judaean law. For this purpose, he seized both barrels from *2 Maccabees* to speak of τὴν ἐμὴν ἀναστροφήν ποτε ἐν τῷ ἰουδαϊσμῷ, "my own former *doggedness* in the *judaizing*" that others had put on the table. His non-Judaean audience presumably had no basis for catching the allusion to *2 Maccabees*, unless Paul's opponents had used the text of crisis as ammunition against him (accusing him of being a new Antiochus). But his meaning is clear enough because he explains it: "*that is*, I was going after the assembly of God with a vengeance, trying to wipe it out" (Gal 1:13). Having invoked ἰουδαϊσμός, he repeats it immediately for effect: "This is what you want? Look, I was far ahead of my peer group in the judaizing," which he glosses this time as: "so completely was I a devotee of the traditions of my ancestors." His point seems clear: no one is now keener on Judaean ancestral law than he *was—before* Christ called him (Gal 1:15).

4 Maccabees, possibly contemporary with Paul, is the only other extant Judaean text that borrows ἰουδαϊσμός from *2 Maccabees* (4 Macc. 4:23). It valorizes the word in the straightforward way that *2 Maccabees* does, whereas Paul finds it the potent *mot juste* for describing his *former* exertions on behalf of Judaean tradition against the threat of Christ-followers—*before* he abruptly joined them in response to God's intervention. This is presumably why Paul never uses ἰουδαϊσμός in the way that scholars do, for "Judaism." That is, he does not use it in the body of Galatians or Romans, to characterize the laws of Moses or Judaean tradition, just where scholars speak of *Judaism*. In Paul's account, his encounter with Christ and commission with The Announcement (τὸ εὐαγγέλιον), which had nothing to do with human input, let alone ancestral tradition, placed his zeal for Judaean tradition behind him (Gal 1:15-17).

Writing decades after Galatians,[29] but well aware of Paul's linguistic moves, Ignatius of Antioch took the decisive step in making ἰουδαϊσμός a durable Christian

---

[29] How many decades after Paul is not of paramount concern here. Timothy D. Barnes in "The Date of Ignatius," *Expo Times* 120 (2008): 119-30, argues for a date in the 140s rather than the traditional date a generation earlier, on the basis of striking literary agreements between Ignatius and the gnostic Ptolemaeus (via Irenaeus).

category,[30] though he did not know that he was doing so. Hearing of judaizing among the Philadelphians of Asia Minor (cf. Rev 3:9), he took a leaf from Paul to object: "If someone explains judaizing to you (Ἐὰν δέ τις ἰουδαϊσμὸν ἑρμηνεύῃ ὑμῖν), don't listen! It is better to hear *christianizing* from a man having circumcision (παρὰ ἀνδρὸς περιτομὴν ἔχοντος χριστιανισμὸν ἀκούειν) than judaizing from a foreskin-type (ἢ παρὰ ἀκροβύστου ἰουδαϊσμόν)" (*Phila.* 6.1). Circumcised or not, everyone should now "talk of Jesus Christ." Anticipating the later writers we noted earlier, Ignatius insists that to bring up laws and customs now is to live among "the tombs of the dead," ensnared by "the ruler of this age"—a Pauline phrase (1 Cor 2:6-8; cf. 2 Cor 4:4). Writing to the Magnesians, he compares judaizing (ἰουδαϊσμός), after Christ's coming, to "ancient and worthless fables" (8.1). Here he replaces the tomb metaphor with that of stinking food past its useful time (*Mag.* 10:1-3), before driving home his point: "It is absurd to talk Jesus Christ and to judaize (ἄτοπόν ἐστιν Ἰησοῦν Χριστὸν λαλεῖν καὶ ἰουδαΐζειν)! For christianizing did not put its trust in judaizing, but judaizing in christianizing (ὁ γὰρ χριστιανισμὸς οὐκ εἰς ἰουδαϊσμὸν ἐπίστευσεν, ἀλλ' ἰουδαϊσμὸς εἰς χριστιανισμόν)." That ἰουδαϊσμός retains a verbal sense in Ignatius is clear because he uses ἰουδαΐζειν and ἰουδαϊσμός as synonyms. He is continuing Paul's creative reuse of *2 Maccabees*. His exaltation of χριστιανισμός as the end of history, however, paved the way for its new use as an abstract noun in Latin (see earlier).

To summarize: Paul and his contemporaries did not know about Judaism. They communicated, instead, using the long-established lexical bank of the Greco-Roman world. This had a clear place for the ancient Judaean *ethnos*, its mother-*polis* Jerusalem, lawgiver Moses, distinctive calendar, festivals, laws, and customs, including circumcision and dietary restrictions. I am not making an argument from silence here, from the mere happenstance that hardly any contemporary texts use ἰουδαϊσμός. Perhaps other texts did use it to mean Judaism, but they have been lost, one might counter. The silence is made both deafening and dispositive, first, by the contrast between the ubiquity of "Judaism" among Christian authors, often in a single text, and its complete absence from such massive corpora as the LXX, the pseudepigrapha, Philo, Josephus, and outsider observers—where the subject matter is precisely what scholars call Judaism. Second, granted that most ancient texts did not survive, the surviving evidence is sufficient for us to trace the development of ἰουδαϊσμός with some confidence, from a rarely needed action-noun to the standard Christian suitcase-label for a system of belief. The new Christian meaning explains the absence of the word from Judaean texts, where it did not and could not have indicated a faith system.

Shaye Cohen's "Jewishness" would not face the same objections *if* we could understand it not as a mere stand-in for the same reified "Judaism" but as something more open and culturally diffuse, by analogy with "Romanness" (cf. *Romanitas*)[31] or perhaps modern "Britishness." These words do not describe a system of belief but rather a vague suite of ascribed traits, values, and behaviors, which differ with each

---

[30] Cf., with a different direction of argument but largely in agreement, Daniel Boyarin, "Why Ignatius Invented Judaism," in *The Ways That Often Parted: Essays in Honor of Joel Marcus* (ed. L. Baron et al.; Atlanta, GA: SBL, 2018), 309–24.

[31] Shaye J. D. Cohen, *The Beginnings of Jewishness: Boundaries, Varieties, Uncertainties* (Berkeley, CA: University of California Press, 1999).

observer.³² Depending on their experience with the British, some might think of Britishness as aristocratic ways, high tea, or excessive diffidence, while others think of vestigial imperialism, others the welfare state embodied by the NHS, still others football hooliganism and knife crime. PWJ scholars appear to move in this direction even with Judaism at times, when they write, "Judaism—*that is*, the Jewish way(s) of life," or say that "Judaism, as a multifaceted, *dynamic cultural development*, took place within *other multifaceted dynamic cultures* in the Hellenistic world." But their insistence on placing Paul and even his foreign converts *within Judaism*, and as constituting "subgroups of Judaism,"³³ explodes that sound historical instinct. The Christians needed and created capsule-words for in-or-out faith systems corresponding to *Christianism*. This matching luggage set was not yet available in the first century. Paul and his contemporaries were therefore "without Judaism."

What Difference Does a Category Make?

When I have discussed such issues with colleagues or published in this vein, the most consistent response has been: "You're being pedantic. Obviously, we need *some* covering term for everything Jewish. *Judaism* is the familiar term, and you don't have a better one."³⁴ This response misses the point, however, that historians do not otherwise feel the need to miniaturize complex cultures with capsule words. At least, I have never heard any historian speak of Romism, Athenism, Egyptism, or Syrism—or lament the lack of such terms. Those who feel this need for Judaeans alone might ask themselves why. Is it because the academic study of Judaea, its people, and literature skews toward the theological and trans-temporal? Are we unconsciously absorbing and preserving old Christian perspectives?

To be sure, we all make compromises for convenience, such as when we use "emperor" for the Roman *princeps*, who, in the first century and a half, could never have used a term corresponding to the normal senses of emperor in English. In many communicative contexts, I have no problem calling my research area "ancient Judaism." It is not a question of pedantry. Communication depends on one's interlocutors and purposes. Using "Judaism" as a real category in historical research on the first century is another matter, with obvious consequences. For once we stipulate that the ancients knew *Judaism*, we inevitably ask, first, what class of things Judaism belonged to (usual answer: it was a species of religion) and then set about characterizing this particular expression of the genus. Scholars in this field have spent huge amounts of time asking, "What *kind of religion* was ancient Judaism: legal, legalistic, progressive, missionary?" Paradoxically, the scholar who did the most to establish the critical-historical study

---

[32] Cf. Louise Revell, *Roman Imperialism and Local Identities* (Cambridge: Cambridge University Press, 2009), 1–39.
[33] Nanos, "Introduction," in Nanos and Zetterholm, *Paul within Judaism*, 9 and 10, respectively (my emphasis).
[34] E.g., Seth Schwartz, "How Many Judaisms Were There? A Critique of Neusner and Smith on Definition and Mason and Boyarin on Categorization," *JAJ* 2 (2011): 203–38, with much more sophistication than I can indicate here.

of Judaism in American universities, Jacob Neusner, stressed more than anyone else the notion of Judaism as a *system*. His mathematical, philosophical, and comparative-religionist inclinations—this last influenced by Jonathan Z. Smith—led Neusner to read each ancient Jewish corpus as the constructions of a discrete "intellectual system."[35] His vision of many "Judaisms" in antiquity provoked Sanders' contrary case for a "common Judaism": not *many systems* but *one system*, one Judaism.[36] These scholars had no interest in preserving the ancient Christian suitcases, certainly not for ancient Christian reasons, but strangely they ended up enshrining them in research nonetheless.

Well before his conflict with Neusner, Sanders challenged age-old Christian readings of Judaism, but he did so by exploring how its "members" understood their place in this "religion."[37] Against long-standing Protestant imaginings, he compellingly argued, Jews were not worried about earning their God's favor, or membership in Judaism. As he famously put it: "A pattern of religion ... is the description of how a religion is perceived by its adherents to function ... of *how getting in and staying in are understood*: the way in which *a religion is understood to admit and retain members* is considered to be the way it 'functions.'" Jews were in by free divine election or choice, not by their efforts to gain entry. They kept the laws (covenant obligations) as a function of membership in this religious system, failure being remedied by repentance and atonement. Whereas Sanders was concerned to clarify how one got in and stayed in, it was only a matter of time before others would take up the corresponding phenomenon of *leaving* the religion of Judaism.[38] Such questions would not arise, however, if one did not impose "Judaism" on first-century texts and real-life conditions. We could then breathe fresher air and spare ourselves the stress of having to fit real people in a fictional category.

Let us try a thought experiment. What would happen if we took a leaf from Martin Goodman's magisterial *Rome and Jerusalem*, which methodically compares these two "ancient civilizations,"[39] and applied our linguistic habit for speaking of Judaea to Rome? Could we ask: "How did one get in and stay in Romism?" Or, "How did one leave Romism?" Such questions would seem absurd, and no one asks them. Why, then, should we not study Judaeans, their mother-*polis*, lawgiver, laws, customs, and individual characters such as Paul in the way we study other contemporary cultures, using the categories familiar to ancient writers?

The lexical categories known to Paul and his contemporaries, which had been around for centuries, permitted practically infinite individual variation. One belonged to a birth group (*genos, ethnos*) that had its peculiar laws and customs but humanity was gloriously diverse, a point that many writers from Herodotus to Julian celebrated. How individual Persians, Romans, or Spartans behaved in relation to their ancestral

---

[35] See Aaron W. Hughes, *Jacob Neusner: An American Jewish Iconoclast* (New York, NY: New York University Press, 2016), 48, 106–8, 137, 145–7.
[36] E. P. Sanders, *Judaism: Practice and Belief, 63 BCE–66 CE* (London: SCM, 1992).
[37] E. P. Sanders, *Paul and Palestinian Judaism* (London: SCM, 1977), 17.
[38] Stephen G. Wilson, *Leaving the Fold: Apostates and Defectors in Antiquity* (Minneapolis, MN: Fortress, 2004).
[39] Martin Goodman, *Rome and Jerusalem: The Clash of Ancient Civilizations* (London: Penguin, 2007).

traditions—how they viewed themselves and how others viewed them—was all to be played for. A Roman or Judaean male who felt perturbed by this variety, or the slovenly attitudes of the *vulgus* (*hoi polloi*, *'ammei ha-aretz*) toward ancestral norms, could always join a group with higher admission requirements: a philosophical school (Stoics, Pharisees, Essenes), priestly college, purity club, particular synagogue, or literary coterie. Formal or informal initiation into such groups was real, sometimes an ordeal. Certainly, one could speak of getting in and staying in such groups. Once admitted among fellow purists, members could safely share their peeves concerning the larger society's descent into the abyss. The larger society could have no such singlemindedness, however. Procreation has no standards.

Before glancing over Paul's letters in pursuit of our real-life historical question of how he presented himself to his groups in relation to Judaean ancestral tradition, it is worth trying to get a sense of the diversity that ancient categories permitted in relation to ancestral tradition, outside of in–out purity groups. Loyalty to one's *ethnos* and *polis* were axiomatic values, as we have seen (cf. Herodotus 3.38). But every literate person knew that new affiliations and changing identities were always possible, whether individual or collective, voluntarily or under compulsion. This kind of thing was not framed as moving in or out of *a religion*, or in the case of Judaea as getting in or out of *Judaism*. How was it framed?

I have mentioned Laconism, or Spartanizing, a famous example of cultural admiration and borrowing. The term referred in the first instance to those who allied with Sparta in the Peloponnesian War. But Sparta's fiercely disciplined way of life would remain highly attractive to modern societies from imperial Britain to Soviet Russia. Ancient admirers included philosophers, who liked its constitution from afar, and the young men who visited Laconia to see it in action—and faced periodic expulsion for the sake of maintaining cultural purity. In the opposite direction, Thucydides and the Spartans accused the Spartan king Pausanias of holding his ancestral laws in contempt, while favoring those of the Persians (1.132.1–2), a charge he did not accept but turned back on them.[40] There were no objective measures of such things. Individuals acted as they saw fit, and sometimes incurred the wrath of opponents for compromising the ancestral traditions. There are surely parallels in modern politics. Herodotus charged the Persian king Cambyses with forsaking his laws *and* everyone else's (3.36–38). The Scythians were a fund of fascination on this score. The reported curiosity of some of their leaders about foreign wisdom led other Scythians to violence. Anacharsis, Toxaris, and Scyles did not cease to be Scythians, or even royals (much less leave a "Scythism"), when they returned home as Athenian citizens or devotees of the Great Mother Cybele. Rather, they were deemed sufficiently defective Scythians to be killed for abandoning their ancestral traditions, or foreignizing as *2 Maccabees* might have put it.[41]

The general assumption was that the world's *ethnē* had become distinct by evolving their customs as they gradually separated from a few root *ethnē*—Dorians and Ionians,

---

[40] Mabel L. Lang, "Scapegoat Pausanias," *CJ* 63 (1967): 79–85.
[41] Herodotus 4.76–80 with Josephus, *Ap.* 2.269; Plutarch, *Banquet of the Seven Sages*; Lucian, *Anacharsis*, *Toxaris*, and *The Scythian*; Diogenes Laertius 1.101–105.

Egyptians and Arabs. Judaeans, like Colchians and others, were assumed to have sprung from Egyptian stock, whereas the originally Arab Idumeans had adopted Judaean laws under compulsion (Strabo 16.2.34), after which they could truly be called Judaeans in some sense (Josephus, *Ant.* 13.258)—while also remaining a distinct *ethnos* (*War* 4.233–82). Members of the Adiabenian royal family risked their lives when they embraced Judaean laws and customs in the 30s CE (*Ant.* 20.17–96) and later fought Romans alongside fellow Judaeans, without losing their identity as Adiabenians.[42] The countless others we hear about who associated with Judaean ways did so in different ways and degrees. Whatever passing Judaean contacts, they had lacked the "curial" authority to declare them "inside or outside Judaism." Such language was not available.

This is, incidentally, one reason why I prefer to render *Ioudaios* as "Judaean" *when I am interpreting ancient texts*. I have never seen anyone render *Ioudaia* other than as Judaea, a simple transliteration, following the principle we normally use for foreign place and people names. Since that regional-ethnic name had the same relation to *Ioudaios* in ancient usage as Syria to Syrian, Egypt to Egyptian, Rome to Roman, Idumea to Idumean, and Samaria to Samarian, since *Ioudaioi* frequently appear in texts juxtaposed with these others, and since the prevailing assumption was that a group's place of origin said much about its character and customs, it seems to me natural to render *Ioudaios* as "Judaean"—*if* my primary interest is in capturing what ancient audiences heard in the term, and not modern convenience. They knew of Judaea and therefore of Judaeans. This pairing also helps us to see that foreigners who emulated or embraced Judaean laws and customs did not join a "religion called Judaism," but allied themselves in some degree with this ancient *ethnos* and its *patrioi nomoi*. Their native *ethnos* identity could not disappear, in spite of such changes in affiliation. That is why Josephus could delight in saying (in effect) of a dead literary opponent who had reinvented himself more than once: "You can take Apion out of Egypt, but you can't

---

[42] With most scholars, Mark Nanos theologizes the Adiabene story in "The Question of Conceptualization: Qualifying Paul's Position on Circumcision in Dialogue with Josephus's Advisors to King Izates," in Nanos and Zetterholm, *Paul within Judaism*, 105–52. Nanos frames it for conversation with Paul (my emphasis): "The portrayal of King Izates sketched by Josephus is related in *a story he purports to have taken place within Diaspora Judaism*" (110). And "*Josephus characterizes the change that the non-Jew Izates makes to living like a Jew or practicing Judaism*"; "Josephus makes no mention of Jewish communities ... very individualistic"; "*Josephus* places the story within a Diaspora setting" (111); "Eleazar is ... likely a Pharisee"; "the *reader is made aware of two conflicting Jewish interpretations of what is faithful*" (116). The highlighted language is all supplied by Nanos, not by Josephus, who knows no "diaspora," Judaism, Pharisee Eleazar, or "two interpretations of what is faithful"—distinctive PWJ terminology, already primed to assimilate Paul. Josephus draws rather from the common Greek lexical bank: "About this time, Helena, queen of the Adiabenians, and her son Izates exchanged their way of life for the customs of the Judaeans (εἰς τὰ Ἰουδαίων ἔθη τὸν βίον μετέβαλον)" (*Ant.* 20.17–96). In *Ant.* 20.48 (the only one of 10 πίστις-cognates in the story Nanos notices), Josephus is restating the lesson of *Antiquities*: that God watches human affairs and rewards those who follow him (*Ant.* 1.14, 20; 10.277–278). As for the alleged individualism: Helena soon visits Jerusalem, sends famine relief for the city, constructs a palace, and plans her burial there (20.49–53, 95). Her sons also send their boys for education there, where they participate fully in Judaean life and eventually, as committed Judaeans, in the coming conflict with Rome (20.71). Their Judaean identity has clear corporate entanglements and is not a matter of private belief or religion. Cf. Mason, "Jews, Judaeans, Judaizing, Judaism: Problems of Categorization in Ancient History," *JSJ* 38 (2007): 506–8, and *Orientation to the History of Roman Judaea* (Eugene, OR: Wipf & Stock, 2016), 209–10.

take the Egyptian out of Apion!" (*Ap.* 2.138–144). Identity was complicated then, as it possibly is now.

Such comings and goings are particularly well known in relation to Judaean culture because of the relative wealth of evidence. Tacitus, Celsus, and Cassius Dio all complain about "those who have abandoned their own ways, professing those of the Judaeans" (Celsus in Origen, *C. Cels.* 5.41; cf. Tacitus, *Hist.* 5.5), with Dio adding that the term "Judaean" is used for both native Judaeans and "all those who emulate their legal precepts, though being of another *ethnos*" (Dio 37.17.1). From the Judaean side, Philo and Josephus talk of the welcome afforded to those who seriously wish to join their *ethnos* and live under their laws. They fully respect the hardships and ruptured family bonds that this can involve (Philo, *Virt.* 102–103; Josephus, *War* 2.463, 560; 7.45; *Apion* 2.280–286). Since Moses' laws reflect the very laws of nature, in Josephus' view (*Ant.* 1.18–23), Abraham the Chaldean could embrace them proleptically long before Moses lived (1.154–168); the Adiabenians complete that work's literary *inclusio* by embracing these laws in the last volume (20.17–96). In the Roman world particularly, the adoption of layered identities was not strange. Rome had extended its citizenship and identity to privileged foreigners, who added it to their existing identities with varying degrees of devotion.[43]

Josephus also recognized the opposite direction of traffic, though he was not pleased about it—about Judaeans who abandoned the laws of Moses or simply failed to follow them. Since the moral lesson of his *Antiquities* is that those who follow Moses' laws find success, whereas those who violate them meet disaster (*Ant.* 1.14, 20), the work furnishes examples of both kinds. Among the defectors and defaulters are various tyrants, rebels, kings including Saul and Herod, and high priests.[44] In Josephus' time, Tiberius Julius Alexander was from the most eminent Judaean family in Alexandria, nephew of Philo and son of a pillar of the Judaean community. Josephus praises this man's actions as governor of Judaea and later of Egypt, but notes matter-of-factly that he "did not persevere in the ancestral customs" (*Ant.* 20.100). No terrible consequence follows in Tiberius' case. Josephus is much more severe toward Antiochus of Antioch, son of the most eminent Judaean in that *polis*, because his defection seriously harmed his compatriots. Unnerved by anti-Judaean sentiment as the war was beginning in 67 CE, Antiochus wanted to prove his Greekness by demonstrating his revulsion toward Judaean customs (τοῦ μεμισηκέναι τὰ τῶν Ἰουδαίων ἔθη). He not only offered Greek-style sacrifices, but advised the authorities to force other Judaeans to do the same, as a test of loyalty to their *polis* of residence, after falsely accusing them of plotting to burn it down (*War* 7.47–53).

A different kind of loyalty question is pondered by Josephus in *War* 2.466–476. There, Judaeans from the south launch indiscriminate reprisals against Syrian *poleis* in retaliation for the massacre of their compatriots in Caesarea. The Judaean minority in Scythopolis join their townsfolk in defending the *polis* against these raids. But as soon

---

[43] Arthur M. Eckstein, *Mediterranean Anarchy, Interstate War, and the Rise of Rome* (Berkeley, CA: University of California Press, 2006), 244–316; Revell, *Roman Imperialism*.

[44] E.g., Nimrod (1.114); Korah (4.15–19); Abimelech (5.234); Hophni and Phineas (5.338–339); Saul (6.262–268); common people (11.40); Alexander Jannaeus (13.377–405); Herod (17.304–308); Drusilla 20.143–144; Ananus II (20.197–203); Ananias and other chief priests (20.204–207).

as the threat has passed, they become suspect as potential spies and traitors, and face a most unjust massacre. Although Josephus presents the Judaean raids as the actions of an *ethnos* made "animal-like" in its vengeful brutality (2.458–460), he curiously also blames the Judaeans of Scythopolis for having killed fellow Judaeans and sided with foreigners (What else could they have done?), actions that placed them "under a curse" and polluted them (2.472–473). He dramatically singles out the best Judaean fighter, Simon, to craft a mini-tragedy: Simon resolved to kill his family and himself, before the Scythopolitans could kill them. To cast Simon's activity as "leaving Judaism" would obscure the tragic tone of Josephus' account, which underscores the real-life struggle of conflicting loyalties. Tiberius Alexander, Antiochus, and Simon were not following different "Judaic systems." They were all Judaeans, who made the unique choices that seemed best in their particular situations. And, of course, we see them only through the literary construction of Josephus, not from an omniscient or even balanced perspective. We cannot ask them how they interpreted Judaean ancestral tradition in relation to their various identities.

Of the many ways in which one could (seem to) let observance of the ancestral laws slide, two others merit attention. The first appears in Philo's famous insistence that knowing the spiritual truth of scripture does not permit one "to dissolve the customs that more exalted and greater men than any of our time devised" (*Migr.* 90). We do not know the real-life situation behind this passage, but it raises the possibility that a purely philosophical approach was leading some Alexandrian Judaeans toward laxity in practically observing the laws. Second, the second chapter of *Wisdom of Solomon*, perhaps also from Alexandria, seems to describe a conflict among Judaeans, between those determined to enjoy life in the present and the "righteous," who accept the constraints of ancestral law, partly in anticipation of the life to come (2.12).[45] In any real human society, there must have been an enormous range of thought and practice, and *perceived* thought and practice, in relation to observance of ancestral custom, as there surely was of Rome's *mos maiorum*. Even civic officials who had to represent the national customs at public events may not have sincerely believed in them,[46] and a Greek's or Roman's enthusiasm for Egyptian or Judaean ways could effectively displace native allegiances. There is no reason to imagine that we would be able to categorize the kaleidoscope of individual possibilities, even if we wished to do so.

In sum, just as there was no Judaism in Paul's day, no authority could decide who was "in" or "out." Just as the choice to join the Judaeans did not obliterate one's Idumean or Adiabenian birth identity, becoming lax in relation to Judaean customs or following Greek or Roman ways to some extent could not stop one being Judaean—even if it caused rupture and scandal with family and friends. Paul was indisputably a Judaean,

---

[45] This standard reading is challenged by Jason Zurawski, "*Paideia*: A Multifarious and Unifying Concept in the Wisdom of Solomon," in *Pedagogy in Ancient Judaism* (ed. Karina M. Hogan; Atlanta, GA: SBL, 2017), 195–214. Even if he is right that this passage does *not* reflect an internal divide between more and less righteous Judaeans (I am not yet convinced), I stand by my general observations about human difference, ancient and modern.

[46] Cicero (*Div.* 2.33 [70]) and Pliny (*Ep.* 4.8) were both members of Rome's prestigious College of Augurs, with no belief at all in the divination behind it. Cf. Polybius 6.56.7–12; Diodorus 1.2.2; 34/35.2.47 on the importance of traditions connected with superstitious belief for public order.

for that was his *ethnos* by birth, and he faced the criticism of compatriots if he seemed so disloyal as to badmouth Judaea's ancestral traditions (Acts 21:21–36). The path he chose, including his posture toward the laws of Moses and ancestral custom, needs to be understood for itself, not as certifying his membership in a system constructed by modern scholarship or late-antique Christians. The next section suggests the beginnings of an approach to the historical Paul in his unique situation.

Paul's *Euangelion* in Relation to Judaeans and Their Ancestral Traditions

In asking how Paul presented himself to his groups, I follow four standard principles of historical research, which I lack the space to defend, namely: begin at the beginning, distinguish rhetoric from true beliefs, do not multiply entities unnecessarily, and work from the known to the unknown. These principles together recommend that we begin with 1 Thess, try to understand *it* (not Paul's psychology or formative influences) as his first audiences might have done, and work from what is clearest to what becomes foggier in his later letters.

The unmissable theme of 1 Thess, the earliest known text by a follower of Christ, is what Paul calls *The Announcement* (τὸ εὐαγγέλιον). He uses this loaded expression six times in this brief letter, glossing it variously as God's, ours, or Christ's. What *was* The Announcement? Before proceeding, we should register the evidential fact, because it is often missed, that the term is strange in ancient discourse and, among early Christian texts, distinctively Pauline. The neuter singular with article, τὸ εὐαγγέλιον, does not appear in pre-Christian authors, including the Septuagint. Even without the article, the singular noun is extremely rare.[47] The point is often missed because scholars have tended to blur cognates as though plural εὐαγγέλια and the cognate verb, which are relatively common in the LXX and the NT, were a mere *tomaeto* and *tomahto* difference. But in English, when someone refers to "messages" we think nothing of it. Messages are part of our daily reality. If, however, a colleague says, "This weekend I'm attending a retreat about *The Message*" (cue eerie music), the impact is completely different. The singular noun and definite article make us want to know: What is *The Message*?

Among the sudden explosion of seventy-six occurrences of εὐαγγέλιον in the NT, sixty appear in Paul and doubtful Paul, fifty-seven of these with the definite article, and often without elaboration as "The Announcement." He obviously expected his letters' audiences to know what he was talking about. By contrast, Luke, John and the Johannines, Hebrews, and reconstructed Q (also Coptic *Thomas*) lack the word altogether. Whatever we make of the outlier 1 Pet 4:17, therefore, εὐαγγέλιον language was evidently not *shared vocabulary* among early Christ-followers.

---

[47] The word was intelligible enough, but usually in the plural ("news"). Even without the article, the singular is rare (Homer, *Od.* 14.152, 166; Josephus, *War* 4.240; Plutarch, *Ages.* 33.4; *Demetr.* 17.6; *Mor.* [*Glor. Ath.*] 347d twice). With the article, it is overwhelmingly Pauline and later Christian; Plutarch has it once with the article, but the article is demonstrative, referring to a report just given, not absolute as in Paul.

This point becomes vividly clear from a tabular comparison of Mark with Matthew and Luke. Mark has a deep investment in εὐαγγέλιον language. It titles itself *The Origin of The Announcement* (1.1) and portrays Jesus himself proclaiming τὸ εὐαγγέλιον in his keynote (1.14, twice), then repeatedly identifying himself with τὸ εὐαγγέλιον (8.35; 10.29; 13.10; 14.9). While salvaging what they can from a largely uncongenial Mark, however, Matthew and Luke methodically remove such language from Jesus' horizon. It belongs with the large body of material they find wrong-headed in Mark—and what motivated them to craft new narratives. To be sure, Matthew retains four occurrences of εὐαγγέλιον, but it is no longer an absolute, self-evident category. Matthew reworks the instances it is kept as "the announcement *of the Reign* [of God]" (4:23; 9:35; 24:14)—this text's *Leitmotif*—or in one case uses it to mean only "this announcement" for the report of a specific incident (26:13). Luke makes no attempt to save the terminology, presumably because the author knows it to belong to the next generation, and expurgates it from Jesus' world.

The simplest deduction from this evidence is that τὸ εὐαγγέλιον was known in the first century to be distinctively Pauline language. This would also explain why Paul referred to his first visit to Philippi and Thessalonica as "the beginning of The Announcement" (Phil 4:15). In the second generation, only the first-known narrative treatment of Jesus' life, Mark, still had sufficient sympathy with Paul's mission to present an interpretation of Jesus' mission in these terms.[48]

Back in 1 Thess, then, Paul's opening thanksgiving declares his confidence that the new Christ-group in this port city has been selected for salvation, given their trusting response to The Announcement in spite of much harassment (1:5). Fortunately for us, he elaborates on the content of The Announcement. Others in Hellas have heard of how this group (a) "turned to God—from mere images to a living and true God" (1:9), (b) "to await his son from the heavens, whom he raised from the dead—(c) Jesus, who is rescuing us from the impending wrath" (1:10). We do not know everything that Paul said during his visit, of course. But given that the remainder of the letter elaborates only these same points, while reiterating that they constitute the heart of The Announcement that Paul brought during his visit (2:2, 4, 8, 9; 3:2), even insisting that Paul has little to add now, we have reason to infer that this was basically The Announcement that he proclaimed.

Even in Paul's incidental remarks, we see that the need to be prepared for Jesus' imminent return dominates The Announcement(e.g., 2:12). He concludes the letter's

---

[48] It cannot be mere coincidence that the later authors remove Mark's other distinctively Pauline emphases (along with τὸ εὐαγγέλιον): the *untrustworthiness of Jesus' family*, including his generally esteemed brother James, the head of the Jerusalem Christ-group (Mark 3:21-35; 6:1-6); the obtuseness of Jesus' first students and especially Peter, though he was James' leading associate in Jerusalem; Jesus' alleged preference for a spiritual family, not connected by natural bonds (3:35; 9:38-41); his alleged rupture with Judaean law (Mark 7:19); the lethal hostility of Judaean leaders toward Jesus *ab initio* (2:1-3:6); and Mark's pervasive sense of apocalyptic imminence, which the author uses Pauline language to create (9:1; 13:30-37). By supplying birth narratives, endorsing Jesus' students (adding redeeming endings to Mark's episodes), situating Jesus in a world of Judaean observance, and delaying or qualifying his Judaean opposition, Matthew and Luke independently reconfigure such unwelcome Pauline themes to yield completely different impressions of a Jesus deeply embedded in Judaean culture and continuous with it—until later ruptures, in Galilee (Matthew) or chiefly in Jerusalem (Luke).

first part by saying that he writes in the hope of strengthening them *so that* they will be "blameless before our God and father at the arrival of our lord Jesus with all his holy ones" (3:13). He then responds to three concerns that have come up after his departure, presumably conveyed via Timothy. For the first and third of these, Paul can only restate what he already told them when he was present. What should you do while waiting for Christ's return? Do *what I told you*, only more (4:1–2): pursue holiness and abstain from sexual sin, especially, each preserving your "vessel" and avoiding lust, while loving each other and minding your business (4:3–12). You ask me, "*When* will it happen?" *As I told you*, we don't know (5:1–2). Just watch, wait, and be prepared, because we aim to be rescued and not face wrath (5:9; cf. 1:10).

The only substantial insight Paul explicitly adds deals with their concern about believers who die before the consummate event. Here he provides information that he claims to have received from the risen Christ (4:15): anyone who dies beforehand will follow Christ's own path, of death followed by resurrection. In fact, the "dead in Christ" will precede *us*, who remain alive, and *we* shall follow to meet them in the clouds. This news should console them (4:16–18). Paul closes the letter by reaffirming the main point (5:23–24): their spirit, mind, and body must be preserved "blamelessly intact at the arrival of our lord Jesus Christ. The one who calls you is trustworthy. He will do this!" The entire letter, brief as it is, thus aims to consolidate Paul's bond with those in Thessalonica who have trusted The Announcement. Having worried that their trust might have faltered, in the face of abuse from their townsfolk (2:17–3:5), he expresses joy at Timothy's good report (3:1–12) and reassures them.

What does this first letter say about Paul's *ethnos*, its laws and customs? Nothing noticeable: no Torah, circumcision, covenant, scripture citations, Judaean tradition, calendar, or diet. It is not clear that anything in that vein would have been relevant to The Announcement. Scholars today know that *Christos* originates from Hebrew *Mashiach* or Messiah, but no such knowledge was necessary to understand this letter's use of *Christos*.[49] Indeed, nothing that Paul says about Christ in this letter requires biblical knowledge. He does not speak in Septuagintal tones about "idols" as a self-evident evil, or mention the second commandment in 1:9–10. He frames his followers' move from mere "representations" (εἴδωλα) to the "living and true" God, in language perfectly intelligible to Greeks. Philosophers had long since contemplated the true God as against mere representations. Greeks also knew about children of gods being restored after their death or removal to the underworld (Dionysus-Osiris, Attis, Persephone). Paul had only to convince such audiences that God had raised the crucified Jesus Christ from death and made him their lord who would soon return for them—a belief that Lucian would ridicule as compelling only to the gullible in his *Passing of Peregrinus*. This Paul succeeded in doing, with at least a few followers, and the claim formed the heart of The Announcement.

Although 1 Thess makes no call on biblical knowledge, its incidental reference to Judaeans is revealing. Expatiating on the abuse that Christ-followers in Hellas must endure before Christ calls them to heaven (1:6; 2:1; 3:3–4), Paul consoles them with

---

[49] This is an evidential fact. Cf. Pliny, *Ep.* 10.96; Tacitus, *Ann.* 15.44; Suetonius, *Claud.* 25.4 (Chrestus); Josephus, *Ant.* 18.63 [whatever the original was]; 20.200.

the thought that they are suffering, from their townsfolk, what earlier Christ-followers including himself faced from *their* compatriots: "the Judaeans, who killed the Lord Jesus and the prophets, and drove us out, and displease God and oppose all humanity, hindering us from speaking to the nations that they might be saved" (2:14–16). This passage vividly depicts a rupture between Christ-followers and their contemporaries, whether Judaean or Greek, who reject the alleged revelation. Scholars of a previous generation, certain that the condign punishment of Jews for rejecting Christ (2:16) must reflect post-70 conditions, declared at least this part of the passage a post-Pauline interpolation. That option has now fallen out of favor, for good reason.[50] Nowadays, the prevailing PWJ momentum in scholarship leads to the assumption that the passage reflects *internal* Jewish conflict.[51] But that is not what it obviously says. If we read only what Paul writes, without resorting to Romans or other material unavailable to his audience in Thessalonica, the point seems clear: all heaven-bound Christ-followers will face "persecution" from the champions of *ethnos*-custom, Judaean and Greek or Thessalonian.

The spectrum of ways in which *Judaean* Christ-followers had reacted to this pressure is another matter, irrelevant to Paul's points to the Thessalonians and not explored here. But he will later charge that some of his Judaean Christ-following opponents, based in Jerusalem, caved in to persecution from other Judaeans, and that this explains their hostility to his mission among non-Judaeans (Gal 6:12). He, by contrast, uses "new creation" language to stress the radical distinction between Christ-following and maintaining any such old commitments: *the old has passed away* (2 Cor 5:17; Gal 6:15).

As far as his surviving letters permit us to judge, Paul remained devoted to The Announcement for the rest of his life. At the end of his undisputed corpus, at least, he still feels the acute need to defend The Announcement (Rom 1:15–16), for which God has uniquely chosen him (1:1). He has by now fully proclaimed The Announcement in the eastern Roman Empire, he says, and so wants to proceed to "the remainder" of the nations, in the west (Rom 15:17–28; 1:13). The Parthian world and points farther east do not offer the same attraction.

If Paul had been free to continue touring The Announcement throughout the Roman Empire, without interference or challenge, perhaps any subsequent letters would have resembled 1 Thessalonians: he gathers a following, leaves town, and sends

---

[50] Birger A. Pearson, "1 Thessalonians 2:13–16: A Deutero-Pauline Interpolation," *HTR* 64 (1971): 79–94.

[51] Sarah E. Rollens, "Inventing Tradition in Thessalonica: The Appropriation of the Past in 1 Thessalonians 2:14–16," *BTB* 46 (2016): 123–32, offers an insightful précis of research. Her own argument, however, illustrates both circular argumentation (pre-70 Christians could not have opposed Jews because they were both "varieties of Judaism," 118) and the multiplication of entities: the passage is "an effort to form the identity of the nascent Thessalonian group, incorporating it into a wider mythic narrative—in this case, the narrative of Deuteronomistic theology ... widespread among other Jewish texts" (129). Rob van Houwelingen, "They Displease God and Are Hostile to Everyone—Antisemitism in 1 Thess 2:14–16?" *Sárospataki Füzetek* 22 (2018): 115–29, arguing that Paul's "sharp criticism of the Jews ... is moderated by the fact that he himself was Jewish" (118) and that Paul does not speak against "Judaism as such" (129), further illustrates the circularity. John C. Hurd, "Paul Ahead of His Time: 1 Thess. 2:13–16," in *Anti-Judaism in Early Christianity* (vol. 1: *Paul and the Gospels*; ed. Peter Richardson and David Granskou; Waterloo: Wilfred Laurier University Press, 1986), 21–36, brought a rare historical sensitivity to the issue.

an emissary for a follow-up visit. Those who remain faithful send back questions with the emissary, which Paul answers in an effort to consolidate the group. Things were not to be so simple, however. This was mainly because other influential Christ-teachers vehemently disagreed with Paul, and to some extent made their influence felt among his groups. If his other letters are notably more complex and problematic than 1 Thess, it is largely because these people were influencing his groups—intentionally or not—with their very different interpretations of Jesus. He would finally write his longest letter, reciprocally, to a group that he did not establish, with a half-apology for interfering in a Christ-association founded on different principles (Rom 15:14–24).

When faced with those challenges from eminent Christ-followers, Paul had to make adjustments and finesse the clear and simple claims of 1 Thess. And as Sanders crucially observed, it was only when facing these later contingencies that he felt compelled to raise the issues of Judaean law and custom—because others had raised them in order to criticize him for alleged misrepresentations of Christ.[52] To what extent his deeper views also changed as he penned his letters remains unclear to us, as it may have been to Paul himself.

1 Corinthians, apparently his next extant letter, already assumes that much has happened since his founding visit there, following a trip south from Thessalonica. He has come and gone, travelling back to Ephesus in Asia, and other teachers have passed through Corinth in the meantime. Or in Paul's words: "I laid a foundation, and another is building over it; let each take care how he builds over it!" (1 Cor 3:10). The over-builders he names are Apollos, elsewhere described as a Judaean thinker and orator from Alexandria (Acts 18:24–28), and the figure most prominent among Jesus' direct students, Cephas (Peter), a Galilean fisherman according to the gospels, who has surprisingly travelled abroad in the Greek world with his wife, Jesus' brothers, and their spouses too (9:5–6). Whatever their intentions may have been, serious rifts have now opened, because elements from Paul's group are tending to prefer what these teachers are saying (1:11–12; 3:22). Paul has already written to the group at least once since his departure (5:9). We know precious little about that lost letter, or much else that was happening, including what exactly Jesus' family members and students taught, or how they viewed their relationships with Paul and each other.

Nevertheless, it seems that Apollos is Paul's most immediate concern, given that he singles him out as the one building on his foundation (3:4–11). Paul also vigorously disparages wisdom and rhetoric (4:6), while apparently punning on Apollos' name (1:19: ἀπολῶ τὴν σοφίαν τῶν σοφῶν). Tellingly, the Corinthians ask Paul, their epistolary contact, when *Apollos* and perhaps the others will return (16:12). It is not clear that they wanted Paul back. It seems that they are not so eager for his return, given that he urgently dispatches Timothy, "my beloved child and trustworthy in the lord, who will remind you of *my ways* in Christ Jesus"—and in a clearly defensive posture *threatens* a follow-up visit, with a stick to enforce discipline (4:17–21). And when he does eventually visit, it is "painful," causing a very serious rift between Paul and the community he established (2 Cor 1:23–2:7).

---

[52] Sanders, *Paul and Palestinian Judaism*, 434–42.

In the febrile atmosphere of 1 Cor, the clearest thread of contention turns on the circumstance that some in the community have come to think of Christ's significance in ways rather different from those of Paul's Announcement. They have come to prefer the notion that following Christ is about finding a kind of fullness, knowledge, and peace in this life, which makes better sense than the misery and suffering Paul predicts before Christ's heavenly return (4:8–13). Other concerns of theirs, which Paul has heard by various means (7:1), would be easy to link up with the same picture, though we cannot join the dots with confidence: whether one should stop engaging with the world in light of Christ's return, as Paul counsels, especially in relation to marriage (ch. 7: he prefers no marriage in light of the imminent end); why they might not eat good meat even if it came to market after temple sacrifices, since there are no real gods other than the true One (chs. 8–10; he prefers not); manifestations of spiritual gifts (chs. 12–14); and the central question of physical resurrection, for Christ and then for his followers—the heart of Paul's Announcement, which some of them now doubt (15:12).

The main point for our purposes is that Judaean law and tradition are still not explicit issues, even in this long and varied letter. Paul cites a few carefully chosen scriptural proof-texts,[53] though these scattered passages, like his quotations of Jesus' sayings and other texts (2:9; 15:32–33), serve his arguments about being "in Christ" and do not resemble midrash, or an attempt to find deeper meaning in scripture as such. They have nothing to do with faithfully living by Torah. If we ask why he includes flashes of scripture at all, or what they might mean to his mainly non-Judaean assembly (12:2), a simple explanation might be that his Judaean rivals had made a great deal of Torah in their teaching, and he felt the need to show that he too could use it, in keeping with his Announcement.

Paul also mentions Judaean holidays that he is observing (16:8). His reference to Passover (5:7) suggests that he shares this major Judaean holiday with his followers. But this might reflect larger Christian practice, in commemorating Christ's death and resurrection at Passover time. We do not know. We must remember that the ancient world knew no default or fallback, secular calendar, as we have today. The Judaean calendar was the one in which Paul had been raised. He could not simply abandon it and still have a way of reckoning time. To reject it, he would have had to adopt the calendar of another *polis*, embracing the sacred festivals and sacrifices of Ephesus, Corinth, or Rome. Why would he do that, especially if he understood Christ's significance from Judaean foundations now supplanted? Just as many ex-Christians still celebrate Christmas and Easter, in some sense, it is not difficult to imagine that the Judaean Paul continued to pattern his life by the calendar in which he was raised, even though he declared Moses' law obsolete. Real life is not an academic seminar or exercise in pure logic.

In Paul's remaining principal letters to groups he has established, this question of Paul's attitude toward Moses' laws becomes ever more prominent, forced onto center stage by these conflicts with others. From Phil 3:2–21 it appears that someone is telling his Christ-followers that they must observe Judaean *nomoi*. In response, Paul makes it

---

[53] E.g., 1 Cor 1:19, 31 (omitting the reference to knowledge from Jer 9:23); 9:9; 10:1–8, 26; 14:2; 15:54–55.

clear as can be that he considers his Judaean past less than worthless now, "on account of the better possession of the knowledge of Christ Jesus my lord." He excoriates the "dogs" who want his groups to be circumcised. What he includes as "loss," or even—a word unfit for church reading—excrement (σκύβαλα), though he *formerly* valued these greatly (3:8), include his Judaean ancestry, circumcision, membership of the Pharisees, and zeal for Torah. None of that matters *now*, he declares (3:9): not because he has begun following a different "Judaism," but because Christ's revelation and imminent return render any such ethnos-nomos heritage irrelevant. All humanity can be rescued now on the same basis, only by commitment to Christ. Confident that "our *politeuma* is in heaven," he rails against the teachers who demand affiliation with an earthly community: their "end is destruction" (3:17–21).

In 2 Cor, Paul is shown as even more distracted by teachers highlighting their authentic Hebrew descent and apostleship, who in his words offer a "different Jesus" (2 Cor 10:12–11:23). They too will meet a horrible end (11:15). This letter or its sequel (2 Cor 1–9), depending on whether one treats 2 Cor as a unity, steps boldly on the Judaizers' turf with a rereading of the fundamental Sinai story. Paul claims Moses himself already realized that Torah's glory was merely temporary and fading—a fact he had to conceal with a covering over his head. Five times in a short space (3:7, 11, 13, 14, 17) Paul repeats that Moses' law has been "nullified" by the greater glory of Christ (ὅτι ἐν Χριστῷ καταργεῖται). Galatians develops the same position, as it seeks to prove *from the law*, for those now enthralled by its observance, that the law is obsolete. Moses' law lasted only until Christ's arrival (Gal 3:1–4:7). "The present Jerusalem ... is in slavery with her children" (4:25).

Paul's letters to his own assemblies, where he asserted a measure of authority even in the face of competition, thus present a coherent picture of the relationship between The Announcement and his ancestral, Judaean traditions. Granted, these letters are by no means uniform in content or tone, and their contingent factors on many matters are evident. Paul must find ever new ways of explaining Christ's return, in the face of high-powered and plausible challenges. For decades, scholars have been developing three main lines of explanation for the differences from one letter to the next: an evolution in his thinking;[54] a "coherent" matrix or core adapted to contingencies;[55] or plain human inconsistency or carelessness.[56] From a historical perspective, however, one might ask why Paul's occasional letters should have to shoulder the burden of "consistency,"[57] a standard we would not dream of applying to Cicero or Pliny.

However that may be, Paul's posture toward his Judaean past in these letters to his own groups does not seem extraordinarily complex or vague. The Announcement is about a radically "new creation: the old has gone away" (2 Cor 5:17; Gal 6:15). He is preparing himself and the chosen (= those who have trusted The Announcement) for evacuation from the impending wrath of God, to be with Christ in heaven—a

---

[54] E.g., Charles H. Buck and Greer Taylor, *Saint Paul: The Development of His Thought* (New York, NY: Scribner, 1969).
[55] E.g., J. Christiaan Beker, *Paul the Apostle: The Triumph of God in Life and Thought* (Philadelphia, PA: Fortress, 1980).
[56] E.g., Heikki Räisänen, *Paul and the Law*, 2nd ed. (Tübingen: Mohr Siebeck, 1987).
[57] Räisänen, *Paul*, xi–xvi.

scenario that would later attract Porphyry's criticism that human bodies do not belong in heavenly spheres.[58] Partly anticipating this objection, perhaps, Paul insists that preparation for heaven requires both a spiritual mode of life, free of carnal attachment, and a final transformation to spirit, following Christ's example, before the upward journey (1 Cor 15:50–53).

Since Paul attached The Announcement to a historical figure whom he had not personally known before his crucifixion, but others had known intimately, his Announcement was certain to put some noses out of joint. After a brief meeting with Peter and Jesus' brother in Jerusalem, he steered clear of the Judaean mother-*polis*. When he returned there after fourteen years, he says, he did so only because of "a revelation" and not from any obligation or summons—though still he worried that these influential Christ-followers would sink his project (Gal 2:2). It is unclear that they ever did accept The Announcement. Even when trying to put the best face on their encounter, Paul can speak only of his promise to Jesus' family and students that he would speak to non-Judaeans only, and "remember the poor" in Jerusalem. With this, they politely shook his hand and sent him off (Gal 2:2–10). The "pillars" themselves also did some travelling, however, as we have seen, and became known to Paul's groups. Whether or not they intended to interfere, their assumption that Christ-followers should follow Judaean laws got around, and they or people influenced by them became quite insistent. In dismissing these claims, Paul used his own formidable knowledge of scripture to make claims about the law's temporary nature and displacement by Christ.

Paul's restriction of Moses' law to a bygone period goes a long way toward explaining his repeated floggings by Judaean compatriots (2 Cor 11:24). Moses' law was the foundation of Judaean life everywhere: the law that Judaean minority communities in many places had a hard-won permission to observe, exempting them from being subject to the prevailing laws in many *poleis*.[59] Yet outside writers occasionally enjoyed ridiculing Moses as a supposed outcast from Egypt: a magician, leper, or deeply antisocial.[60] Judaeans did not need one of their own now seeming to join in such deprecations, just as they did not need Antiochus of Antioch undermining their legitimacy there (Josephus, *War* 7, earlier), especially given that Paul was basing his claims on the post-mortem appearances of a Judaean crucified in Jerusalem.

Even Acts, though generally a calming and homogenizing narrative, claims that when Judaeans from Asia spotted Paul near Jerusalem's temple, they were outraged because he was "teaching everyone everywhere against the people, the law, and this place" (Acts 21:28). The same text claims that Christ-following Judaeans, who insisted on maintaining Judaean law, were under the impression that Paul was teaching "all Judaeans living among the nations *defection from Moses*: advising them not to circumcise their children or continue in the customs" (21:21). These impressions

---

[58] Porphyry (vel sim.) in Macarius Magnes, *Apocr.* 4.2; in Hoffmann, *Against the Christians*, 68–9.
[59] Virtually every page of Josephus' *Antiquities* and *Against Apion*, composed for Roman audiences in the first instance, is about the excellence of Moses' laws as those governing Judaean life. Outside observers never doubted that Moses was the lawgiver under whose ordinances Judaeans everywhere lived, e.g.: Hecataeus of Abdera in Diodorus 40.3.38; Apollonius Molon in Josephus, *Apion* 1.145; Diodorus 34–35.1.1–5; Strabo, *Geog.* 16.2.34–46; Tacitus, *Hist.* 5.2–4.
[60] See Apollonius Molon in Josephus, *Apion* 1.145 and Tacitus, *Hist.* 5.2–4.

are difficult to explain historically as the invention of this author. Left with only tiny fragments from Paul's life, we do not have clear examples of what he said to other Judaeans, unless the letter to the Romans fits that bill. But already to the Corinthians he implies that he did talk with Judaeans when the opportunity arose, and when he did so he adapted his language for the sake of The Announcement:

> While being free from all, I have enslaved myself to all, so that I might win more. To the Judaeans I became *as a Judaean*, that I might win Judaeans; *to those under law as one under law*, though I am *certainly not under law myself*, that I might win those under law; to the law-less as law-less—though I certainly am not law-less with God, but in the "law of Christ"—that I might win the law-less. To the weak I became weak, that I might win the weak. I became *all things to all people* so that *by all means* I might save some. And I do all that *because of The Announcement*, so that I might be a partaker in it with others. (1 Cor 9:19–23)

It is hard to see how Paul could have put more starkly the primacy of The Announcement and the resulting irrelevance of all other norms. Feeling an imperative to "rescue" as many as possible, he persuades Judaeans and foreigners in *whatever language will work*, though he claims no attachment except to The Announcement—and is certainly not "under law."

I can almost hear any colleagues who may still be reading saying, "Yes, but what about *Romans*?" The question I proposed at the outset concerned Paul's letters to the *groups he founded*. Even there, my interest is not in his internal thoughts or formative influences, which can only be conjectured, but in how his letters present his relationship to Judaean ancestral law. When Paul comes to write Romans, by contrast his proclamation of The Announcement in the east is over (Rom 15:18–28). Rome had apparently not been on his itinerary in declaring The Announcement, in part because the Christ group there was established by others. But now his plans have changed. Since he has decided to go as far as Spain to reach "the remainder" of non-Judaeans, he *can* hope to visit Rome without causing offence and with due respect, purely as a passing-through point, since he must pass that way anyway. His groups in Philippi, Thessalonica, Corinth, or Galatia did not know his letter to the Romans, however, and that is why I have ignored it while trying to understand his correspondence with them.

That said, the Romans reflex is so powerful in scholarship, even all-consuming, that some readers will think I am cheating if I ignore this unusual text. So I shall make a brief effort. Following our principle of stressing what is clearest, we see immediately that Romans continues to present Paul as uniquely linked with The Announcement (1:1, 9). He explains that "according to my Announcement" Christ will return to judge the world (2:16), ties The Announcement to his work among the nations (10:16; 11:28; 15:16, 19), and ends with a greeting to the group in Rome based on "my Announcement" (16:25). What his audience itself believes about Christ, tellingly, he *cannot* call The Announcement, but rather "your kind of teaching" or "the teaching you learned" (6:17; 16:17). Indeed, he will bring his Announcement when he visits, *because he is not ashamed of it* (1:15–16). He writes partly in preparation for that visit, but also for more urgent reasons. Heading first to Jerusalem, to convey the financial gift he has raised in Hellas, from his own assemblies, he appeals to the Roman for their support in ensuring that the gift will be accepted, and for their intercessions to ensure that he will be protected from "unbelievers" or unpersuaded in Judaea (15:25–32).

Why seek the support of Roman Christ-followers before heading to Jerusalem? Since Romans assumes Judaean perspectives, knowledge of texts, and even technical terms (3:25), uniquely calls Abraham "*our* physical ancestor" (4:1), addresses the audience *as* Judaeans who know the law, and adopts "we" language with them (2:17, 23, 27; 3:9; 7:1), while consistently speaking of Gentiles in the third person (even at 11:13, telling his audience "Now I am speaking to the nations/Gentiles"), and since the letter hardly makes a claim without a scriptural proof-texts, it seems to me that these Christ-followers are Judaeans.

That is why, uncharacteristically falling over himself to be polite with a group he did not establish (1:11–12), Paul bobs and weaves to defend The Announcement from specifically *Judaean* criticisms. Circumcision and Judaean identity have *enormous* value, he stresses (3:1-2)—although none with respect to salvation in Christ (3:30). Is the law finished with, or is it sin? Perish the thought! (3:31; 7:12)—although it points to Christ and otherwise is irrelevant (3:21; 4:14; 10:4). Has God abandoned Israel? Absolutely not! (9:2-6a)—but then again, not all "Israel" are *really* Israel, are they? (9:6b). God's choice of Israel is irrevocable, and so *all* Israel will be saved—at least when they cease to oppose The Announcement (11:25-32).

The two-covenant (*Sonderweg*) reading of Rom 11:26—all Judaeans will be saved as such, without following Christ—might make sense if the line is taken by itself, at Paul's moment of writing, deducing from the formulation in this verse alone. If exegetes of this persuasion are right about that, however, perhaps they would agree that an editor would have advised Paul to express himself much more clearly, without all the distracting build-up of chapters 1 through 8 or such remarks as at 11:14: "might save *some* of them"). Again, it is hard to imagine another historical figure (cf. Churchill, Roosevelt, Tony Blair) with whom we would pull out one remark, from one letter or speech, and when he was trying everything to woo a particular group insist that this was *the foundation* of his thinking in spite of all evidence to the contrary. For the overwhelming evidence of both Paul's other letters and of Romans itself points, as we have seen, in a different direction. Paul considers it rather important to follow Christ, as he has done.

Although this arguably last letter is clearly preoccupied with Judaean issues, most scholars understand it to have been written primarily for Gentiles.[61] I cannot follow

---

[61] W. G. Kümmel, *Introduction to the New Testament* (trans. H. C. Kee; Nashville, TN: Abingdon, 1975), 309: "essentially a debate between the Pauline gospel and Judaism, so that the conclusion seems obvious that the readers were Jewish Christians," *except* that "the letter contains statements which indicate specifically that the community was Gentile Christian," and "Any attempt to gain a picture of the readers of Rom[ans] must be made from this established point of view." Cf. Andrew D. Das, *Solving the Romans Debate* (Minneapolis, MN: Fortress, 2007) and Neil Elliott, *The Rhetoric of Romans: Argumentative Constraint and Strategy and Paul's Dialogue with Judaism* (Minneapolis, MN: Fortress, 2007), both of which highlight the Jewish content but insist on a gentile audience. Alleged proof of a gentile audience is found in Rom 1.5-6, 13; some translations embed

this reasoning, finding it much easier to understand Romans as a case study of the principles Paul boasts of in 1 Cor 9:19–23 (earlier). For our question, however, it does not matter greatly whether Romans' audience comprised Judaeans or devotees of Jupiter Optimus Maximus: first, because he did not write the letter to his own groups, and second, because "Judaism" does not appear. As for Paul's relationship with his ancestral traditions, while saying every reassuring thing he can about Israel and the law of Moses in this unusual letter, he still clings to The Announcement, which declares salvation through Christ alone for Judaeans and Greeks on the same basis.

From Solution to Problem

Although I depart substantially from Sanders' approach to Paul in avoiding "Judaism" or "patterns of religion," and in not assuming that Paul had to be a coherent thinker,[62] Sanders' picture of Paul's relationship to his ancestral tradition seems to me to explain what Paul says to his "assemblies" better than the NP can. He claimed that his encounter(s) with the risen Christ had transformed his life; without that transformative experience, Paul would have remained happily devoted to his ancestral tradition, and persecuting Christ-followers. Following the divine encounter, however, all that mattered was union with Christ and preparing for his return, meanwhile fulfilling his unique mission to bring The Announcement to the nations. To be "in Christ" was to be a "new creation," which rendered existing structures and allegiances, laws and customs, without point or purpose. Whereas Sanders' Paul followed a "pattern of religion" very different from Judaism's covenantal nomism, I consider "Judaism" a historical distraction. But I share Sanders' impression that Paul's encounter with Christ, and not scriptural exegesis or the like, led him to jettison all earth-bound law and custom. Precisely that claim to be free from *nomoi* would become central in outsider criticism of Christ-followers, and among such figures as Tertullian, Minucius Felix, and Origen in the following decades (in the first section in this chapter).

Dunn's 1982 lecture launched "The New Perspective on Paul," we have seen, but in a roundabout way. He first allows that, among the many contributions to Pauline studies of past decades, only Sanders' *Paul and Palestinian Judaism* deserves the accolade of a "new perspective on Paul."[63] This makes it sound as though Sanders' view *is* the new perspective of the title. So the reader is surprised to discover that Dunn then

---

this assumption (NRSV, NIV, ESV). But in the first passage, Paul mentions his own work among the nations (ἐν πᾶσιν τοῖς ἔθνεσιν; cf. Gal 1:16; 2:2; Acts 15:12; 21:19) and before ingratiatingly comparing his audience, "*among whom you also* are called of/for Christ" (ἐν οἷς ἐστε καὶ ὑμεῖς κλητοὶ Ἰησοῦ Χριστοῦ; cf. 1 Pet 2:12). He says only that he and they are likewise among (ἐν) the nations (cf. Acts 21:21 on Judaeans: τοὺς κατὰ τὰ ἔθνη πάντας Ἰουδαίους). In 1:13 Paul writes προεθέμην ἐλθεῖν πρὸς ὑμᾶς … ἵνα τινὰ καρπὸν σχῶ καὶ ἐν ὑμῖν καθὼς καὶ ἐν τοῖς λοιποῖς ἔθνεσιν. Although scholars usually read τοῖς λοιποῖς ἔθνεσιν as "[to] the *other* gentiles" (in addition to *you*), the ordinary sense of τοῖς λοιποῖς is "[to] those *remaining*, the rest." Given Paul's plan to stop in Rome en route to the west, it is easier to see there as a distinction between the Romans and the remainder of the Gentiles he plans to reach; cf. Steve Mason, *Josephus, Judea, and Christian Origins: Methods and Categories* (Peabody, MA: Hendrickson, 2009), 303–28.

[62] Sanders, *Paul and Palestinian Judaism*, 433.
[63] James D. G. Dunn, "The New Perspective on Paul," *BJRL* 65 (1983): 95–122.

applauds everything in Sanders' book *except* its view of Paul. This view Dunn considers retrograde, inferior even to the old Lutheran Paul.[64] An even bigger surprise is Dunn's reason: "The Lutheran Paul has been replaced by an *idiosyncratic* Paul who in *arbitrary* and *irrational* manner turns his face against the glory and greatness of Judaism's covenant theology and *abandons Judaism simply because it is not Christianity*."[65] Dunn imagines Paul as only one of a class of Jews who became Christ-followers, who must all have had similar reasons for doing so.[66] This assumption leads him to reject Sanders' "arbitrary and abrupt discontinuity between Paul's gospel and Jewish past." Dunn prefers to see Paul as reasoning himself into following Christ from scripture, as a Jew concerned only about the too-narrow "nationalist and racial" character of contemporary Judaism. Being committed to ancestral tradition, Dunn proposes, Paul saw Christ as a means of dropping the "badges" of Jewish exclusivity. "Logic," "argument," and "corollaries" appear more than half a dozen times each in the famous lecture's latter part.

But the ancient recipients of Paul's letters, who were perhaps more willing than modern professors to believe that God spoke to people, might not have found Paul's move (according to Sanders) so strange. Is it arbitrary or irrational to do what God tells you? The author of Acts actually thematizes *necessary obedience* to divine instruction, irrespective of human preference, to explain Christian origins—and uses Paul as Exhibit A (9:3–19; 26:19). Should Paul have remonstrated with the divine presence: "Well I'm flattered, but could you offer a seminar for me and my Jewish friends? *If you can convince us* that this is all grounded in scripture, *and* if we can all be apostles (I wouldn't wish to be idiosyncratic), I'll consider your offer"? Dunn's assumption that Paul was one of a class, the members of which must have followed Christ from similar reasoning, seems to me controverted by nearly every line from Phil 3:2 through Gal 6, with Romans in the bargain. Paul's claims of personal selection, revelation, and unique authority leap out everywhere: "When the one who had set me apart from my mother's womb and called me ... was pleased to reveal his son in me, that I might proclaim him among the nations, I did not consult with flesh and blood" (Gal 1:15–16). "Am I not an apostle? Have I not seen Jesus ...? Are you not my work in the lord? ... You are the seal of my apostleship!" (1 Cor 9:1). "Last of all ... he appeared to me. ... I am what I am ... I struggled far more than all of them [apostles] put together' (15:8, 10). "I reckon myself in no way behind the oh-so-grand apostles" (2 Cor 11:5). No less, Paul speaks pervasively of abrupt change, novelty, and disjunction: "If one is in Christ, it's a new creation. The old things went away. Look: new things have come to be!" (Gal 6:15). He *formerly* pursued the ancestral traditions with zeal, but now regards those who read scripture without Christ as veiled and blinded by "the god of this age" (2 Cor 3:17–4:4). If Paul's Announcement had been more in the vein of "I'm OK, you're OK," or "You know, I've discovered a new reading of Isaiah," it would surely not have generated such urgency—or intense controversy.

---

[64] Dunn, "New Perspective," 102–3.
[65] Ibid.," 109.
[66] Ibid., 101 (my emphasis): "Paul was by no means the only Jew who became a Christian and it is difficult to see such an *arbitrary* jump from one 'system' to another commending itself quite as much as it ... did to *so many of his fellow Jews*."

Giambattista Vico (1668–1744), founder of a modern philosophy of history, warned against five prejudices that ensnare historians. The third, "the conceit of the scholars," meant "delight in fancying an inaccessible esoteric wisdom among the ancients, coinciding miraculously with the opinions professed by each one of themselves [the modern scholars], which they dress in the garb of antiquity in order to enforce their acceptance."[67] That is to say, we imagine that the ancients thought as we do, ignoring their unavoidable weirdness as figures from an alien past. Classicists and biblical exegetes—I say this as a fully complicit commentator—are especially prone to this fallacy because of the great distance between us and the world we study and yet the very hominess of "Judaeo-Christian" tradition. We feel that we should understand it intuitively and feel at home in it. Dunn's call for a reasonable, scholarly Paul seems to me to embody this pull, which we all feel in some way.

Conclusion

Many, perhaps most historical questions are worth pursuing even if we cannot definitively answer them. When we investigate why an actor in the past did something, or why an event occurred, we are immersing ourselves in their world to rethink their thoughts and situations. Since history is first of all the act of investigating, nothing is lost and much is gained by this effort to live imaginatively in the foreign world of the past, whether we ever figure things out completely or not. Whether Paul was inside or outside "Judaism" is, by contrast, a pointless historical question in my view. This is *not* because it cannot be answered, but because even trying to answer it, merely framing such a question, takes us away from the ancient world, away from Paul's world. Discussing the issue requires us to find out *from each other* what *we* mean by "Judaism"—a common-room discussion requiring several levels of abstraction.

In this essay I have tried to examine with readers a different and simpler question, which is susceptible to at least partial (dis)confirmation: "How did Paul present himself to the groups of Christ-followers he established, in relation to Judaean law, custom, and culture?" Paul was a Judaean by *ethnos*, and that he could not change. He was indelibly circumcised, and he continued to follow at least some key moments in the Judaean calendar. The degree to which he "remained in the ancestral customs" of the Judaeans, as Josephus might have put it, is a different matter. Since most of what we all do comes from custom or habit, not rational analysis before each action, even if we could watch Paul acting in certain contexts we might not know what he was thinking or how he reconciled his thought with his actions. Where we *can* make some progress is with Paul's *self-representation* to his "in Christ" groups in letters.

From this it emerges, first, that he was sure of having been singled out by God, and son Christ, to prepare the chosen among the nations for rescue to heaven. Second,

---

[67] This is Benedetto Croce's summary, in *The Philosophy of Giambattista Vico* (trans. R. G. Collingwood; New York, NY: Macmillan, 1913), 157, of passages from Vico's *Scienza Nuova* (1744), accessible in English in Thomas G. Bergin and Max H. Fisch, eds., *The New Science of Giambattista Vico* (Ithaca, NY: Cornell University Press, 1948), such as I.vii (59); II.iv (127–128), and III (330).

"The Announcement" he lays out to his groups lacked any Judaean requirements and required no biblical knowledge. Third, in response to those who thought that he *should* include Judaean content, he responded with a firm "No." This was not because he had a different Judaism or because his groups were Gentiles. It was because, for him, being in Christ rendered every *nomos*, of Greeks or of Judaeans, a dead letter. Moses' law too had served only until Christ. Paul was emphatically not "under law." Fourth, Paul declared as vividly as one could imagine his abandonment of the zeal he formerly had for his ancestral traditions. Fifth, he was happy to eat with non-Judaeans in a way that leading Judaean Christ-followers—Peter, Paul's associate Barnabas, and a group from Jesus' brother James—could not accept. Sixth, as word about these points got around, from Rome to Jerusalem, Paul's Announcement caused deep offence to other Judaeans, whether Christ-followers or not. Seventh, Paul faced a rough reception from Judaeans everywhere, which included repeated whippings, because of The Announcement.

These indications present a fairly unified picture, though still beginning and partial, of one Judaean who consciously abandoned his ancestral custom. He did this not for the more common reasons of laxity, intermarriage, or attraction to the ways of another *ethnos*, however, but because he claimed an encounter with the resurrected figure of Jesus Christ, which in his view displaced the *ethnos-polis-nomos* foundations of ancient identity. This radical departure from the long-established, essential-seeming categories of life would require successive generations of Christ-followers in Paul's trajectory—by no means the only Christian trajectory—to explain themselves, when Christ did not return to evacuate them. Their predicament remained awkward until perhaps already Tertullian and Origen in anticipation, but certainly Eusebius and his successors, managed to turn the tables and reform the social-political lexicon in light of Christianity's ascendancy, so as to value this faith-based identity over *ethnos*- and *polis*-affiliation.

2

A Displaced Jew: The Specific Nature of Paul's Earthly Identity

Leif Vaage

In his capacity as a missionary, Maurice Leenhardt once suggested to a New Caledonian elder that Christianity had introduced the notion of spirit (esprit) into Canaque thought. "Spirit? Bah!" the old man objected: "You didn't bring us the spirit. We already knew the spirit existed. We have always acted in accord with the spirit. What you've brought us is the body."[1]

Defining the specific nature of the enduring relationship between Paul's apostolic adventures "in Christ" and their social origin within "Second Temple Judaism" has been a core conviction—or at least a chief concern—of Terence L. Donaldson for much of his scholarly career.[2] The same cannot be said of me; at least not until quite recently. Perhaps late can still be better than never. In any case, in this essay I now join my long-time friend and colleague in his evermore popular scholarly effort to find Paul anew within what once was deemed to be of old. At issue is what I shall be calling Paul's earthly identity.

This essay summarizes the main argument of a larger monograph that still is under construction, whose working title also is: "Paul: A Displaced Jew." The monograph explores the multiple ways in which the question of the early Christian apostle's Jewish identity complicates not only many aspects of traditional Pauline scholarship but also some conventional habits of Jewish historiography. In addition, this question serves to expose how deeply imbricated both enterprises are in certain decidedly modern political projects.[3]

---

[1] See Marshall Sahlins, *What Kinship Is—And Is Not* (Chicago, IL: The University of Chicago Press, 2013) 19; further, Maurice Leenhardt, *Do Kamo* (Chicago, IL: The University of Chicago Press, 1979), 164.

[2] Cf. Terence L. Donaldson, *Paul and the Gentiles: Remapping the Apostle's Convictional World* (Minneapolis, MN: Fortress, 1997); also Donaldson, *Judaism and the Gentiles: Jewish Patterns of Universalism (to 135 CE)* (Waco, TX: Baylor University Press, 2007).

[3] As a summary statement of the monograph, the present essay does not include all the supporting references that will be provided there for many of the claims to follow.

Both this essay and the monograph that it summarizes are being written within the framework of another even larger project that will be, for want of a better term, a biography of the same erstwhile Paul. The larger project gathers together the results of an extended inquiry into the implied "historical" author of the "less inauthentic" canonical letters of Paul, which I have conducted as a pair of doctoral seminars over the last 20 years or so as part of the Advanced Degree program of the Toronto School of Theology where Prof. Donaldson has been giving courses on the same set of issues, albeit in a somewhat different direction. He and others will decide whether here, at last, our paths finally coincide or definitively diverge.[4]

Introduction: Stating the Obvious

In the context of the ancient Mediterranean world, Paul was obviously *Ioudaios*. This social identity, moreover, never became a problem for him. At no point did Paul ever experience the fact that he was this kind of a human being as anything other than a self-evident truth about him as well as, arguably, the sign of a certain privilege. One could therefore begin to wonder how and why the question of Paul "within Judaism" now is deemed to be a necessary and/or important topic to discuss.

At the same time, however, as someone who obviously was *Ioudaios* Paul also came to think—under the aegis of an experience that he called "Christ"—that this "fleshly" identity—which is how he described being *Ioudaios*—was not the last word to be spoken about him (just as the "Gentile" identity of many of Paul's eventual coreligionists was likewise not the last word to be said about them, at least not by Paul). In fact, the whole debate about social "identity" in these terms would have been for Paul essentially beside the point were it not that it kept coming up in the developing and ongoing squabbling about what it meant sociopolitically to be a manifestation of "Israel" or "heir of Abraham," and the like.

Again, all of these affirmations would be, in my opinion, so many statements of the obvious. But they obviously are not that, at least not as I have stated them, since they continue to elicit too much discussion to be declared simply a truth that goes without saying. What, then, would be finally at stake in a putative non-debate that nonetheless remains somehow debatable? How can the early Christian apostle Paul have been both indubitably *Ioudaios* and yet apparently not infrequently only questionably so?

Part of the problem here has to do with how we translate the ancient Greek word *Ioudaios*.[5] If Paul obviously was such a person, it is not equally clear what it concretely meant to be that sort of a human being in the context of the ancient Mediterranean world. And even when a definition for the word has been determined, the question

---

[4] Again, all of the reasons for the specific *Paulusbild* underlying the argument of this essay cannot be rehearsed here. But it should become clear, especially in the conclusion, why my understanding of the specific nature of Paul's earthly identity has not a little to do with the social location in which— for entirely other, though equally exegetical, reasons—I would place the runagate Jew.

[5] Cf. *Jew and Judean: A MARGINALIA Forum on Politics and Historiography in the Translation of Ancient Texts*, ed. Timothy Michael Law and Charles Halton (The Marginalia Review of Books/ Marginalia/Los Angeles Review of Books, August 26, 2014).

then swiftly becomes whether or not Paul himself "really" was a straightforward instance of that kind of ancient person. Or, if you will, how will we have to understand the extant discourse in Paul's name in order to make it "fit" our definition of someone who obviously was *Ioudaios*?

Scholars who think that they basically know what it meant to be a "Jew" in antiquity typically have not taken Paul to be a very good example of that identity. At best, Paul would be an unstable example of it, whether he is deemed to be a "radical Jew" (Boyarin) or a "very unusual Jew" (Cohen) or "not ... representative of Judaean views" (Mason) or an "anomalous Jew" (Bird).[6] None of these characterizations of Paul, however, reflects his own conviction that he was, in fact, a fully realized instance of the same and therefore ought to be viewed as such.

What Paul Said about Himself as *Ioudaios*

What did Paul say about himself as someone who would be obviously *Ioudaios*? The answer to this question does not resolve the larger one about what it normally or generally meant to be such a person in Mediterranean antiquity. But it should help us to clarify what Paul thought that it meant in his regard. And it may be that in clarifying this question, we shall find ourselves able to think more broadly about the issue of Jewish identity as such and even perhaps the topic of social identity itself.

On the relatively few occasions when Paul does characterize those who would be *Ioudaioi* or "Israel" as a distinct social group, he speaks of them as a *genos*. Notably, Paul never uses the word *ethnos* to describe these persons. And though he does occasionally use the word *laos*, it seems to be always only because the biblical text (LXX) that he is citing has used it.

Thus, for example, when, in Phil 3:5, Paul describes himself with respect to his "flesh" (*en sarki*) he states that this means: "from the *genos* of Israel, the *phylē* of Benjamin." Or in Gal 1:14 after referring to his earlier prowess *en Ioudaismō*, Paul goes on to compare himself with others of the same age "in my *genos*" (see, further, 2 Cor 11:26). And in Rom 9:3 at the beginning of an otherwise exceptional discussion of the destiny of "Israel" vis-à-vis the benefits of knowing Christ, those who are "my brothers (and sisters) ... according to the flesh" are said by Paul to constitute "my *syggeneia*."[7]

Thus the terminology that Paul uses throughout his published correspondence to characterize the social group to which he belonged as someone who obviously was *Ioudaios* is remarkably consistent. Everyone whom the category of "Israel" or the term

---

[6] See Daniel Boyarin, *A Radical Jew: Paul and the Politics of Identity* (Berkeley, CA: University of California Press, 1994); Shaye J. D. Cohen, *From the Maccabees to the Mishnah*, 3rd ed. (Louisville, KY: Westminster John Knox, 2014), 29; also 165–7; Steve Mason, "Jews, Judaeans, Judaizing, Judaism: Problems of Categorization in Ancient History," *JSJ* 38 (2007): 457–512, p. 495 n. 83; Michael F. Bird, *An Anomalous Jew: Paul among Jews, Greeks, and Romans* (Grand Rapids, MI: Eerdmans, 2016).

[7] Presumably those called in Rom 16:7, 11, 21 "my *syggeneia*," viz. "*syggeneis*," also were members of the same social group.

Ioudaios would describe is, for Paul, a member of this *genos*. How to translate *genos* then becomes the next problem.

The problem is not, however, whether such a term (*genos*) could have been used in antiquity as an equivalent expression for the word *ethnos* in the sense of specified social group. Rather, the question is whether or not on the lips of Paul—or from his pen or from that of his secretary—such a word (*ethnos*) is what Paul meant when he used the other term (*genos*).[8]

Only in Rom 9:3 are we given, perhaps, a little more information whereby we could define a little more precisely the specific social group that Paul called his *genos*. This would be a social group known "according to the flesh" (*kata sarka*).[9] But what made "Jewish" flesh—for Paul—different from other "kinds" of human flesh? Said otherwise, what was it about that flesh that revealed "us" to be distinctively "Jews" while everyone else's flesh would be contrariwise "Gentile," which is to say non-Jewish flesh?[10]

On these terms alone, however, the conversation becomes almost instantly a viciously circular line of reasoning. The social group of the *Ioudaioi* is distinguished by a peculiar kind of "flesh." That "flesh" is then what makes them *Ioudaioi*.

Indeed, were it not for Paul's initial statement about "us Jews" in Gal 2:15, there would be no other clearly marked exit from the tautological labyrinth he otherwise rehearses. But in Gal 2:15, through its exceptional use of the word *physis* in the phrase: *hêmeis physei Ioudaioi*, we are given the extra datum that will enable us to know with a little more precision how exactly Paul understood himself to be such a creature. For Paul, to be *Ioudaios* was a matter of "nature." It was, in other words, a question of the kind of "body" that he was. And in Paul's case, this body would be defined even more specifically by the peculiar kind of "flesh" that it displayed.[11]

For this reason, Paul's identity as someone who obviously was *Ioudaios* could remain intact (at least from Paul's point of view) despite the fact that Paul otherwise came to lack or no longer to practice many or most or even all of the things that a properly *ethnic* identity typically would have entailed. At least if Steve Mason's list of ingredients for the latter kind of identity has any merit, it usually involved or required the assertion of a designated home place with specific "ancestral traditions (τὰ πάτρια)" or "customs, norms, conventions, mores, laws (νόμοι, ἔθη, νόμιμα)" to be exercised in its name. In the case of the *Ioudaioi*, these "ancestral traditions" would have been those that were practiced by the people then living in *Ioudaia* aka *Israel*.

---

[8] Otherwise the Greek word *genos* (as also the Latin *genus*) would alone tell us next to nothing about what Paul thought that he was specifically (qua specie) as a "Jew"—except, of course, that Paul did imagine that being *Ioudaios* meant membership in a defined collectivity of some sort.

[9] Although if this were the only other statement that we had to clarify how Paul obviously was *Ioudaios*, the end-result would not be very different since to speak of "flesh" alone merely restates the problem to be clarified.

[10] Before jumping to the conclusion that the telling indicator must be circumcision, since this was not uniquely a Jewish practice there is an even more obvious question to be asked, namely: How can this be so, especially for Paul, if "flesh" (*sarx*) was understood elsewhere by him to constitute an impediment to knowing a more divine life, both for Jews and for Gentiles? Meant here is the oft-rehearsed Pauline opposition between that which is *kata sarka* and that which is *kata pneuma*.

[11] I recognize that the meaning of each of the terms in this equation—nature: body: flesh—is hardly self-evident or even obviously distinct vis-à-vis the others. The point here is simply to notice that these are the terms in which Paul presents himself as someone who obviously was *Ioudaios*.

None of this, however, seems to have played much of a role in articulating Paul's own sense of himself as someone who was obviously *Ioudaios*. Beyond declaring such traditions to be effectively beside the point, at least for Gentile life in Christ, Paul's reading of his ethnic group's "charter stories (μῦθοι)" hardly reflected the more usual understanding(s) of those representative texts. And had the reproduction of its mores been deemed by Paul to be a crucial element of that which made him indubitably *Ioudaios*, it would then become basically impossible to explain how he could remain a "Jew" when he refused, on the one hand, to oblige Gentiles "in Christ" to "live Jewishly" while repeatedly exhorting them, on the other hand, to "imitate me."

Let me therefore suggest a different explanation. It was possible for Paul to speak as he did "in Christ" without thereby ceasing to be obviously *Ioudaios* because, *pace* Mason, the latter identity had, for Paul, basically nothing to do with claiming any sort of permanent or divinely ordained homeland at the eastern end of the Mediterranean basin or with maintaining one or another of its customary practices. Instead, Paul's social identity as a person who obviously was *Ioudaios* described, for Paul, the kind of physical body that he was with its attendant flesh.[12]

So what exactly did it mean for Paul to say, in Gal 2:15, *hêmeis physei Ioudaioi*? A simple way to answer this question is to look at how Paul uses the language of *physis* elsewhere in his published correspondence. It turns out that this language is not very common in Pauline parlance. Beyond Gal 2:15, the word *physis* is used only one other time in Paul's letter to the Galatians (4:8) where it serves to distinguish between true and false divinities, defining a contrast between, on the one hand, "the God" and, on the other hand, "the gods that with respect to their nature (*physei*) are not really gods (*mê ousin*)."

In other words, there would be one kind of *physis* that characterizes—in an otherwise unspecified manner—the only truly divine *theos*. And there would be another, decidedly different, heavenly or chthonic kind of *physis* that belongs to every other so-called god. Since those who have the latter kind of *physis* also typically are called *theoi*, they might seem to be equally divine. But according to Paul, this simply is not true.[13] And for that reason, it could make no sense to Paul that the Galatians having come to know "in Christ" the only God whose *physis* actually is divine, now were turning back (let alone in that God's name) to a life that would be (at least for Paul) something else altogether.

Similarly for Paul, the difference between men and women was a function of their respective *physis*. Both men and women otherwise would each be a manifestation or variable species of a larger encompassing genus, which is *anthrôpos*. But their visible peculiarities were due to a distinctive *physis*.[14] Thus Paul can state, for example, in 1 Cor 11:14 as if it were a logical derivative of this distinguishing *physis*—that is, what

---

[12] This flesh typically—though not always (see 1 Cor 5:3–5; 2 Cor 12:2–4)—went most places with Paul and did whatever else he might be doing at the time.

[13] Because Paul and others of his "Jewish" kind took it for granted that the God of Israel as the true and living *theos* was not to be confused with any other so-called god that really was an "idol."

[14] My intention here is only to describe the way in which this kind of language was used by Paul. My claim is that Paul's use of this language has a specific logic or intelligibility even if its veracity may not finally be defensible.

it taught—that a woman properly has long hair while a man properly does not. Or in Rom 1:26–27, the same conviction allows Paul negatively to assess sexual behavior whose "natural" mode the women and men in question are not practicing. Thus they are said to be doing something *para physin*. This would "only" mean, however, that whatever they are doing does not reflect the *physikên chrêsin* that Paul and his implied audience explicitly took to be peculiar to female flesh and by implication or *mutatis mutandis* also indicated for its male counterpart.

Thus Paul uses the language of *physis* on the relatively few occasions when he does so essentially to underscore what would have been, for him, further statements of the obvious, or the kind of matter-of-fact distinctions that would go without saying in ancient Israelite daily life, beginning with the difference between the Israelite God who really was divine aka true and living and all the other so-called gods aka idols that really were not. Thus the language of *physis* was used by Paul also to distinguish between the male kind of human being that had a penis and the female kind that did not. Hence the term *physis* named for Paul what he otherwise assumed that everyone already knew and was therefore not in dispute.[15]

Likewise Paul distinguished between those who were *physei Ioudaioi* (Gal 2:15) and everyone else whom he describes elsewhere (Rom 2:27) as being *hê ek physeôs akrobustia*.[16] In the case of the latter reference (Rom 2:27) since Paul's interlocutor (*su*, viz. *se*) here is explicitly identified previously and subsequently as someone who is *Ioudaios* (see Rom 2:17; also 2:28–29) the opposing substantive must therefore logically refer to Gentiles or someone who is not *Ioudaios*. Thus both Jew and non-Jew would be explicitly described by Paul as being so due to their respective *physis*.

That said, none of this language is finally free of internal contradiction. Thus, for example, if we were to agree that the first phrase "Jews by nature" in Gal 2:15 concretely means a circumcised male body; this same practice—circumcision on the eighth day after birth—must assume that the eventually circumcised infant (male) body also once was "uncircumcised by nature," namely at birth and for a few days afterward. And in this case, the term used in Rom 2:27 to describe those who categorically are not Jews also would be applicable to those who otherwise shortly would become Jews through the act of circumcision and who therefore cannot be said, strictly speaking, to be "Jews by birth" and thus "by nature." Again, they would only become so sometime (8 days) after birth; which, however, is precisely not what Paul typically is understood to be saying about himself and other *Ioudaioi* in Gal 2:15; to wit, that they always somehow were "essentially" so.

---

[15] In other words, Paul's use of the term *physis* would claim for the epistemological prejudice that is always enshrined within such language the substance of an ontological truth. Let me hasten to clarify at this point that I do not think that there actually is any such thing as specifically "Jewish flesh." The notion of a "Jewish gene" belongs to the history of modern racism and has no biological basis; although there obviously is a long-standing discursive tradition that posits a fundamental distinction between those who are "Jews" and those who are not, which then has been further elaborated through notions of their divine "election," etc. It is this tradition that I mean to describe with the phrase "epistemological prejudice."

[16] Cf. Rom 2:14. The ambiguity in question is whether the term *physei* should be taken with the participial phrase that it stands next to here or with the following verb and its direct object.

In fact, it would be quite impossible to reconcile what Paul says in Gal 2:15 about "us Jews by nature" with his later statement in Rom 2:28–29 about who is "really" a Jew if we were to take the phrase "Jews by nature" in Gal 2:15 to mean something like the ethnic definition of Jewish identity as lifelong participation in a certain social and ritual life. For if we were to interpret the phrase *hêmeis physei Ioudaioi* in Gal 2:15 to mean something like "we who have lived a Jewish life from the time that we were born," this identity would be flatly denied in Rom 2:28–29 as being basically irrelevant to the true meaning of the term *Ioudaios*. For in Rom 2:28–29 Paul claims that whatever it might mean to be *Ioudaios*—including the practice of "circumcision" (*peritomê*), which may or may not be considered by Paul to have been a necessary feature of this identity—the "real" Jew finally cannot be known "visibly" (*en tô phanerô*) or "visibly in flesh" (*en tô phanerô en sarki*) but only "invisibly" (*en tô kryptô*) or "spiritually, not literally" (*en pneumati ou grammati*). Thus either Paul would have abandoned, in Rom 2:17–29, his previous claim to be "naturally" a Jew or he meant something else, in Gal 2:15, with the phrase "Jews by nature" than the usual (scholarly) understanding of that statement, which has generally taken it to be a description of a lifelong "ethnic" identity.

In Rom 11:13–24, which is explicitly addressed to "you ... Gentiles" (11:13), not a little of the argument that is made here regarding the relationship between the salvation of the Gentiles and the future of Israel proceeds on the basis of an analogy derived from viticulture; specifically, the practice of grafting different vines together. The argument as a whole cannot be said only to succeed. Indeed, it falters—if it does not simply fail—in more than one respect.[17]

Nonetheless, whatever success the argument does enjoy will depend entirely on the language of *physis* used to describe both "Jew" and "Gentile" as if each of the two kinds of human being had a distinct "nature." Each one—just as the other binary distinctions drawn by Paul between male and female, slave and free—would be as unlike the other as a "wild olive tree" (*agrielaios*; Rom 11:17, 24) was thought to be different from a "cultivated olive tree" (*kallielaios*; Rom 11:24) and/or the "olive tree" as such (*eleia*; Rom 11:17, 24).

Again, all of this may finally prove to be neither internally coherent nor botanically intelligible. But it is rhetorically clear, I think, what Paul thereby is claiming: at least, it makes apparent what Paul took for granted and therewith also what he sought to dispute. The default conviction should come as no surprise: Jews are one thing, Gentiles another. And for this reason, when Paul then goes on to speak about the possibility of the two nonetheless becoming equally part of a divine *tertium quid*, Paul describes those who are not Gentiles (because they are Jews) as those who would be "naturally" (though perhaps for other reasons not) included in this new growth (*kata physin*; Rom 11:21, 24) while those who are Gentiles (because they are not Jews) would be those who "naturally" are excluded from it (*ek tês kata physin exekopês agrielaiou*; Rom 11:24) and therefore only able to be "unnaturally" conjoined to the same new growth (*para physin*; Rom 11:24).

---

[17] See, e.g., the problem of the logical connection, or flat contradiction, between what is said in Rom 11:15 and then immediately afterward in Rom 11:16; also the shifting significance of being "cut (broken) off" in Rom 11:17, 19, 22, 24.

Whatever persuasive force the agricultural image ultimately possesses, it only works on the assumption that Jews are essentially *x* versus the Gentile *y*. Once again, it would be precisely this kind of a sharp and absolute distinction that the language of *physis* as deployed by Paul typically articulates as if it were a self-evident truth.

What, then, does the statement *hêmeis physei Ioudaioi* in Gal 2:15 mean? It means, I think, exactly what it says. Some of "us" who call ourselves and/or are called *Ioudaioi* would be this by virtue of our *physis*, which is to say some invisible *je-ne-sais-quoi* aspect or quality that everyone else—those whom "we *Ioudaioi*" call Gentiles—were not supposed to have while those who are not *Ioudaioi* are essentially or reciprocally something else, to wit, "sinners" (for want of a better term) just as men and women likewise were taken to be two distinct species of the one earthly creature called *anthrôpos*.

For this reason, Paul could hardly stop being *Ioudaios* any more than he was able to stop being "male" or one of the two kinds (male and female) of the two kinds (Jewish and Gentile) of human being (*anthrôpos*) into which Paul's Israelite world was divided. Paul was obviously a Jew and not a Gentile for the same reason that no one would have doubted (he hoped) that he was a man and not a woman.[18] As if these self-descriptions were straightforward facts like up versus down or right versus left, Paul therefore described himself in Gal 2:15 as one of those who was undeniably, indelibly, constitutively, ontologically, "naturally," invisibly, don't-ask-me-how-I-know-this-but-decidedly *Ioudaioi*.

What then displaced the self-evidence of this "fleshly" identity for Paul was an experience of "spirit" although that experience never erased or cancelled out in any way the continuing—albeit now limited—truth of such an identity. As long as Paul remained the "flesh and blood" body that he thus far always had been, he was obviously and wholly *Ioudaios*. In fact, Paul was persuaded that the experience of "spirit" that eventually displaced this earthly "fleshly" identity that he naturally received from his (Hebrew) mother's womb—as if the former possibility somehow always had been a constitutive component of his incarnate existence as a "Jew." Nonetheless, at the point in this incarnate existence when the God who was supposed to have designated Paul's patently Jewish body for such a purpose "chose ... to unveil his son in me" (Gal 1:15-16) Paul came to know his Jewish flesh differently. While he never denied it as such—to wit, his body's obvious Jewishness or the fact that Paul like others of his kind plainly was a Hebrew, Israelite, seed of Abraham, Benjaminite, and so on—Paul also claimed simultaneously another identity for himself.

This other identity was as someone in whom the fleshly "I" no longer lived. Instead, according to Paul, it was now "Christ [who] lives in me" (Gal 2:20). And this apparently made all the difference (at least to Paul) since it implied that the self-evident truth of his own flesh no longer articulated sufficiently the truth of the world in which Paul now found himself. That truth was an identity beyond or above or in excess of the mundane facts of his own "nature."[19]

---

[18] Even though it is quite clear that both terms "Jew" and "male" could polemically be subtracted from the social identity of someone who otherwise "obviously" was one or both of them.

[19] Lest we think, however, that this extraordinary truth was merely a function of Paul having drifted somehow into the realm of the metaphysical, it is important to remember the correlative claim made

What Shall We Say about All This?

This is the point, I think, at which our habitual myopia regarding the historical strangeness or peculiarity or uniqueness (if you want) of our own modern North Atlantic late-capitalist nationalist sense of human identity comes to the fore. At least, we still seem to take it for granted as if it were a self-evident fact that the individual physical body would be the basis for having any sort of social identity at all; as if that material entity somehow were matter-of-factly the obvious framework for defining who a person essentially is. But this is hardly so clear—at least not if Marshall Sahlins' reading of a wide range of anthropological literature is to be taken into account.[20] Cross-culturally speaking, it simply is not true that the individual physical body alone or the genealogical circumstances of one's "birth" and the distinguishing features of one's peculiar "flesh" would suffice in most human communities to explain who one actually—socially—"is."

At the same time, it appears to be true that at least for the last few centuries across Western Europe and North America—whether under the aegis of the Cartesian *cogito* or as a governing assumption of liberal democratic nation-states; in the form of explicit racism or as the emergent right to gender-election; whether as a basic tenet of post-WWII consumer society or within a generalized cultural anxiety (*tabu*) about death as an experience of totally meaningless loss[21]—it has become broadly assumed (however exceptional this assumption may be shown to be historically) that the individual physical body would constitute the principal (theoretical) framework within which different issues of social and personal identity are to be defined and debated.

Moreover, since the individual physical body is understood within this frame of reference to be a discrete or functionally independent (however complex) organic whole—how else to say that it actually "ex-ists" as such?—we also appear to think (certainly in political practice) that a person's "real" identity can only be singular; hence, for example, the proliferating tendency to defend a previously denied right to be recognized as decidedly x or y. A person with more than one identity must therefore be either lying as a fraud or is sick, for example, with a borderline or multiple personality disorder.

To be sure, the preceding paragraph does not adequately represent ongoing scholarly debates about the socially constructed character of all human identities including their inherent vagueness or malleability or lingering uncertainty. But my purpose here is not to comment on this growing complexity of the academic use of the category of "identity." Instead, I am trying to underscore that within the growing complexity, there yet prevails an unquestioned assumption about the putative fact that

---

by Paul that the displacing identity equally took place "in me" (Gal 1:16; 6:17; further, 4:6, 14), which is to say: in the same "me" that otherwise still was "naturally Jewish."

[20] I depend here on Marshall Sahlins' review of the pertinent anthropological literature.

[21] See Norbert Elias, *De døendes ensomhet* (trans. Niels Magnus Bugge; Oslo: Pax, 1984; German original: *Über die Einsamkeit der Sterbenden in unseren Tagen*); also Philippe Ariès, *Western Attitudes toward Death: From the Middle Ages to the Present* (trans. Patricia M. Ranum; Baltimore, MD: The Johns Hopkins University Press, 1974).

each person somehow would be more or less continuous with and thereby limited to the life that is that person's individual physical body.[22]

Again, that unquestioned assumption may strike us as a statement of the obvious. But Marshall Sahlins' theoretical survey of a wide range of anthropological literature on the topic of "kinship" once more would make it plain that, in fact, most human beings have not understood themselves to exist as someone in particular in this manner. While the specific features of a given person's "flesh" obviously would play some role in defining who that person is, the same flesh has not always or even usually determined this person's operative or governing identity in a given social context.

That is why, to cut to the chase, Daniel Boyarin in *A Radical Jew* essentially misconstrues, in my opinion, the significance of Paul's discourse about himself as a Jew in Christ. Because Boyarin basically equates the later rabbinical emphasis on the enduring opacity of the written sign aka the letter of the law including the practice of circumcision with a decidedly (post-) modern focus on the physical body as the locus for having a specific social identity together with other practices of signification, Boyarin has no choice but to understand Paul's displacement of the telling nature of his own flesh as the result of his adoption of a Hellenistic "universalizing" hermeneutic.

But Paul's own sense of himself as someone who obviously was *Ioudaios* is not unlike Boyarin's account of a "carnal Israel."[23] For both Paul and Boyarin, being *Ioudaios* is a function of the flesh. Where Boyarin and Paul would differ from one another is Boyarin's apparent assumption that such an embodied identity—being "Jewish"—cannot coexist with another that claims "in Christ there is no Jew or Greek." For Boyarin, it seems that there can only be the truth of the flesh, viz. its refusal, whereas, for Paul, there would be both that truth and another that neither contested nor observed it.[24]

Why does Boyarin insist as he does—both traditionally and nervously—on the role of the flesh for being Jewish? There is likely more than one reason for this emphasis. What makes it traditional is the degree to which Boyarin reiterates what the rabbinical reasoning enshrined in the Talmudim actually teaches. Boyarin's nervousness in reaffirming this perspective has everything to do with the way in which that reasoning now inevitably becomes entangled with the recent history of the Jews—both before and after 1948—in which such a definition of being "Jewish" has tended to support a view of the Jews as constituting a separate "race" of human being.

---

[22] The extent to which this equation strikes the reader as a statement of the obvious only proves my point. Cognitive science, conventional medical treatment, one or another form of personal therapy, to name but a few of the modern modes of explaining human experience to its current practitioners, all take for granted that the individual physical body ultimately defines the basic parameters of whatever a human being essentially is. Said otherwise, there is supposedly no human life apart from or beyond or in excess of the material conglomerate that is that person's physical "flesh."

[23] Cf. Daniel Boyarin, *Carnal Israel: Reading Sex in Talmudic Culture* (Berkeley, CA: University of California Press, 1993).

[24] With this intentionally paradoxical statement, I wish to depict Paul in a manner akin to José Rabasa's characterization of the Zapatista insurgency as a movement capable of inhabiting simultaneously two quite different worlds: the dominant contemporary one articulated, e.g., via the internet as well as another with deep roots in Mesoamerican antiquity. See José Rabasa, *Without History: Subaltern Studies, the Zapatista Insurgency, and the Specter of History* (Pittsburgh, PA: University of Pittsburgh Press, 2010).

In other words, it would be the same reason why Shlomo Sand, for example, who otherwise does not share with Boyarin any desire to be an "orthodox" practitioner of traditional Judaism (unsuccessfully) has tried to stop being such a "Jew," which is the basis for citizenship in the modern State of Israel; again, not unlike Boyarin, who *mutatis mutandis* has advocated a "diasporic" existence and therewith precisely not identification with the modern State of Israel as the better way to lead an explicitly Jewish life.[25] Even more strikingly, Shaye Cohen—who, like Boyarin, is an observant Jew, but, unlike Boyarin and certainly unlike Sand, maintains this identity in alliance with the modern State of Israel—singles out at the end of his seminal work *The Beginning of Jewishness* the problem for present-day Judaism represented by converts: namely, by those who have chosen to practice Judaism without having been born of a Jewish mother. According to Cohen, their situation represents a continuing challenge to "the mores of the contemporary Jewish community" since, lacking a "Jewish" birth, such people can never become bona-fide "Jews," which is to say be regarded as "equal to the native born," despite their evident commitment to enacting a Jewish life.[26]

What would connect all three scholars—who, again, are otherwise unlikely ever to be confused with one another—is their shared preoccupation with the lingering racist legacy of every definition of Jewish identity based on having "Jewish flesh."[27] At the same time, these three scholars all appear to share the same decidedly modern conviction that being "Jewish" necessarily excludes also being someone else who would not be a function of the same identity, to wit, a "non-Jewish" person.[28]

By contrast, the main reason why Paul could think as he seems to have done about himself as someone who obviously was *Ioudaios* while simultaneously being "in Christ," that is, why Paul was able to imagine that he could still have Jewish flesh without continuing any longer to be governed by the mundane distinction between Jew and Gentile (or slave and free, male and female)—had everything to do with Paul's discovery (or, if you will, his self-dis-closure) of an ability (attributed to the experience of having received a certain "spirit") to be more than one thing at a time. In other

---

[25] See Shlomo Sand, *How I Stopped Being a Jew* (trans. David Fernback; London: Verso, 2014); also Sand, *The Invention of the Jewish People* (trans. Yael Lotan; London: Verso, 2009); and Sand, *The Invention of the Land of Israel: From Holy Land to Homeland* (trans. Geremy Forman; London: Verso, 2012).

[26] See Shaye J. D. Cohen, *The Beginnings of Jewishness: Boundaries, Varieties, Uncertainties* (Berkeley, CA: University of California Press, 1999), 349 n. 6.

[27] One takes up or rejects what once was and still may be used to put down or to privilege. This is not merely a "reaction-formation" but belongs to the politics of survival and resistance and thus is worthy of consideration. At the same time, it does not mean that such a reading of things is inevitably or necessarily persuasive.

[28] That is why, e.g., Sand must try to "stop" being "Jewish" when he opposes the modern State of Israel's definition of this identity. Similarly Boyarin's advocacy of a "diasporic" existence for contemporary Jews really only "works" if and when it takes place in an otherwise officially "secular" social and political environment, or where one's identity as a "Jew" or "Christian" or "Muslim" effectively is limited to matters of private or personal concern. Thus it seems to me to be unlikely that Boyarin "really" thinks of Paul as actually embodying another equally legitimate way of being properly "Jewish," however much Boyarin may welcome him under the aegis of a "reading" as an erstwhile critic of Jewish ethnocentrism vis-à-vis contemporary debates among Jews about how best to be such a person. Meanwhile, Shaye Cohen clearly does not view Paul as being in any way a representative "Jew" even if Cohen also begrudgingly acknowledges that Paul obviously was a product of (one of) the multiple Judaisms existing "between the Maccabees and the Mishna."

words, Paul knew himself yet to be carnally a "Jew" while ceasing "pneumatically" to be solely defined by that fleshly identity within the same earthly body.

This was possible because, for Paul, being human—to wit, the kind of creature denominated by the Greek term *anthrôpos*—was (as it appears to have been for most human beings both before and after Paul) a multiform existence. By "multiform" I do not mean merely a complex "intersectional" mode of singular existence. Instead, I mean something more like what I earlier called being an earthly body with heavenly or cosmic connections.[29] A given human being could thus belong—equally or unequally—to more than one world at a time, constituting at least potentially a compound entity made up of earthly flesh and heavenly spirit.[30]

Having said all of the above, it needs to be underscored immediately that none of it would properly undercut in any way the limited truth of the "flesh" as a defining feature of a social identity. In this regard, Boyarin and others make a salient point when they critique a not uncommon (Christian) reading of the discourse of Paul, which would have it arguing that the flesh has ceased to matter "in Christ," being made thereby essentially irrelevant. There has been a dominant (Christian) tradition that understands Paul's advocacy of an excessive possibility "in Christ" to be true apart from whatever a given body's "flesh" might be as such—as if "being in Christ" were something "universal" that therefore somehow could be known independently of all the singularities describing one's existence as a "Jew" or "Greek," slave or free, woman and man.[31] Against this kind of "allegorical" rendering of Paul's discourse, it plainly is pertinent to recall the role that the physical body plays in defining who someone is, including Paul and his followers "in Christ." Every human being has "flesh" that says something of importance to that person's earthly identity. Indeed, without some such flesh, it was evidently inconceivable for Paul to imagine that anyone actually could be a person at all.[32]

Thus it cannot be said that Paul somehow understood himself to be "a Hebrew from Hebrews" (Phil 3:5; cf. 2 Cor 11:22) in any way that failed to take seriously the specific

---

[29] Cf. Teresa Brennan, *History after Lacan* (London: Routledge, 1993), 81.

[30] Or, if you will, human beings combine a biological "nature" with another artificial (linguistic) "culture." We all exist as instances of whatever human being is through a certain individuated arrangement of otherwise thoroughly interchangeable "stuff," though always and only within an encompassing intangible web of shifting social "relations." As a human being, one is therefore never uniquely whatever the individual physical body alone might entail. Again, this understanding of how each human being is constituted would not be unique to Paul. In fact, I think that it describes how most human beings historically have understood themselves to be concretely someone. The "flesh" of the physical body is obviously a telling part of this picture. But it is not the only or even the most important consideration when determining who someone finally is. Hence in the epigraph at the beginning of this essay, the New Caledonian elder's dismissal of the claim that Christianity had introduced the notion of spirit (*esprit*) into Canaque thought. It had already been perfectly clear to the elder that the individual physical body alone hardly defines the parameters of a given person's embodied social existence.

[31] Cf. the introduction to Denise Kimber Buell, *Why This New Race: Ethnic Reasoning in Early Christianity* (New York, NY: Columbia University Press, 2005).

[32] This is why Paul in 1 Cor 15 cannot believe that some would say that there is no resurrection of the dead. Without some kind of ongoing (albeit altered) bodily "substance"—even if now (unlike 1 Thess 4:15–17) it cannot be the "corruptible" matter of "flesh and blood" itself (see 1 Cor 15:50)—there would be no point for Paul in the evangelical promise of another more "glorious" existence for that earthly creature that is a human being.

nature of that flesh. Indeed, it was the very "nature" of this flesh that made Paul—in his eyes—obviously one of the *Ioudaioi*. Nothing Paul said about being "in Christ" ever questioned that fact. What Paul did question, however, was the sufficiency of this fact to name everything else that the same earthly body yet might be. The truth of Paul's Jewish flesh remained intact. It never was denied or erased. But its truth was displaced or re-described through an experience of another equally possible identity for the same existence. This other identity Paul called "heavenly citizenship" (Phil 3:20).

Obviously, much more would need to be said adequately to explain the equation just drawn between the experience of being "in Christ" and the possession of "heavenly citizenship" for Paul since such an equation seems to require something like the possibility of embodying two ontologically distinct identities simultaneously. Paul was still a free male *Hebraios ex Hebraiôn* and yet claimed already to be also a supra-individual extra- or hyper-physical denizen of the heavens. And to compound matters even further, this second identity was somehow supposed to have become wholly (if not fully) present in that body of enduring Jewish flesh as the experience of a certain "spirit" (*pneuma*). For the moment, however, I have merely tried to state as clearly as possible what Paul literally said about himself.

The focus of this essay is on the first of Paul's two identities: to wit, Paul's earthly existence as someone who obviously was *Ioudaios*.[33] I have insisted on two key conclusions in this regard: (1) that Paul's Jewish identity did not prevent him from becoming a Jew "in Christ" who no longer would be governed by the distinction between Jew and non-Jew; and (2) that "in Christ" Paul's Jewish identity—understood to describe the kind of "flesh" that Paul's physical body was supposed to display—never ceased to articulate the substance of this flesh-and-blood human being.

The coeval truth of these two claims means that, while Paul understood himself to be certainly *Ioudaios* as long as he remained on earth, he did not understand this identity to prevent him from simultaneously and already becoming a citizen of another "heavenly" polity in which that "fleshly" identity would be rendered of secondary importance even if and as it never was annulled or diminished as such. I have already acknowledged that the very possibility of such a "doubleness" is extremely difficult to imagine within the cultural (identity) politics of late capitalist North Atlantic (post-)modernity. At the same time, I am obviously trying to hold together two aspects of Paul's self-understanding that usually are opposed to one another.

For this reason, I have argued that Paul remained from the beginning to the end of his early Christian apostolic life indubitably and even proudly *Ioudaios*. At the same time, he did not make of that identity—despite his own equation of it with his fleshly "nature"—the exclusive definition of who he was. Thus Paul claimed as "carnal" fact a Jewish identity that is basically equivalent to the one that Boyarin otherwise ascribes to the ensuing rabbinical tradition; yet Paul, unlike Boyarin, disavowed the ability of this fact to disqualify the correlative and discrepant truth about himself "in Christ."

---

[33] My terminology here lacks rigor or stands in need of a more adequate vocabulary since Paul's own sense of himself as a Jew who simultaneously was "in Christ" and thus already a "citizen of heaven" also describes an earthly possibility; its heavenly character is simply that which made it not what the more conventional earthly identity typically entailed.

This latter truth displaced without undoing Paul's "fleshly" identity, thereby enabling, theoretically, a practice of non-integrative solidarity with the other kind(s) of human beings in the world, both then and in the time(s) to come.

What shall we call this? How shall we explain it—if it is not merely to be dismissed as the wishful or inchoate thinking of someone who finally makes no sense as stated? How could and why should we take at face value such contradictory statements about a Jewish identity that was hardly stable, let alone confirmed, as such?

For discussion of any Jewish identity after the Holocaust, which includes the subsequent establishment of the modern State of Israel, the peril remains to end up positioning Paul's description of himself as someone who indubitably was *Ioudaios* on the side of whatever is deemed to have been "normal" social life in antiquity, thereby inevitably turning Paul's sense of himself as a "Jew" into a "normalizing" posture, which is to say a more restrictive, less expansive, more demanding mode of social existence. And this, in turn, will have us almost immediately or at least implicitly lapsing back into a description of Paul's other experience "in Christ" as a response to whatever must have been wrong or dissatisfying with his former identity. And thus Paul would become, for the umpteenth time, yet again the originating archetype or architect of an all-too-familiar Christian supersessionism.

And even if I have no desire to support such a manoeuver and say so here explicitly, which I now do, one would still have to conclude correctly that such a disclaimer hardly obviates the ideological danger at hand. Moreover, I have no ready solution to the ongoing political conundrum that results from imagining a person like Paul, as I also want to do, as someone who would not simply have been another "normal" Second Temple "Jew."

I do not think that any sort of Christian supercessionism is acceptable. And neither do I think—in this case, for specifically exegetical reasons on the basis of "what Paul himself said" about himself as someone who would be obviously *Ioudaios* as was argued in the second section of the present essay—that Paul was this "Jew" in accordance with any current "ethnic" definition of that identity. Paul was clearly not "Jewish" in the modern Zionist racialized "Israeli" sense of the word.

In fact, I want to argue that it is basically wrong to confuse Paul's sense of himself as "carnally" a Jew with any notion of Jewish "ethnicity," let alone with the latter term's underlying echo of "race." Again, much more obviously will need to be said in order to explain why I am not only not persuaded but, in fact, also increasingly disquieted by the growing scholarly effort to use such language—namely "ethnicity"—in order to characterize Paul's erstwhile identity as a "Jew."[34] Suffice it to say for the time being that

---

[34] The language of "ethnicity" might be helpful—although it still would be anachronistic and ethnocentric—to characterize the later development that took place within second- and third-century CE Christianity whereby those who were now "Christians" came to understand themselves as constituting a distinct "people." See Buell, *Why This New Race?* See also David G. Horrell, *Becoming Christian: Essays on 1 Peter and the Making of Christian Identity* (London: Bloomsbury, 2013). One could think of this later development as being, in effect, simply the logical extension of an earlier description of local groups "in Christ" as each constituting an *ekklēsia*. But none of this would have, in my opinion, anything to do exegetically with the writings of Paul. Cf. Denise Kimber Buell and Caroline Johnson Hodge, "The Politics of Interpretation: The Rhetoric of Race and Ethnicity in Paul," *JBL* 123/2 (2004): 235–51; also Caroline Johnson Hodge, *If Sons, Then Heirs: A Study of Kinship and Ethnicity in the Letters of Paul* (Oxford: Oxford University Press, 2007).

the category of "ethnicity" seems to me to belong inherently to a distinctly modern kind of nationalist politics that obliges each individual human body to become "really" only one kind of (complex) carnal subject.

However changeable or "unfixed" the definition of a given ethnicity might be, the term itself tends to reify human beings as each ultimately able to be only one more instance of a given body-type. In fact, this is how the modern nation-state has come routinely to define its particular "people"—those who would make up its official citizenry—arguing on this basis for a specific homeland that would correspond to that specified subset of human beings, legislating how the members of the same group ought to live together and also thereby designating those who will never belong to this group.[35]

But this is not what it has meant historically for most human beings to understand themselves as part of a given "people." At least this is how, again, I would construe the historiographical import of Marshall Sahlins' theoretical essay on the anthropological category of "kinship," which he defines as a sense of "mutual being." My "kin" are those people without whom my singular life effectively becomes unimaginable, threatening without them to unravel into a kind of living death, a form of existence in which the kinless "I" no longer would be anyone at all.

Such kinship is not a biological fact. But it is an anthropological one. In other—Aristotelian—words, we would all be, as it were, "by nature" inherently social creatures. And therefore all of us have a certain social group to which we understand ourselves properly to belong. In the case of Paul, this "people" were the *Ioudaioi*. And they, in turn, were, for Paul, his "kinfolk" (a word that derives, in fact, from the ancient Greek term—*genos*—that Paul usually used to describe them). Thus, when Paul describes himself as among those who were *physei Ioudaioi*, or as someone who was *Hebraios ex Hebraiôn*, he is speaking—not biologically, but anthropologically—in the key of ancestry. And that is why—even if he had wanted to do so—it would have made no sense for him or for anyone else to imagine that he could somehow cease to be *Ioudaios*, given that his parents and grandparents were all Israelites, of the tribe of Benjamin, and the like.

With regard to Paul's own "Jewish" identity, I think that it is this simple. Paul was *Ioudaios* because this was one of the names used by his "people" to describe themselves. The same people were not, however, what we now might call an "ethnic" group but, rather, the much more limited set of Paul's "kinfolk," those with whom Paul knew, as it were, in his own flesh, as his own flesh, a sense of "mutual being."

The sense of belonging to such a social group—those who were *physei Ioudaios*—was profound, to be sure. In fact, it is the kind of feeling that appears to be basic to all human life and therefore would be as ordinary a sentiment as it could be. For this

---

[35] Even though none of this has ever described very well—no matter how much power it may have possessed at a given time and place—the always much more heterogeneous configuration of human life "on the ground," including the category's own designated sphere of influence. Not even the social life of one human family is adequately or concretely described when understood to be only an instance in miniature of a given "ethnicity." What the term does describe more or less accurately, at least as far as it goes, is the ideological and bureaucratic mechanisms of modern political power whereby the concept of the "nation-state" corresponding to a specific "people" would be endowed with some identifiable substance, to wit, color as race, sound as speech, taste as food, mass as land, etc.

reason, to underscore Paul's "Jewish" identity is, in one sense, merely to restate the obvious fact that, yes, of course, Paul, too, was a human being, which means that he, too, claimed a specified set of ancestors. And he never stopped claiming to be their descendant as long as he continued to display the earthly flesh that their most recent avatars, to wit, Paul's parents, had produced once upon a time.

For Paul, however, as important as it was to affirm this, it did not resolve the question of his political identity.

Conclusion: Letting the Cat Out of the Bag

The question therefore becomes, once again, why Paul's earthly identity as someone who obviously was "carnally" *Ioudaios* did not remain his only identity. In other words, why did the early Christian apostle eventually welcome or acknowledge and continue to explore another possible identity for himself in excess of his ancestral one? Obviously not everyone who, like Paul, was *Ioudaios* did this. But, for some reason, Paul did, claiming for himself in addition a "heavenly citizenship" whose most notable effect would be to render Paul's earthly (ancestral) identity neither irrelevant nor nugatory but decidedly displaced from center stage.

I would argue—very schematically—that the main reason why Paul's ancestral identity did not remain the only self he knew had everything to do with Paul's "subaltern" social status. Finding himself also "in Christ" was appealing because it provided a way out of some of the constraints and deprivations that otherwise evidently had marked his all too earthly flesh. These constraints and deprivations, just to be clear, had nothing to do with being *Ioudaios*. But, like that ancestral identity, those constraints and deprivations also were a function of Paul's earthly flesh. By contrast, the experience of "Christ" was understood by Paul to take him out of the regime of the flesh into another possible mode of existence, which Paul described as having a "heavenly" nature, not least of all because it entailed, for Paul, an experience of "spirit" (*pneuma*; see, e.g., Gal 3:2).

The problem now becomes what exactly Paul's subaltern "flesh" had known together with its evident "Jewishness." Once more, this problem has nothing specifically to do with "Jewishness" as such since for Paul the possession of this kind of "flesh" was effectively synonymous with his own existence as a human being on the face of the earth. But evidently that flesh did not describe or circumscribe for Paul the only kind of life that also a human body of this kind could and ought to be able to know.[36]

It is notable, in my opinion, that Paul's statements about himself as a person who obviously was *Ioudaios* did not include any claim to social power on the basis of that identity.[37] He does not register, for example, any obvious sense of identification with any of the Jewish authorities in Jerusalem. (This is an image of Paul provided only

---

[36] If, however, we can only imagine "flesh" as the framework for a human existence; and if, moreover, we continue to maintain the very modern assumption that the proper identity of this fleshly body finally can only be one thing, to wit, a singular whole; then I think that we will never find ourselves in a position to grasp how Paul could claim to be what he said that he was: namely, both indubitably a "Jew" and yet equally a citizen of a world no longer trading in these terms.

[37] At least not beyond the kind of power that comes with belonging to a given social group; in Paul's case, this group was those who claimed to be Abraham's inheritors.

by the book of Acts.) It is, moreover, hardly clear (*pace* Acts) that Paul's earlier life *en Ioudaismô* had anything to do with those same powers. At most, Paul admits to a previous "zealotry" on behalf of "my ancestral traditions" (Gal 1:14). And when Paul eventually came to speak "in Christ," it was from a body that, though still "naturally" Jewish, patently was not in control of very much else, including its own possible mistreatment by "the unpersuaded" in Jerusalem (Rom 15:31).

What, then, does this mean? Simply stated, Paul was a weak Jew. Not weakly Jewish but a socially weak Jew, evidently without a lot of power to begin with, and then increasingly less and less. In other words, a subaltern Jew: hardly among those who "called the shots." In fact, Paul was not very "successful" at all, at least not in any conventional sense of the term, and certainly not if we take seriously what he sometimes claimed to be: namely, another working stiff, toiling "night and day" with his hands, and thus situated at the lowest end of the ancient social spectrum.[38] Said otherwise, Paul was a poor Jew, whose ostensible "freedom" meant only that no one else was involved in procuring his daily bread.

Being *Ioudaios* therefore did not mean for Paul the enjoyment of any obvious social privilege—whatever the promises once made to his ancestor Abraham might have been. This did not mean, yet again, that Paul's Jewish identity was not important to him. It plainly did "matter" to Paul; indeed, quite literally—just as being, for example, a "Vaage" matters to me. It defined Paul's family of origin, the matrix of his earthly identity, his social site in the world. But being *Ioudaios* did not make Paul *eo ipso* a man with social power. It did not make him "strong" in any immediate or other way. Instead, it described simply and sufficiently how he got the sort of "skin" he was "in" and thus who his "kinfolk" were.

The same fact, however, also makes it clear that not all *Ioudaioi* were created equal; certainly not with respect to the practice of leisure with its literary delights and political "perks." And for that same reason, being *Ioudaios* would not have answered all the questions or concerns that a person such as Paul conceivably might have any more than being Greek or Roman or a "Vaage" would. In other words, being *Ioudaios* did not necessarily "save" you from all your other afflictions especially if and when you were a "poor" one as Paul apparently was. With Paul, you might be proudly *Ioudaios* but simultaneously find yourself welcoming "in Christ" a heretofore unthinkable "salvation." And this would be not because you were looking to be "saved" from "Judaism" but, rather, because being *Ioudaios* did not encompass everything that was your life. It did not define the only identity you might hope to desire. It was not the only problem to be addressed.

Not surprisingly, not all *Ioudaioi* agreed with Paul that a "Jew" actually could do or think what Paul had done and said. But Paul obviously did insisting "in Christ" that he still belonged to the ancestral group that he called those who were *physei Ioudaioi*. This is, conceivably, what ought to make him at least an interesting historical point of reference for contemporary thinking about Jewishness; although it also likely will be the reason why those who insist on an ethno-geographical understanding of this identity will continue to dismiss him as an insignificant runagate.

---

[38] See, e.g., Catherine Jones, "Theatre of Shame: The Impact of Paul's Manual Labour on His Apostleship in Corinth" (Ph.D. diss.; University of St. Michael's College, 2013).

3

The New Creation Motif in Romans 8:18–27 in Light of the Book of *Jubilees*

Ronald Charles

At the end of his lengthy argument (chapters 1-8), Paul's focus shifts from the redemption of human beings to the redemption of the created order. He sees a connection between the state of human beings and the state of the created order, both in that sin has negative consequences for creation and in that the full redemption of God's children will be the occasion for the renewal of creation. This then leads to two questions that are worth pondering: (1) How is one to understand the shift in his argument (i.e., to the new creation)? (2) How does this shift fit with the argument to this point? The aim of this chapter is to study the new creation motif in Rom 8:18–27 in light of one selected "apocalyptic" text (*Jubilees*).[1] The interconnected themes of creation, sin, people of God, and new creation are present both in this particular pseudepigraphal work as well as in Paul's epistle to the Romans. Hence, the rationale for selecting it for the analysis undertaken herein.[2] A comparison/contrast with *Jubilees* problematizes a two-covenant/*Sonderweg* reading of Paul, since "new creation" theme suggests a radical reformulation of identity not only for Gentiles but also for Jews.[3]

---

[1] The type of literature *Jubilees* represents (Rewritten Bible) is fairly different from other texts dubbed apocalyptic. Only two chapters in *Jubilees* (chapter 1 and 23) really fit this particular genre; it is, nevertheless, usually included in this category. John J. Collins thinks that "it may be regarded as a marginal member of the genre apocalypse, on the 'fuzzy edge' of the genre, without claiming that this is its only generic affiliation." See Collins, ed., *Apocalypse: The Morphology of a Genre* (Semeia 14; Missoula, MT: Scholars Press, 1979), 754. See also Todd R. Hanneken, *The Subversion of the Apocalypses in the Book of Jubilees* (Early Judaism and Its Literature 34; Atlanta, GA: SBL, 2012). For a meticulous and recent study of *Jubilees* see James C. VanderKam, *Jubilees: A Commentary in Two Volumes* (Hermeneia series; Minneapolis, MN: Fortress, 2018).

[2] For a thorough treatment on the redemption of creation in Romans (particularly in Rom 8:19–22) in light of a broader spectrum of Jewish apocalyptic literature see Harry Alan Hahne, *The Corruption and Redemption of Creation: Nature in Romans 8.19–22 and Jewish Apocalyptic Literature* (London: T&T Clark, 2006).

[3] I am always very impressed by Terry's careful scholarship, especially in how he probes difficult questions. On the *Sonderweg* (two-covenant) question, see his "Jewish Christianity, Israel's Stumbling and the *Sonderweg* Reading of Paul," *JSNT* 29 (2006): 27–54. I am eternally grateful to have studied with him, both at the Masters and Ph.D. level in Toronto. I could not have asked for a better, and very patient, scholar-mentor. The present chapter is a revised version of a seminar paper for a class I took with him as a graduate student.

Jubilees

"The (Book) of *Jubilees*" or "The Little Genesis" according to the Greek, Syriac, Latin, and later Ethiopic witnesses is a work most likely written between 161 and 140 BCE.[4] It is generally maintained that the text was written in Hebrew.[5] According to O. S. Wintermute, "the author of *Jubilees* belonged to the Hasidic or Essene branch of Judaism."[6] The literary device used is in the form of a revelation to Moses by the angel of the Presence. The book is a retelling/reappropriation of the history of Israel that is given in Genesis to the early chapters of Exodus. It often reproduces parts of Genesis and Exodus, while also recasting, adding, and eliminating parts of the biblical narratives. The author of the book aims to instruct and to encourage his contemporaries to cling on to the law by obeying it because the present time is critical. The author saw the covenantal laws as a basic expression of Israel's distinctiveness, and obeying them as the proper response "for maintaining a proper relationship with the God of the covenant."[7] It is important to notice that obedience to the law in *Jubilees* is presented as the proper response of the covenantal people to the God of the covenant and not as the cause of salvation. It is because they are the elect of God that they need to be holy, to separate themselves from the non-Jews and obey the commandments (mostly the ones that govern one's behavior toward God). The ethnic-religious identity manifested in the keeping of the law is presented by the author of *Jubilees* as the paradigm for measuring all of humanity's acceptability to God. The law maintains preeminence over all. The author of *Jubilees* presents the view that it is more than necessary to keep both themselves and the traditions pure from defilement. At times, one might have the tendency to consider the author of *Jubilees* as a preacher of work righteousness because of his emphasis on being obedient to the law. However, as E. P. Sanders cautioned, "despite the strict legalism of one sort, the author's view is not the kind of legalism which is summed up in the phrase 'works righteousness,' for salvation depends on the grace of God."[8] The author uses elaborated narrative detail, and even the insertion of new episodes, to convey his message. He also draws from the patriarchal narratives to derive specific laws and *halakhot*, and he presents these as immutable laws, which

---

[4] See James H Charlesworth, *The Old Testament Pseudepigrapha*, Vol. 2 (Garden City NY: Doubleday, 1983), 44; George W. E. Nickelsburg, *Jewish Literature Between the Bible and the Mishnah: A Historical and Literary Introduction* (Minneapolis, MN: Fortress, 2005), 69–73. See also John C. Endres, *Biblical Interpretation in the Book of Jubilees* (CBQ Monograph Series 18; Washington, DC: Catholic Biblical Association of America, 1987); Sidnie White Crawford, *Rewriting Scripture in Second Temple Times* (Grand Rapids, MI: Eerdmans, 2008).

[5] See James C. VanderKam, *The Book of Jubilees* (Sheffield: Sheffield Academic Press, 2001), 13.

[6] See Charlesworth, *The Old Testament Pseudepigrapha*, Vol. 2, 45.

[7] James C. VanderKam, *An Introduction to Early Judaism* (Grand Rapids, MI: Eerdmans, 2001), 97.

[8] See E. P. Sanders, *Paul and Palestinian Judaism: A Comparison of Patterns of Religion* (Philadelphia, PA: Fortress Press, 1977), 383. Covenantal nomism is Sanders' famous phrase in regard to what was common in Second Temple Judaism. Covenantal nomism, simply stated, means that one has to live within the parameters of the covenant by acknowledging its standards. In other words, Second Temple Judaism was far from being "legalistic" since the real issue was fidelity to the covenant, especially in a time of widespread apostasy. Sanders' contribution is that righteousness is not just work righteousness, as often understood in some theological circles, but righteousness with regard to the Jewish covenant. See also D. A. Carson et al., eds., *Justification and Variegated Nomism: Volume 1—The Complexities of Second-Temple Judaism* (Grand Rapids, MI: Baker, 2001).

are often said to be inscribed on the heavenly tablets (3:31; 4:32; 16:29). The whole narrative is set within a chronological structure using weeks and *"Jubilees"* (7-year periods or weeks of years and units of 49 years) as the framework.[9]

Theology

For the author of *Jubilees*, God is the God who has chosen a people for himself to serve him in righteousness. The covenant that God establishes with his chosen people began with love, and the people of the covenant have to love God and keep his commands.[10] Their faith comes not as a result of abstract logic but out of experience with the covenantal God. Faith is seen as trust and commitment to the covenant relationship between God and the people of the covenant. God's covenant with Abraham is based on God's grace to provide land and nationhood to Abraham's descendants. God has freely chosen one man and his descendants through whom "all the families of the earth will be blessed" (*Jub.* 12:23). Abraham believed and trusted in God and it was reckoned to him as faithfulness. Faith and obedience are, in this sense, two sides of the same coin. Thus the one calling himself a Jew must exercise his faith in God and the Torah so that he or she may remain faithful to the covenant. The faith and obedience required of the people of God has also a creational ideal of commitment to God the creator, rather than the created order. If Adam and Eve failed to remain in this setting of believing-obedience, Israel must avoid this path by living in complete devotion to Yahweh. Their salvation must be seen not in any meritorious work but in love, in obedience, in a heart entirely devoted to pleasing God. E. P. Sanders is on target when he concludes that in the book of *Jubilees*:

> Salvation is given graciously by God in his establishing the covenant with the fathers, a covenant which he will not forsake (I.18); individuals may, however, be excluded from Israel if they sin in such a way as to spurn the covenant itself. Those who are faithful and do not sin in such a way and who confess and repent for their transgressions constitute a kind of "true Israel," although the term is not employed.[11]

---

[9] The translator of this book in *The Old Testament Pseudepigrapha* states this in the footnote to the title: "In order to provide a chronological framework for dealing with events covering a long period of time, the author has used a system based on multiples of seven, the number of days in the week. Seven years are treated as a week of years, and seven weeks of years equal a jubilee." See Charlesworth, *The Old Testament Pseudepigrapha*, Vol. 2, 52 n. 1b.

[10] It is interesting to note how the author interprets the role of covenants in the Genesis-Exodus accounts and how to him humanity, or even animals, do not seem to occupy any part in God's covenantal interest. Rather, the focus of the various covenants is deemed to be solely directed toward Israel. On more on the understanding of covenant in *Jubilees* see, among others, Annie Jaubert, *La notion d'alliance dans le Judaïsme* (Patristica Sorbonensia 6; Paris: Seuil, 1963), 90–115; Betsy Halpern-Amaru, *Rewriting the Bible: Land and Covenant in Post-Biblical Jewish Literature* (Valley Forge, PA:Trinity Press International, 1994), 25–54; Jacques T. A. G. M. van Ruiten, "The Covenant of Noah in Jubilees 6.1-38," in *The Concept of the Covenant in the Second Temple Period* (ed. Stanley Porter and Jacqueline de Roo; JSJSup 71; Leiden: Brill, 2003), 167–90; William Gilders, "The Concept of Covenant in Jubilees," in Boccaccini and Ibba, *Mosaic Torah*, 178–92; and Ari Mermelstein, *Creation, Covenant, and the Beginnings of Judaism: Reconceiving Historical Time in the Second Temple Period* (JSJSup 168; Leiden: Brill, 2014), 88–132.

[11] *Paul and Palestinian Judaism*, 370–1.

God sustains both creation and humanity in his covenantal relationship with his people. God showed his foreknowledge of the future on different occasions. For example, the author of *Jubilees* speaks of God as the speaker of the prophetic words (chapter 1), and these words become facts that are present in the foreknowledge of God. The message of the book of *Jubilees* may be summarized as follows: the present historical situation is one of corruption, but the faithfulness of God in electing a people and keeping them safe will usher in the coming judgment of the apostate Jews and the wicked gentiles at the dawn of the new creation. This anticipates the next point to be treated: eschatology in the book of *Jubilees*.

Eschatology in *Jubilees*

The present situation of the world is one of corruption and sin. Every being on earth had been corrupted/contaminated. Israel has turned away from the directives of Torah to follow the ways of the wicked peoples of the nations. The temple cult has become so corrupt that it no longer can be considered as authentic. Israel has forsaken the festivals, the covenant, and God himself. There is no hope for the present as the covenantal people stand in corruption and in disobedience to God. The present is characterized by despair and evil. It has lost its intrinsic value. However, in spite of Israel's unfaithfulness, God remains faithful. Those who are unfaithful should heed the message of the faithfulness of God and confess both their sins and the sins of their ancestors so that they may partake in the eschatological hope. The only hope is in an imminent and final intervention of God to vindicate the righteous who keep the law. The faithful ones of the nation will rise and, with strength from God, will put everyone (unfaithful Israelites and wicked Gentiles) to the sword. They will be the zealots who use the sword of the Lord. Earlier, it appeared that the Maccabean warriors were the hope of Israel, but as it turned out, they became corrupted and defiled even the Holy of Holies. Consequently, there will be an even greater onslaught from the Gentiles. In the battles of this war, the faithful will eventually emerge triumphant. All Israel's foes will then be put to the sword.[12]

The Corruption of Creation

In the book of *Jubilees*, the corruption of creation is due to the fall, which has repercussions for the natural world.[13] One of the effects is that the normal human lifespan is shortened (*Jub.* 4:30; 23:12). Most frequently, sin brings to the world corruption, disease, death, decay, suffering, and sorrow. The story of the fall of the flood in *Jubilees* expresses the idea that it is the fall in the superhuman or semi-divine realm that most readily explains the presence of evil in the world. Wintermute suggests that "the author of *Jubilees* teaches us three things about evil: (1) It is superhuman;

---

[12] The Book of *Jubilees* may also be understood in the context of Jewish/Judean self-definition in and around the Maccabean Crisis. One might find it also helpful to read *Jubilees* in concert with later works such as *2 Bar.* and *4 Ezra* regarding the fall and Torah.

[13] See later for more precision.

(2) but it is not caused by God; (3) therefore it comes from the angelic world, which has suffered a breach from God's good order."[14] Sin also brings about major disruptions in the orderly operation of the natural world. Animals' original nature change and so they began to rebel against humans and lose the ability to speak. *Jubilees* 3:28 reads: "On that day the mouth of all the beasts and cattle and birds and whatever walked or moved was stopped from speaking because all of them used to speak with one another with one speech and one language (τὰ θηρία καὶ τὰ τετράποδα καὶ τὰ ἑρπετὰ ... ὁμόφωνα εἶναι πρὸ τῆς παραβάσεως τοῖς πρωτοπλάστοις· διότι ... ὁ ὄφις ἀνθρωπίνῃ φωνῇ ἐλάλησε τῇ Εὔᾳ)."[15] The earth itself was corrupted by the fall as a result of increasing sin. *Jubilees* further reads: "Behold, the land itself will be corrupted on account of all their deeds, and there will be no seed of the vine, and there will be no oil because their works are entirely faithless" (*Jub*. 23:18). Cosmic irregularities occur during times of extensive sin, such as during the pre-flood era and in the last days. These cosmic changes include earthquakes, widespread crop failure, plagues, birth defects, and disturbances among animals. Some of these changes in the natural world are based on Gen. 3:16-19, which discusses the pain of women in childbearing. The curse on the ground requires hard labor to grow crops (*Jub*. 3:25; 4:28) and death is the certain human fate (*Jub*. 4:3). *Jubilees* 23:13-14 describes the increasing futility of life due to the deterioration of the world from human sin:

> Plague came upon plague, and wound upon wound, and affliction upon affliction, and evil report upon evil report, and sickness upon sickness, and every evil judgment of this sort one upon another: sickness, and downfall, and sleet, and hail, and frost, and fever, and chills, and stupor, and famine, and death ... And all of this will come in the evil generation which sins in the land.

In spite of the corruption of the present moment one may live with the hope that restoration will happen in the new age and the new creation.[16]

The New Age and the New Creation

The new age is seen as the true return from exile. Only those who confess their guilt will enjoy that return. The end of the exile and the coming of a new creation involve judgment upon the Gentiles and unfaithful Israelites alike, as well as blessings to those who are faithful and obedient. Then, they will be restored to health and live long and extraordinary ages in a new creation that brings the world back to its lost paradise status. In the victory of Judah, the destiny of Israel is realized. The Levites will rule over a nation whose true happiness is centered in the Temple on Mt. Zion, in keeping Torah, and in celebrating the festivals of the restored calendar. The hearts of the people will be

---

[14] Charlesworth, *The Old Testament Pseudepigrapha*, Vol. 2, 47.
[15] *OTP* 2, trans. Wintermute, 60. The Greek text is from the Online Critical Pseudepigrapha.
[16] In spite of the bleak description of the present age, the author seems to entertain the possibility that the new age has already begun; that he was living in the early period of the eschaton. In chapter 23 he seems to be describing some events of his own time. For more on this, see T. Hanneken, *The Subversion of the Apocalypses in the book of Jubilees* (Atlanta: SBL, 2012).

transformed so that never again will they desire to stray from the covenant. Annually, they will come to Jerusalem to renew the covenant on Mt. Zion in the purified Temple, from which blessings will flow over the entire earth. Humans will live out their lives in peace and health, and when they die, they will rest in peace knowing that God has remembered his promises to Israel, driven out the enemy, vanquished the wicked angels, and established Israel in her glory. *Jubilees* 1:29 is well worth quoting at length:

> And the angel of the presence who went before the camp of Israel took the tables of the divisions of the years from the time of the creation of the law and testimony of their weeks (of years), according to the jubilees, year by year throughout the full number of jubilees, from [the day of creation until] the day of the new creation when the heaven and earth and all their creatures shall be renewed according to the powers of the heaven and according to the whole nature of earth, until the sanctuary of the LORD is created in Jerusalem upon Mount Zion. And all the lights will be renewed for healing and peace and blessing for all the elect of Israel and in order that it may be thus from that day and unto all the days of the earth.[17]

In this verse there is a movement from creation to new creation that is quite explicit. The heavens and the earth shall be renewed but it is a renewal that is not sudden. R. H. Charles observes that "this renewal of the creation is not to be instantaneous and catastrophic, but gradual, and its progress to be conditioned ethically by the conduct of Israel."[18] Because the renewal of the creation is gradual in *Jubilees*, there is reason to hesitate when considering a two-age type of eschatology in this work. Charles notes that according to the author of *Jubilees*, God is to renew His creation at three distinct periods.[19] The first occasion was the Deluge when He destroyed all that was corrupt (v.11) and "made for all His works a new and righteous nature."[20] The next renewal, to synchronize with the foundation of the Jewish community in Jacob, which should "serve to lay the foundations of the heaven and to strengthen the earth and to renew all the luminaries which are in the firmament;"[21] and the third is "when God's sanctuary and the Messianic Kingdom are established amongst men."[22] The final renewal will set in, "when the heavens and the earth shall be renewed" and "all the luminaries shall be renewed."[23] According to the author of *Jubilees* there are special locations of God's dwelling in the new creation: "For the Lord has four places on the earth, the Garden of Eden, and the Mount of the East, and this mountain on which thou art this day, Mount Sinai, and Mount Zion (which) will be sanctified in the new creation for a sanctification of the earth; through it the earth will be sanctified from all (its) guilt and its uncleanness throughout the generations of the world" (4:26). The blessedness

---

[17] *OTP* 2, trans. Wintermute, 54–5.
[18] R. H. Charles, *The Book of Jubilees or The Little Genesis* (Jerusalem: Makor, 1972; orig. pub.: London: Black, 1902), 9.
[19] Ibid.
[20] Ibid., 10.
[21] Ibid.
[22] Ibid.
[23] Ibid.

of the new creation will be accompanied by a renewed study of the law. We read in 23:26, "And in those days the children will begin to study the laws, and to seek the commandments, and to return to the paths of righteousness." In the new creation human beings will be able to attain the number of years originally designed for them. *Jubilees* 23:27–29 states:

> And the days will begin to grow many and increase amongst those children of men, till their days draw nigh to one thousand years, and to a greater number of years than (before) was the number of the days. 28. And there will be no old man, nor one who is not satisfied with his days, for all will be as children and youths. 29. And all their days they will complete and live in peace and in joy, and there will be no Satan nor any evil destroyer; for all their days will be days of blessing and healing.

At times we have the impression that in this new creation there is hope not only for Israel but also for the whole world. We recall that in *Jub.* 19:25 the seed of Abraham and Jacob will be blessed so that "they will serve to establish heaven and to strengthen the earth and to renew all of the lights which are above the firmament." In 22:13 Abraham prays that his seed would have the same new creation blessings "with which he [God] blessed Noah and Adam," so that they might be a blessing in and for all the earth. In this sense, there is a multiple blessing by God focused on Israel "in the earth" and "for the earth" in the eschatological age.

Summary

In *Jubilees* we find that the Hebrew Bible faith is alive and well during the second century BCE. Its themes and concerns indicate that very well. The present situation of the world is marred by corruption and sin but it is progressively being renewed. In spite of Israel's unfaithfulness, God has remained faithful and his faithfulness would some day make a place for Jews (and Gentiles?)[24] in a renewed world as the Hebrew Bible writers had anticipated. God will bring the end of the exile and introduce the coming of a new era. Then, there will be judgment upon the Gentiles and unfaithful Israelites alike. All Israel's enemies will be put to death and the nation will be restored to health in a renewal as wide as the creation itself. The hearts of the people will be

---

[24] It is difficult to make a decision one way or the other. It is true that there seems to be hope for the whole world in the book but the negative view of the Gentiles in *Jubilees* (e.g., *Jub.* 31:20) makes it hard to see little sign of hope for them in the new creation. They seem, ultimately, to be preordained for doom, whereas only God's people are envisioned to benefit from God's blessings in the eschatological age. See in particular Christian Frevel, "'Separate Yourself from the Gentiles' (Jub. 22:16). Intermarriage in the Book of Jubilees," in *Mixed Marriages: Intermarriage and Group Identity in the Second Temple Period* (ed. C. Frevel; New York, NY: T&T Clark, 2011), 220–50; Christine E. Hayes, *Gentile Impurities and Jewish Identities: Intermarriage and Conversion from the Bible to the Talmud* (Oxford: Oxford University Press, 2002). Donaldson presents a very complex and nuanced picture of how various Jewish texts mulled over how gentiles could relate to the Jewish God in his magisterial *Judaism and the Gentiles: Jewish Patterns of Universalism (to 135 CE)* (Waco, TX: Baylor University Press, 2007).

transformed and they will live in peace and health. This new creation comes with a renewed interest in the study of Torah and the people will, at last, be able to attain the number of years originally designed for them. The future hope offered in *Jubilees* is for the faithful who are obedient to the law. For the author of *Jubilees*, it is God's love for Israel, his faithfulness to them, his demand for obedience and fidelity, his power to do what he promises to do, and his willingness to forgive the repentant that can usher in a new creation without sin and corruption. *Jubilees* ought to be seen also as an encouragement to Jews of the second century BCE that the promises of God will be fulfilled after all, not in this age but in the next, at the dawn of the new creation. As previously stated, "The Little Genesis" is a retelling or reappropriation of the history of Israel as given in Genesis to the early chapters of Exodus. It is because they are the elect of God that they need to be holy, to separate themselves from the Gentiles and obey the commandments. The ethnic-religious identity markers are strong. The author of *Jubilees* presents the view that it is more than necessary to keep both themselves and the traditions pure from defilement.

Let us now turn our attention to Paul's epistle to the Romans to see how the apostle to the *ethnē* presents the new creation motif.

Romans

The aim here is not to present an in-depth study of Romans, but to highlight how the theme of new creation develops in the letter. The comparison with *Jubilees* is to show how this particular work can shed light on the creation motif in Paul's letter to the Romans. The comparison with *Jubilees* also helps in addressing the nexus of new creation language and the reformulation of ethnic identity in Paul's theology.[25]

The introduction to Romans tells us a great deal about its whole purpose. Paul presents himself as one who has been appointed as an apocalyptic prophet to a proper place and for a particular eschatological task in the series of events to be accomplished in the final days of this world.[26] He is called and separated to proclaim the good news

---

[25] To situate Paul's letters firmly within a new creation framework see T. Ryan Jackson, *New Creation in Paul's Letters: A Study of the Historical and Social Setting of a Pauline Concept* (WUNT 2.272; Tübingen: Mohr Siebeck, 2010).

[26] In terms of the historiography concerning Paul and apocalyptic thought there are three names that stand out: Albert Schweitzer, Ernst Käsemann, and J. Christiaan Beker. Schweitzer raises awareness among NT scholars of the importance of eschatology (fused here with apocalyptic) in Paul's thought. Käsemann brings an awareness of the apocalyptic dimension in Paul's thought to mainstream NT scholarship. Beker carries this agenda further by showing how close apocalyptic thought is to the heart of Paul's theology. For him, "Paul's theology is deliberately cast in apocalyptic terms." See J. Christiaan Beker, *Paul's Apocalyptic Gospel: The Coming Triumph of God* (Minneapolis, MN: Fortress Press, 1982), 136. The main points of Paul's teaching constitute his apocalyptic theology; and it is within the apocalyptic context that he makes the claim that the eschaton has arrived with the advent, death, and resurrection of Christ, all of which have introduced the age of the Spirit. In other words, the conceptual framework of Paul's theology is cosmic and/or apocalyptic: his main concern is with a new creation. Therefore, the "main door" of his theology is not forensic, though there is a forensic element within it (as in Jewish apocalyptic). As they follow the apocalyptic model, the main arguments of Paul's preaching can be reduced to the following: (a) the advent of Christ in the fullness of the time; (b) his death and resurrection; (c) the Spirit; (d) the revelation of the

to those outside of the covenant with no claim to grace in the eyes of Judaism. God has "granted him the eschatological mission to proclaim salvation in Christ to all the nations. If he does not preach, the eschatological kingdom will not come to happen."[27] Through their adoption into the Davidic/Abrahamic lineage, the Gentiles are set apart and established as children of God, belonging and sharing in the Abrahamic blessings.[28] By working to turn non-Jews away from their gods to Israel's deity, "Paul worked as well, beneath a canopy of biblical promises, for the redemption of his own people."[29]

In sum, from the beginning of Romans, Paul presents the argument that it is in his proclamation of the message of Christ that the new creation comes.

New Creation in Romans 1–8: A Brief Overview

The following brief overview is in order to show (1) that there is an apocalyptic substructure to Paul's argument in Romans and (2) that the new creation theme of Rom 8:18–27 is the climax of the argument that has preceded it (rather than chapters 1–4 or 5–7).

Morna D. Hooker has convincingly argued that one has to read Rom 1 in light of the story of Adam as told in Gen 1–3.[30] Adam, thus, is a type of the idolater that Paul is addressing in Rom 1 because he serves the creature rather than the creator. Hooker observes, "It is from this confusion between God and the things which he had made that idolatry springs."[31] The nature of idolatry then consists in confusing the creator and the created things and beings. Romans 1:18 states, "For the wrath of God is revealed (Ἀποκαλύπτεται γὰρ ὀργὴ θεοῦ) from heaven against all ungodliness and unrighteousness of men, who suppress the truth in unrighteousness." The present tense of Ἀποκαλύπτεται points to what is being revealed by the Christ-event, that is, that the turn of the ages has been inaugurated by Christ in the midst of the eschatological present,[32] while Christ-followers, alongside with creation, await in eager expectation for the fulfilment of what is to come (8:18–23). And in 1:19–20 Paul specifies that Gentiles and Jews alike have failed to respond appropriately to the knowledge of God. The Gentiles and the Jews are guilty of idolatry, and it is from their idols that they must turn to serve the living and the true God in order for them to be participants in God's new creation. For this reason, Paul goes back to creation and back to Adam who denies perceiving God's eternal power in creation (v. 20). According to Douglas J. Moo, "The adjectives 'all' and 'every' that he [Paul] uses throughout serve to place Israel on

---

mystery; (e) the formation of a new people. A significant confirmation of the apocalyptic character of Paul's preaching and theology is found in Rom 8:18–27.

[27] Anton Fridrichsen, *The Apostle and His Message* (Uppsala: A. -B. Lundequistska, 1947), 3.
[28] See Brendan Byrne, *"Sons of God" — "Seed of Abraham": A Study of the Idea of the Sonship of God of all Christians in Paul against the Jewish Background* (AnBib 83; Rome: Biblical Institute, 1979), 111–27.
[29] Paula Fredriksen, *Paul: The Pagans' Apostle* (New Haven, CT: Yale University Press, 2017), 166.
[30] M. D. Hooker, *NTS* 6 (1959–60): 297–306; cf. Hooker, "A Further Note on Romans 1," *NTS* 13 (1966–7): 181–3.
[31] See M. Hooker, "Adam in Romans 1,"' in *From Adam to Christ* (Cambridge: Cambridge University Press, 1990), 73–85.
[32] See Ernst Käsemann, *Commentary on Romans* (trans. and ed. Geoffrey W. Bromiley; Grand Rapids, MI: Eerdmans, 1980), 35.

par with other peoples."[33] Paul's different images give a particular picture of what it means to be in the old creation. In Romans, he uses the same motif of the universal unrighteousness of human beings in the sight of God in order to articulate the divine remaking, redoing, and recreating of the cosmos through Christ.

The new humanity, the name of Christ and being in Christ, is what characterizes the new creation and restructures the new world in his image.[34] The new creation images in Romans show that creation theology is fundamentally significant for understanding the driving force of Paul's missionary message.[35] Because there is a new creation, the whole conception of being a Jew, with a set of "identity markers" rooted in Torah, undergoes a radical redefinition. Jesus is understood as the head of the cosmos and, as such, it is by virtue of being "in him," not "in the law" (Rom 2:12) that those in him become "the doers of the law, οἱ ποιηταὶ νόμου" (Rom 2:13). Paul insists that "God shows no partiality" (Rom 2:9–11), and he argues that God's judgment is not based on the possession of the Torah (Rom 2:12–16), which would have presumably conferred some special privileges to particular individuals in Israel in terms of salvation. Rather, in line with a widely accepted sapiential aphorism, Paul advances that God will repay according to each one's deeds (Rom 2:6; cf. Prov 24:12b; LXX PS 61:13b).[36] Paul thus "reinterprets and refashions Jewishness and true circumcision in terms of new creation realities. The true Jew is one who is circumcised in the heart by the work of the Holy Spirit in him (2:29a), and so what is of importance is not circumcision but the new creation (cf. Gal 6:15)."[37]

The thrust of chapter 3 is that none (Jews or non-Jews) is righteous. The point is not that some are better than others or that some are not so bad after all. Paul is not making a distinction between the wicked and the righteous, implying that all are accountable to God, but not all are guilty before him. In fact, he is saying quite the opposite. The verdict is clear in Paul's understanding: all are guilty before God. Paul's polemic is clear: The Jews are no better than the Gentiles when it comes to God's righteousness. Paul's usage of different images gives us a picture of what he considers humanity to look like outside of Christ and what it is to be in the old creation. By pointing to the

---

[33] Douglas J. Moo, *Romans 1–8* (Chicago, IL: Moody Press, 1991), 202.

[34] For T. L. Donaldson, Paul's Christ is "an eschatological figure; his resurrection represents the firstfruits of the general resurrection (1 Cor 15:20), so that Christians are those for whom the age to come has begun to dawn." See Donaldson, *Paul and the Gentiles. Remapping the Apostle's Convictional World* (Minneapolis, MN: Fortress, 1997), 197.

[35] Certainly one cannot neglect the rhetorical strategies employed by Paul in his letter, and one needs to indicate that Paul is also trying to bring about something in the Roman community. It is also important to take into account the historical setting of the letter, its specific goal, without treating it as a witness that gives direct access to Paul's theology and Paul's mind. See among others Stanley K. Stowers, *A Rereading of Romans: Justice, Jews and Gentiles* (New Haven, CT: Yale University Press, 1994), and Thomas H. Tobin, *Paul's Rhetoric in Its Contexts: The Argument of Romans* (Peabody, MA: Hendrickson, 2004). See also, Samuel Vollenweider, *Freiheit als neue Schöpfung. Eine Untersuchung zu Eleutheria bei Paulus und in seiner Umwelt* (Göttingen: Vandenhoeck und Ruprecht, 1989); Jean-Noël Aletti, *Israël et la Loi dans la lettre aux Romains* (Paris: Cerf, 1998); A. Dettwiler et al., *Paul, une théologie en construction* (Le Monde de la Bible, 51; Genève: Labot et Fides, 2004).

[36] See Robert Jewett, *Romans: A Commentary* (Hermeneia: A Critical and Historical Commentary on the Bible; Minneapolis, MN: Fortress Press, 2006), 204.

[37] See R. Tannehill, *Dying and Rising with Christ* (Berlin: de Gruyter, 1967), 65.

dark side of the tableau, he points to the light he believed was revealed in Jesus as God's Messiah.

Paul, in Rom 5-8, is dealing with Creation typology. Romans 5-8 speaks on how God has solved the Adam problem and therefore the problem of the world. It demonstrates how Jesus' faithful act of obedience solved Adam's and the world's problem. The result is a new creation through the covenant renewal in Jesus. What is at stake in Rom 5 is salvation in the broadest sense—the new creation inaugurated and consummated—and the necessity of perseverance until the old creation is thoroughly displaced by the new. Romans 5:1-11 exhibits that "the whole sweep of human history is embraced by the two epochs instituted by Adam and Christ."[38] As Anders Nygren observes, "Adam is the head of the old aeon, the age of *death*; Christ is the head of the new aeon, the age of *life*."[39] Paul, who reads everything Christologically, shows how the work of Christ—the second Adam—is greater than the work of the first Adam. At the head of old and new creations respectively are the first and the last Adam. In this sense, E. Käsemann is correct in stating:

> Decisive in the interpretation of our text ... is not the comparison of two heads of a generation, but of two figures, in sharp dualism, who alone inaugurated a world of perdition and salvation, so that they cannot be listed in a series of ancestors. In this dualistic contrast, Christ and Adam are now the bearers of destiny for the world determined by them.[40]

Adam defines the old creation whereas Christ represents the new creation. Christ's obedience guarantees the obedience and perseverance of those who believe in him. Paul's understanding of Jesus, whom he categorized as "the second Adam" who came to undo what the first Adam has done, in the sense of rectifying the sinfulness of the first human, is not and has not been shared by many interpreters.[41] In keeping with this cosmic/salvation-historical perspective, Paul sets the events of Israel's first exodus and exile in contrast to the second exodus and exile of the latter-day people.[42] Coming

---

[38] James D. G. Dunn, *Romans 9-16* (Word Biblical Commentary 38; Carlisle: Authentic Media, 1988), 1. 271.

[39] A. Nygren, *Commentary on Romans* (Philadelphia, PA: Fortress Press, 1972), 210.

[40] Käsemann, *Commentary on Romans*, 142-3.

[41] Augustine pushed Paul's understanding further by reading Rom 5:12 as referring to original sin, which is not what the text states. Elaine Pagels makes Augustine's idiosyncratic interpretation clear and all the more problematic when she states, "The Greek text reads, 'Through one man [or "because of one man" δι' ἑνὸς ἀνθρώπου] sin entered the world, and through sin, death; and thus death came upon all men, *in that* [ἐφ' ᾧ] all sinned.'" John Chrysostom, like most Christians, took this to mean that Adam's sin brought death into the world, and death came upon all because "*all* sinned." But Augustine read the passage in Latin, and so either ignored or was unaware of the connotations of the Greek original; thus he misread the last phrase as referring to Adam. Augustine insisted that it meant that "death came upon all men, *in whom* all sinned"—that the sin of that "one man," Adam, brought upon humanity not only universal death but also universal, and inevitable, sin. See E. Pagels, *Eve, Adam, and the Serpent* (New York, NY: Vintage, 1988), 109.

[42] In this regard, N. T. Wright asserts, "Forgiveness of sins is another way of saying 'return from exile.'" See N. T. Wright, *Jesus and the Victory of God: Christian Origins and the Question of God* (Minneapolis, MN: Fortress Press, 1996), 268-9. For Wright, "this is, patently, the point also of Jeremiah's famous promise [31-34], holding out the composite hope of covenant renewal, return from exile, the renewal of the heart, the internalization of Torah, and the forgiveness of sins" (269).

out from exile, like conveying the idea of the exodus and baptism, is the perfect image for the whole argument in Rom 5. This is clear in light of the parallel between the old creation and the new humanity in Christ. Israel was in bondage in Egypt under the tyranny of Pharaoh; so are those redeemed in the last days. Moses was chosen by God to lead Israel out of Egypt to the promised land. Likewise, Jesus is the one who is sent to lead his people through a second exodus. Moses and the people had to go through the water to the wilderness. Jesus and the new people of God go through the event of baptism by water before they experience the hardships of the wilderness of this life.[43] The symbolism of water as cleansing and judgment speaks of eschatological realities in new creation/new exodus language. The exile came to an end as Jesus came to play the role that was ascribed to Adam and then to Israel in a way to undo what they did. Christ inaugurated the new era, but the fulfillment of the kingdom of God is yet to experience its glorious consummation. In chapter 6, law, sin, and death characterize the old creation, whereas the new creation is grace, righteousness, and life. In Rom 6:17–18, Paul says: "Thanks be to God that you who once were slaves of sin have become obedient from the heart to the pattern of teaching to which you were committed, and, being set free from sin, become enslaved to righteousness."

The overlapping of the two worlds (Rom 7) creates struggles and temptations for the believer; it is a life lived between two creations. Those in Christ live in the new creation while still surrounded by the sin and effects of the old creation. Those in Christ certainly and already live in a new reality by virtue of being in him, but they eagerly await the redemption of their bodies (Rom 8:23). It is because of this wait and hope that there is now—always taken eschatologically in Paul—no condemnation for those in Christ Jesus (Rom 8:1). They groan within themselves while awaiting the redemption of their bodies (8:23). They are in Christ, but they still need the help of the Spirit to intercede for them with inexpressible groanings (8:26). It is with this narrative substructure of Rom 1–8 that one may understand the whole creation motif developed in Rom 8:18–27 in light of a Jewish work such as *Jubilees*.[44]

From Wright's conclusion, one can infer that, in Paul's understanding, Jesus is the true Israelite, who, on the cross went into exile bearing the sins of his people. However, in his resurrection he returned from exile. Thus, those who are united in him by faith are delivered from the exile of sin and its ensuing effects. Only those who confess their guilt will enjoy that return. The end of the exile and the coming of a new creation involve judgment upon the Gentiles and unfaithful Israelites alike and blessings to the faithful obedient ones. See also Sylvia Keesmaat C., *Paul and His story: (Re) Interpreting the Exodus Tradition* (Sheffield: Sheffield Academic Press, 1999), particularly chapter 4, and Michael F. Bird, "Jesus and the Continuing Exile of Israel in the Writings of N.T. Wright," *JSHJ* 13 (2015): 209–31.

[43] We must keep in mind that from a *Heilsgeschichte* perspective the wilderness is not so much a locality on the map of the Middle East as "the place of God's mighty acts, significant for all believers of all times and places." See Ulrich Mauser, *Christ in the Wilderness, the Wilderness Theme in the Second Gospel and Its Basis in the Biblical Tradition* (London: SCM Press, 1963), 14.

[44] For more nuance and discussion on the apocalyptic framework of Paul's world see Klaus Koch, *The Rediscovery of Apocalyptic* (London: SCM, 1972); Christopher Rowland, *The Open Heaven: A Study of Apocalyptic in Judaism and Early Christianity* (London: SPCK, 1982); R. Barry Matlock, *Unveiling the Apocalyptic Paul: Paul's Interpreters and the Rhetoric of Criticism* (Sheffield: Sheffield Academic Press, 1996); Frederick J. Murphy, *Apocalypticism in the Bible and Its World: A Comprehensive Introduction* (Grand Rapids, MI: Baker Academic, 2012); Ben C. Blackwell et al., eds., *Paul and the Apocalyptic Imagination* (Minneapolis, MN: Fortress, 2016); James P. Davies, *Paul among*

Romans 8:18–27 in Light of *Jubilees*

As previously addressed, "The Little Genesis" is a retelling or reappropriation of the history of Israel as given in Genesis to the early chapters of Exodus. The author's use of Genesis helps him to set covenantal theology within the context of election. It is because they are the elect of God that they need to be holy, separate themselves from the Gentiles, and obey the commandments (mostly the ones that govern human's behavior to God). The ethnic-religious identity markers are strong. The author of *Jubilees* presents the view that it is more than necessary to keep both themselves and the traditions pure from defilement.

The grand narrative of Genesis is also important to Paul in Romans. However, contrary to the ideals of *Jubilees*, Paul places the Jews on par with the non-Jews. For him, the non-Jews have come short of the will of God in their rejection of Jesus as the promised Messiah (Rom 1:18–23), as have the Jews in their boasting in the Torah while transgressing it (Rom 2:17–24). Paul emphasizes that Jews and non-Jews are under sin (Rom 3:9–20). He also stresses that, through *pistis*, God's blessing promised to Abraham—who exercised his faith/trust in God—is for both the circumcised (the Jews) and the uncircumcised (the non-Jews) (Rom 4:1–9). According to Paul, the righteousness of God is made manifest only by means of the obedience of faith of all the nations to a person presented as the *telos* of Torah. Paul's view, in this sense, is contrary to the intention of the author of *Jubilees* calling on the Jews to exercise faith in God and Torah so that one may remain faithful to the covenant. The only hope for Paul is not in the clinging to the law but to Christ. Recall that in the book of *Jubilees* creation suffers and is corrupted because of sin, and that has effected several changes in the natural world. The ecology suffers and strange phenomena appear in the cosmos.[45] The destinies of creation and human beings are also closely related, according to Paul. Creation is groaning as we groan together with it. As Jeremy Punts states, "Groaning is not tantamount to resigned patience, but participatory resistance aimed at the future realisation of new reality. It means creation is to be re-created, to be made over!"[46] Paul does not see everything in this present age as bleak as does the author of *Jubilees*.[47] For Paul, Christ has inaugurated the "presence of the future."[48] Everything holds together in Jesus who has, by his death and resurrection, brought the creation to its very end and purpose. Jesus is the one who puts the whole universe under his power and has introduced the new creation.

Romans 8:18–27 looks forward to a renovation of the present creation. There is nothing in this passage that suggests the destruction of the world and the creation

---

the Apocalypses? An Evaluation of the "Apocalyptic Paul" in the Context of Jewish and Christian Apocalyptic Literature (London: T&T Clark International, 2016).

[45] Jubilees retells the narrative in Gen 3, but it does not have the power it gains in Paul. In fact, the reference to the sins of the evil generation in *Jub.* 23:15 sounds much more like the aftermath of the sin of the Watchers (like Gen 6 in the Bible) since the great sin story in this time and location was that of the Watchers, and not of Adam and Eve.

[46] Jeremy Punt, *Postcolonial Biblical Interpretation: Reframing Paul* (Leiden: Brill 2016), 207.

[47] This statement should be qualified with the caveat that for the author of *Jubilees* the end has begun but there are glimmers of hope even in the present.

[48] I am borrowing from George E. Ladd's title, *The Presence of the Future: The Eschatology of Biblical Realism* (Grand Rapids, MI: Eerdmans, 1996).

of a new world. It is not the corruptible world that is destroyed, but the corruptible aspects of the world, which are part of the old age. What is present in the passage is the renewing of this world to a world that is pleasant to the Creator. We read in Rom 8:18, "I consider that our present sufferings (τὰ παθήματα τοῦ νῦν καιροῦ) are not worth comparing with the glory that will be revealed (τὴν μέλλουσαν δόξαν ἀποκαλυφθῆναι) in us." The phrases "present sufferings" and "glory that will be revealed" correspond to the time frame: this age and the age to come. The future is a glorious one, and one that Paul prays and hopes for. Romans 8:18–27 looks forward to the eschatological glory of creation, but it does not describe in detail the future changes in the transformed creation.[49] Creation has hope and awaits eagerly the future changes (vv. 19–20), which would be unlikely if the world was going to be destroyed and recreated anew. The present creation will be delivered from its slavery to corruption and futility and it will be set free to share in the glory of the glorified children of God (v. 21).[50] Thus creation will be able to fulfill the purposes for which it was created, but which were blocked by the damage that human sin brought to the created order. Even though the present plight of creation is due to one man's disobedience, the redemption of creation will not involve a return to the lost paradise, but rather creation will gain more than it lost. The natural world will share in the greater glory of the resurrected and glorified children of God. The basic premise here is that the threat of chaos to the originally good creation is an ever-present opportunity for God to demonstrate his theodicy by always redeeming life from the grip of chaos. New creation to Paul is about the rejection of the old creation, with its idolatry and its standards of living and being in the world and for the world, and the remaking/reconciling the world to its creator by means of Christ.

Most interpreters agree that the words "the creation was subjected to frustration, not by its own choice, but by the will of the one who subjected it" refer to Gen 3:17–19 as the cause of such a condition. In that passage, God cursed the earth because of Adam's sin: "cursed is the ground because of you." Sin brings to the world corruption, disease, death, decay, suffering and sorrow. In the end, for Paul, creation will share in the freedom of the glory of the children of God (Rom 8:21). In this manner, both Paul and the author of *Jubilees* presuppose that there is an intrinsic and genuine link between creation (the cosmos) and humanity. When humanity is redeemed, the material world, which humanity has dominion over, will also become what God intends it to be. In other words, there is a real interconnectedness between the earth and humans groaning together. For Paul, redemption includes creation. Creation will

---

[49] See Karina Martin Hogan, "The Apocalyptic Eschatology of Romans: Creation, Judgment, Resurrection, and Glory," in *The Jewish Apocalyptic Tradition and the Shaping of New Testament Thought* (ed. Benjamin E. Reynolds and Loren T. Stuckenbruck; Minneapolis, MN: Fortress Press, 2017), 205–31. In this chapter, Hogan endeavors to show how the apocalyptic themes of creation, resurrection, judgment, and glory function in Romans, with particular attention to *4 Ezra* and *2 Baruch*. Hogan's contribution presents some similarities to what I am doing here in the sense that she focuses on points of contact between Paul in Romans with some Jewish apocalyptic works. See also Moyer Hubbard, *New Creation in Paul's Letters and Thought* (Cambridge: Cambridge University Press, 2002), especially 26–53, where he addresses the connections between Paul's new creation language in relation to the book of *Jubilees*.

[50] It is as if Paul has siphoned creation anew into an ongoing aspect of the present, and the destruction then becomes not the *ekpurosis* of all things, but the burning away of the corruptible.

enjoy complete freedom when corruption ends and when it shares the eschatological glory of the children of God.

In Rom 8:18–27 the children of God suffer with creation and their redemption is securing the hope of redemption for the cosmos. It is only when they appear in their eschatological glory that creation will finally be delivered from its bondage and decay. The creation is already in the process of redemption in Paul through the redeemed humanity in Christ. As Paula Fredriksen puts it, "Christ as God's eschatological champion redeems the whole cosmos, of which Israel is certainly a part (Rom 8–15); Christ's Parousia coincides with the raising of the dead, among whom certainly number Jews."[51] Its final deliverance will come in the revealing of the children of God and then, and only then, will creation completely be delivered from its present futility and corruption.

The nationalistic covenant presented in *Jubilees*, in Paul's understanding, is being replaced by a new covenant in Jesus, the Christ. The knowledge of God is the experience of the new creation and is the act of God causing his word to abide in his people formed of both Jews and non-Jews. The author of *Jubilees* has an eschatology that is more a renewal of the old creation than a sharp two-age one. The present creation is corrupt and is progressively being renewed from the old. God, in his faithfulness, will make a place for all (albeit mostly Jews) in this renewed world as the prophetic writers anticipated. This new creation comes with a renewed interest in the study of the Torah and people will at last be able to attain the number of years originally designed for them. The future hope offered in *Jubilees* is for the repentant and the obedient person to usher in a new creation where sin and corruption will be no more. Romans 8:18–27 shares the eschatological standpoint of the book of *Jubilees*. One fundamental difference is that Rom 8:18–27 refers to what will happen at a basic level without being much interested in the details of what the new creation will be like. For Paul, what is of utmost importance is that there will be an end to the state of affairs of this present evil world and to the futility that creation is now experiencing (8:20). Creation will be set free from its slavery to corruption, and the natural world will be transformed through the freedom of the glory of the children of God (v. 21). At last, creation will be able to function according to the purpose for which it was created, but which was thwarted by sin. Christ's death marked the defeat of sin that is the ruler of this age. The Christ-event (death and resurrection) effected the shift of the two ages. However, for Paul, the realities of the earth are not yet done with and this is well captured in Rom 8:19 when he says that creation is "waiting in eager expectation for the sons of God to be revealed (ἡ γὰρ ἀποκαραδοκία τῆς κτίσεως τὴν ἀποκάλυψιν τῶν υἱῶν τοῦ θεοῦ ἀπεκδέχεται)." There is an eschatological tension that is experienced by the new creation community because they are, in fact, living in two creations at the same time. The logical development of this thought from Paul is that those in Christ are to walk by the Spirit and not according to the patterns of this evil world. Paul believes that the

---

[51] Fredriksen, *Paul: The Pagans' Apostle*, 234 n. 64. This statement from Paula comes as a response to the arguments advanced by the proponents of the Sonderweg position (e.g., Lloyd Gaston, John Gager). See also, Terence L. Donaldson, "Jewish Christianity, Israel's Stumbling and the *Sonderweg* Reading of Paul," *JSNT* 29.1 (2006): 27–54.

new has dawned in the midst of the old and that those in Christ must live accordingly. To be in Christ is to live a transformed life and participate in the new creation; it is to receive the promise of the Spirit and assume the quality of life that characterizes the new eon of God's dealings with the human race, a veritable resurrection from the dead. To be in Christ for Paul means that nothing can separate the believers from the love of God (Rom 8:39). Paul's goal in preaching, then, at least in Romans, is to place his converts in union with Christ so that they may live in Christ and in hope within the new creation that is already a reality of world history, while awaiting eagerly with patience and endurance (ἀπεκδεχόμεθα δι' ὑπομονῆς, 8:25) for its final consummation. The apostle personifies the cosmos to show that it is already in the process of new creation "in hope that the creation itself will be liberated from its bondage to decay and brought into the glorious freedom of the children of God" (ἐφ' ἐλπίδι ὅτι καὶ αὐτὴ ἡ κτίσις ἐλευθερωθήσεται ἀπὸ τῆς δουλείας τῆς φθορᾶς εἰς τὴν ἐλευθερίαν τῆς δόξης τῶν τέκνων τοῦ θεοῦ, 8:20–21). Paul's hope for creation is rooted in the presence of the future, which is soon to appear in its full measure.

Conclusion

Paul's use of liberation language with respect to the "new creation" motif in Romans is revealing. It shows how his future hope is linked to what has already transpired in Christ's death and resurrection in anticipation of what is yet to come, namely the redemption of the believer's body and the liberation of creation from slavery to liberation. The motif of new creation is not unique to him. The comparison presented in this work with the book of *Jubilees* shows that there are both similarities and differences. However, Paul develops the new creation ideas in fresh ways and with new content. Romans 8:18–27 forms a climax in the letter. It shows how the hopes expressed in the Hebrew Scriptures and in the book of *Jubilees* find their resolution in the renewal of all creation by God's great act of setting everything free. The cosmos will be redeemed to share in the freedom of the glory of the children of God, where there will be no more suffering nor death, but joy everlasting. Romans 8:18–27 also shows us that Paul's theology is steeped in the covenant theology and in the Genesis/Exodus narrative, while being fundamentally restructured and reoriented around the resurrection of Jesus, whom he considers to be Israel's long awaited Christ. It is a theology that calls for what Paul envisions as new creation communities—composed of both Jews and non-Jews redeemed by Christ as the messiah son of David—to take the whole of created reality seriously, in learning to live presently in light of the future, where God's new creation momentarily floods their existence in anticipation of what is to come.

4

Did Paul Think in Terms of Two-Age Dualism?

L. Ann Jervis

For what is the privilege of the scholarly life except to question what is accepted. Or, in one of Terry Donaldson's characteristic witticisms: "If God had meant us to question what is taken for granted, God would have created us." In this study in honor of my colleague and friend I question one of the orthodoxies in Pauline study: that Paul's temporal thought is shaped by a Jewish dualistic two-age architecture.[1] More specifically, I question whether Paul modified an inherited Jewish apocalyptic two-age dualism: after Christ the ages overlap.[2]

Though this scholarly understanding of Paul's defining structure for believer-specific time is relatively recent,[3] it is now ubiquitous; and it is held by those I deeply respect.[4]

---

[1] E. DeWitt Burton declared influentially, "There is no doubt that Paul held the current Jewish doctrine of the two ages" in *A Critical and Exegetical Commentary on the Epistle to the Galatians* (Edinburgh: T&T Clark, 1920; repr. 1977), 14. D. E. Aune states that Paul's "eschatological or apocalyptic thought ... is generally accepted as firmly rooted in Judaism" (215). "In apocalyptic eschatology, the primary dualism is temporal, involving a distinction between 'this age' and 'the age to come'": "Anthropological Duality in the Eschatology of 2 Cor 4:16–5:10," in *Paul Beyond the Judaism/Hellenism Divide* (ed. T. Engberg-Pedersen; Louisville, KY: Westminster John Knox, 2001), 217.

[2] A. T. Lincoln's exemplary study of heaven in Paul claims that the apostle modified the two-age schema that he inherited from apocalyptic. See his *Paradise Now and Not Yet. Studies in the Role of the Heavenly Dimension in Paul's Thought with Special Reference to His Eschatology* (Cambridge: Cambridge University Press, 1981), 170–4. Paul believed that after Christ the ages overlap (173, 193). Recognizing that the two ages idea is found in apocalyptic and other Jewish works, N. T. Wright states: "one of the standard Jewish ways of addressing the problem of the creator and the cosmos was to speak in terms of two epochs of world history: the present age and the age to come ... Paul's specific contribution to this overarching narrative is to insist that the 'coming age' has already been inaugurated (though not yet completed) through Jesus:" Wright, *Paul and the Faithfulness of God* (Minneapolis, MN: Fortress Press, 2013), 476, 7.

[3] A. Schweitzer is typically credited with being the founding father of modern scholarship's trend to source Paul's thinking in Jewish eschatological concepts. See Schweitzer, *The Mysticism of Paul the Apostle* (trans. W. Montgomery; Baltimore, MD: The Johns Hopkins University Press, 1931). It should be remembered, however, that Schweitzer was influenced by R. Kabisch who had proposed that Paul transferred his Jewish apocalyptic two-age framework into his interpretation of Jesus. See Kabisch, *Eschatologie des Paulus in ihren Zusammenhängen mit dem Gesamtbegriff des Paulinismus* (Göttingen: Vandenhoek & Ruprecht, 1893).

[4] T. L. Donaldson assumes it when he describes Paul's Christ as "an eschatological figure; his resurrection represents the first fruits of the general resurrection (1 Cor 15:20), so that Christians are those for whom the age to come has begun to dawn." Donaldson, *Paul and the Gentiles. Remapping the Apostle's Convictional World* (Minneapolis, MN: Fortress, 1997), 197.

Interpretation in the last century or more of Paul's eschatology, soteriology, ethics, and theology very typically assumes an overlapping two-eon design to Paul's thought. Even scholars who have serious disagreements regarding Paul's view of time—salvation history versus apocalyptic interpreters—agree on this point: Paul thought that those in Christ live two overlapping ages.[5] The most common interpretative tropes for this now standard view are as follows: "overlap of the ages,"[6] "eschatological tension";[7] and "already/not yet."[8]

Despite this scholarly consensus, I query whether Paul conceived that the temporal structure for believers' lives is shaped by two ages at once: the evil age that will be obliterated and the other age that God has inaugurated in Jesus Christ. My approach here will not be to investigate Jewish apocalyptic literature itself to see if indeed it had a dualistic two-age temporal structure.[9] Nor will it be to interrogate whether Paul's thought should be understood to be rooted in Jewish apocalyptic. My approach is to start again and apart from the current operating framework.

I look at the *prima facie* evidence of Paul's letters,[10] and ask what it offers concerning Paul's conception of believers' temporal location. The assumed modified two-age schema will be a foil but not the only focus. That is, I am interested in two

---

[5] The salvation historical interpreter J. D. G. Dunn writes that Paul thinks that "the ages overlap." Dunn, *The Theology of Paul the Apostle* (Grand Rapids, MI: Eerdmans, 1999), 464. Dunn goes on: "the beginning of the age to come is pulled back into the present age…but the present age has not yet ended, and will persist until the Parousia" (464). The apocalyptic interpreter M. de Boer describes Paul as thinking that "believers live neither in the old age nor in the new: they live at the juncture of the ages where the forces of the new age … are in an ongoing struggle with the forces of the old age." Dunn, *Galatians* (Louisville, KY: Westminster John Knox, 2011), 34.

[6] Wright, for instance, takes Gal 1:4 to be a "clear statement of the 'two ages' belief, together with an equally clear statement of the particular Pauline claim that these ages now *overlap*." Wright, *Paul and the Faithfulness of God*, 477, italics his.

[7] See Dunn, *Theology*, 461–98.

[8] B. Blackwell rightly states, "Paul's soteriology is frequently characterized as being 'already/not yet'" in *Christosis: Engaging Paul's Soteriology with His Patristic Interpreters* (Grand Rapids, MI: Eerdmans, 2011), 112. O. Cullmann is among those who popularized this view; see his *Salvation in History* (New York, NY: Harper and Row, 1965), 255.

[9] There has already been important push back to Pauline interpreters' perspective on Jewish apocalyptic, in particular that it had a widespread and straightforward dualistic conception of successive ages. L. T. Stuckenbruck argues that "the 'already' principle of evil's defeat and the 'not yet' of its manifest destruction was an *existing* framework that Paul could take for granted" (254). "Demonic powers … are not thought to be destroyed as much as they can be managed by pious Jews who already could understand themselves as living in a time between God's proleptic establishment of control over evil and the effective defeat of it at the end." Stuckenbruck, "Posturing 'Apocalyptic' in Pauline Theology: How Much Contrast to Jewish Tradition?" in *The Myth of the Rebellious Angels. Studies in Second Temple Judaism and New Testament Texts* (Tübingen: Mohr Siebeck, 2014), 240–56; italics mine. J. P. Davies observes that in Jewish apocalyptic the idea of two ages is not as universal or fundamental as Pauline apocalyptic interpreters assume. Davies adds that the "motif of 'two ages' is not a theme unique to apocalyptic thought"; in fact, the dualism of the ages is found widely in Second Temple Jewish thought. It is, then, not an identity marker for apocalyptic. See Davies, *Paul among the Apocalypses. An Evaluation of the "Apocalyptic" Paul in the Context of Jewish and Christian Apocalyptic Literature* (London: Bloomsbury T&T Clark, 2016), 82; R. B. Matlock questions whether there is anything like the apocalyptic tradition in Judaism that apocalyptic interpretation of Paul presumes. Matlock, *Unveiling the Apocalyptic Paul. Paul's Interpreters and the Rhetoric of Criticism* (Sheffield: Sheffield Academic Press, 1996).

[10] I take as authentic Romans, 1 and 2 Corinthians, Galatians, Philippians, Colossians, 1 Thessalonians, and Philemon.

matters: whether there is adequate evidence in Paul's epistolary remains to warrant the prevalent assumption that his thought was shaped by an inherited apocalyptic temporal dualism and, if not, what concept might have framed his thinking about believers' time.

My investigation requires leaving aside previous scholarly assumptions and claims about Paul's rootedness in Jewish apocalyptic two-age thinking for the sake of investigating the epistolary data afresh.

Let us begin by noting the obvious: Paul never states, as do for instance, Matthew and Ephesians, that there is "this age" and "the age to come" (Matt 12:32, Eph 1:21); nor does he declare, like *4 Ezra*, that "the Most High has made not one age but two" (7:50). This fact may be acknowledged by scholars but it is then quickly cleared away. For instance, Leander Keck writes that Paul "never states the [two ages] idea fully: yet his allusions to it show how deeply ingrained it is in his thought."[11]

Interpreters regularly claim that since Paul speaks of this age, he must surely have thought there was another. As J. L. Martyn avers with regard to Gal. 1:4, "to speak of the present evil age is obviously to imply that there is another age (or something like another age), and indeed, from writings and traditions of Paul's time we know that there was a conceptual frame of reference positing *two ages*."[12]

Pauline commentary and interpretation typically supply "age to come" or "new age" as if they are synonyms for Paul's own terminology, "new creation."[13] (A few do stick with Paul's own language.)[14]

In what follows I will look, necessarily briefly, synthetically, and without adequate argument at Paul's use of "this age," [15] and "new creation." Does it point to the current scholarly conclusion that he thought that the lives of believers are shaped by two ages, one of which overlaps the other, creating an already/not yet existence for those in Christ?

This/the age: A necessarily brief exegetical rehearsal of the occurrences of this/the age (αἰών) demonstrates that Paul believes that his converts live (or can live) apart from it. *Where* Paul thinks they live is part of our exegetical investigation.

In Gal 1:4 Paul announces that Christ's giving of himself for our sins was so that, in Martyn's translation, Christ "might snatch us out of the grasp of the present evil

---

[11] Leander Keck, "Paul and Apocalyptic Theology," in *Christ's First Theologian. The Shape of Paul's Thought* (Waco, TX: Baylor University Press, 2015), 75–88, 83.

[12] J. L. Martyn, *Galatians* (New York, NY: Doubleday, 1997), 98 (italics his). Martyn goes on to say that this "is a scheme fundamental to apocalyptic thought."

[13] E.g., R. B. Hays, "Apocalyptic *Poiesis* in Galatians," in *Galatians and Christian Theology* (ed. M. Elliott et al.; Grand Rapids, MI: Baker Academic, 2014), 203. See M. V. Hubbard, *New Creation in Paul's Letters and Thought* (Cambridge: Cambridge University Press, 2002) for critique of equating "new creation" with the apocalyptic new age. Interpreters also supply "the old age" when talking about Paul's supposed two-age schema, though Paul himself talks only about this age. See, e.g., de Boer, *Galatians*, 34; J. P. Sampley, *Walking between the Time* (Minneapolis, MN: Fortress, 1991), 11.

[14] E.g., Martyn uses "new creation." though by fitting it into an apocalyptic two-age scheme, he effectively identifies new creation with the new age. Commendably (though perhaps without realizing it, complicating his own argument) Martyn describes new creation as embodied in Christ, the church, and the Israel of God in *Galatians*, 573f.

[15] Exploration of whether Paul is speaking about this age or the new age when he refers to νῦν καιρός and καιρός is also necessary. Likewise, since αἰών and κόσμος signify the same concept in Paul, κόσμος too should be investigated. For obvious reasons this study cannot be included here.

age."¹⁶ I take the aorist subjunctive ἐξέληται to indicate present liberation of believers out of the evil age.¹⁷ It is to be noted that Paul does not here state *where* believers are liberated to.

Consequently, I propose that, given the prevalence of Paul's claim that believers live in union with Christ,¹⁸ we might reasonably assume that though he does not say it out loud in Gal 1:4, Paul thought believers are those who have been *liberated out of the present evil age and so are found in Christ*. In Gal 1:4, in the absence of a description of what believers are liberated into, I contend that the most likely scenario is Christ.

I recognize the thorny patch into which I have wandered: the controversy over what concept might control the apostle's use of other concepts. I cannot here argue the case that the best candidate for the concept that coheres his various other monumental ones (for instance, justification by faith, covenant, the apocalypse of God's Son) is Paul's concept of union with Christ. I will, however, state that I take this concept to be the apostle's theological center of gravity. Or, as C. Campbell puts it: "union with Christ is … an essential theme that serves to connect the various elements of Paul's theology."¹⁹ I interpret Paul on the basis of the long-observed abundance of his references to the concept of union with Christ. Unlike evidence for some of the other candidates for his theological center, these references are not only abundant but are also spread across his letters.

This is also not the place to enter fully into the debate on the meaning of the union phrase that has triggered the most discussion: ἐν Χριστῷ.²⁰ Some of the more influential interpretations follow. A. Deissmann proposed that it indicates a literal location, that of "Christ-intimacy … Christ in him, he in Christ."²¹ W. Bousset asserted that Paul thought that the "believer is taken up in [Christ's] being."²² A. Schweitzer stated that Paul's phrase signifies his mysticism, which is "the sharing by the Elect in the same

---

[16] Martyn, *Galatians*, 95.
[17] Cf. F. F. Bruce, who, though he takes for granted that Paul thought in terms of two ages, recognizes that "here … is Paul's 'realized eschatology.' Temporally, the age to come, the resurrection age, still lies in the future; spiritually, believers in Christ have here and now been made partakers of it … they have … been delivered from the control of the powers which dominate the present age." Bruce, *Galatians* (Grand Rapids, MI: Eerdmans, 1982), 76.
[18] The choice of the term "union" is meant to cover the range of Pauline expression: in Christ, with Christ, Christ in believers, etc. See C. Campbell for a fine study of the history of scholarship that recognizes the centrality of union with Christ in Paul, as well as for thorough organization of the concept, *Paul and Union with Christ. An Exegetical and Theological Study* (Grand Rapids, MI: Zondervan, 2012). Campbell investigates various phrases such as ἐν Χριστῷ, εἰς Χριστόν, σὺν αὐτῷ (where the pronoun refers to Christ) and διὰ Χριστοῦ, and wisely determines that the shorthand for these concepts is union with Christ. For Campbell this is an umbrella concept meant to signify also participation, identification, and incorporation.
[19] Ibid., 444.
[20] In addition to C. Campbell, *Paul and Union with Christ*, see the fine analyses and contributions by G. Macaskill, *Union with Christ in the New Testament* (Oxford: Oxford University Press, 2013), 17–41; M. Novenson, *Christ among the Messiahs. Christ Language in Paul and Messiah Language in Ancient Judaism* (Oxford: Oxford University Press, 2012), 119–26; and the essays in *"In Christ" in Paul. Explorations in Paul's Theology of Union and Participation* (ed. M. J. Thate et al.; Tübingen: Mohr Siebeck, 2014).
[21] A. Deissmann, *Paul: A Study in Social and Religious History* (trans. W. E. Wilson; New York, NY: Harper &Brothers, 1912, 1957), 140.
[22] W. Bousset, *Kyrios Christos. A History of the Belief in Christ from the Beginnings of Christianity to Irenaeus* (trans. J. E. Steely; Nashville, TN: Abingdon Press, 1970), 166.

corporeity with Christ."[23] N. T. Wright claims that what Paul means by ἐν Χριστῷ is to be in the covenant community, for Jesus as the Messiah "sums up his people in himself, so that what is true of him is true of them."[24] M. Gorman alleges that Paul's participatory language indicates that "to be one with Christ is to be one with God; … to be in Christ is to be in God."[25]

Here I can only state that I agree with C. Campbell's statement that the phrase "has a range of usage determined by the elasticity of the preposition ἐν … [and so] it does not convey a fixed meaning every time it occurs."[26] Yet that it is "reasonable to regard the spatial sense of the preposition to be primary, and this should be our first consideration when analyzing each instance."[27]

Paul, in my opinion, employs his language's locative sense to signify what E. P. Sanders could only call a "new category of perception."[28] By ἐν Χριστῷ Paul points to his perplexing and generative insight that Christ is more than a corporate personality manifested in the church,[29] more even than "the revelation of God's own fidelity, love and holiness."[30] Christ for Paul is even more than G. Macaskill's wise interpretation of Paul's meaning: "a sphere (or state) of existence that is eschatological and that has come to realization in, and through, the incarnational narrative of the crucified and risen Son, sent by the Father."[31]

I take Paul to mean by ἐν Χριστῷ that those who are in Christ are in a *being* who occupies and creates a particular location and lives in a particular time. A. J. M. Wedderburn's careful study notes that Paul's use of ἐν Χριστῷ is "surprising in that 'Christ' and 'Lord' are not the sort of words that can easily be classified" according to normal grammatical usage.[32] For, Wedderburn asserts, Christ "is not a time or a place … in the normal senses of these terms."[33] Perhaps, however, for Paul Christ is a being who has and is a location and who lives a temporality.

Interestingly, some who claim that Paul thought apocalyptically assert that, in line with Jewish thinking, the new age for Paul is both spatial and temporal.[34] This might

---

[23] Schweitzer, *Mysticism of Paul*, 125.
[24] N. T. Wright, *Climax of the Covenant. Christ and the Law in Pauline Theology* (Minneapolis, MN: Fortress, 1993), 48.
[25] M. Gorman, *Inhabiting the Cruciform God. Kenosis, Justification, and Theosis in Paul's Narrative Soteriology* (Grand Rapids, MI: Eerdmans, 2009), 4.
[26] Campbell, *Paul and Union with Christ*, 26.
[27] Ibid., 73.
[28] E. P. Sanders famously wrote: "I must confess that I do not have a new category of perception to propose here. This does not mean, however, that Paul did not have one." Sanders, *Paul and Palestinian Judaism. A Comparison of Patterns of Religion* (Philadelphia, PA: Fortress, 1977), 522–3.
[29] Schweitzer writes that being in Christ is "being partakers in the Mystical Body of Christ" (*Mysticism*, 123); this is a "collective and objective event" (123). Wright's regular claim is that to be in Christ is to be part of the new covenant people. Interestingly, both Schweitzer and Wright are heavily invested in claiming that Paul's participatory language is a reworking of Messianic expectations.
[30] Gorman, *Inhabiting the Cruciform God*, 93.
[31] Macaskill, *Union with Christ*, 249. Macaskill also notes rightly that this eschatological state is actualized by the Spirit who conforms those in it to the likeness of Christ, see 249.
[32] A. J. M. Wedderburn, "Some Observations on Paul's Use of the Phrases 'In Christ' and 'With Christ,'" *JSNT* 25 (1985): 83–97, 87–8.
[33] Ibid., 88.
[34] E.g., de Boer writes, "in Jewish cosmological apocalyptic eschatology, the two ages are not simply, or even primarily temporal categories … they are also spatial categories, referring to two spheres or orbs of power," in *Galatians*, 33.

lead us to imagine that Paul is simply placing Christ in the role of his inherited new age hope. (Something comparable to W. D. Davies' proposal that Christ replaced Torah in Paul's religious schema.)

If so, it is highly important to note that the concept that most would suppose Paul to have equated with the new age—"new creation"—is, Paul says, *in Christ* (2 Cor 5:17), and not the other way around. Furthermore, the apostle says that for him Christ's cross has crucified the cosmos, with the result that all that matters is "new creation."[35] It is no longer he who lives but Christ who lives in him (Gal 2:20).

If "new creation" is meant to signify the new age (though, as we will see below, I challenge that), this is a strange presentation of the connection of Christ to it. "New creation" is *in Christ* and is created by Christ's cross in which Paul shares. It is Christ and not "new creation" (new age) that holds Paul's gaze. And, furthermore, the apostle does not attempt to connect any dots between Jewish expectation (whether apocalyptic expectations or not) and his declarations about the relationship between Christ and Christ's cross to "new creation" (understood as new age). Though there have been influential proposals about the conceptual antecedents with which Paul works, these do not convince.[36]

What we find is *not* that Christ is a stand in for the expected new age. For Paul, Christ is very definitely a *being* in whom people may live. Unlike the new age, the risen Christ loves, Christ intercedes, Christ will come again, and so on. For Paul the being of Christ risen is presently active, and is expected to participate in future God-directed events such as the Parousia. This bears little resemblance to the idea of the new age in which the righteous and elect live in eternal undisturbed glory under divine aegis.[37] Paul asserts that believers live not in a new age but in the being of Christ.

---

[35] See later, where I point out that cosmos and eon are interchangeable for Paul.

[36] Schweitzer asserted that Paul's 'in Christ' theme is sourced in Jewish eschatology. According to Schweitzer, Jewish eschatology conceived "of the preordained union of those who are elect to the Messianic Kingdom with one another and with the Messiah" (*Mysticism*, 101). Novenson rightly observes that it "has been well documented since, [that] substantiating this theory from the sources presents serious problems" (*Christ among the Messiahs*, 122). Wright appeals to the idea of kingship in ancient Israel that "the king and the people are bound together" (*Climax of the Covenant*, 46). Moreover, the way Paul made sense of Christ's resurrection in light of his Pharisaic expectations contributed to Paul's participation in the Christ concept. Paul the Pharisee believed that resurrection would happen to all of Israel at the end. When he came to believe that it had happened to Jesus, "it meant at once that *Israel's God had done for Jesus what it had been supposed he would do for Israel* ... He was, in effect, Israel in Person. And it was precisely *as Messiah* that he therefore represented his people": Wright, *Paul and the Faithfulness of God*, 827–8 (italics original). Wright's assertion is, however, based on only a small slice of Jewish scripture (Samuel-Kings), a problem to which he himself alludes: "while these texts are not sufficient in and of themselves to suggest that such language was familiar in the first century, it does a least suggest a matrix of ideas out of which a fresh incorporative usage could grow, namely, that of the king representing the people," in Wright, *Climax of the Covenant*, 47.

[37] See, e.g., the Enochic description of the age that follows "that day" for those who are saved: "the righteous and elect *shall never thenceforward see the face of the sinners and unrighteous. And the Lord of Spirits shall abide over them, and with that Son of man shall they eat and lie down and rise up for ever and ever. And the righteous and elect shall have risen from the earth, and ceased to be of downcast countenance. And they shall have been clothed with garments of glory, And these shall be the garments of life from the Lord of Spirits*": 1 Enoch 62.13–16.

Paul's letters themselves do not ask us to imagine that he used two-age thinking to make meaning of Christ, nor that he has made sense of an inherited temporal dualism in light of Christ. Rather, it is Christ untouched by two-age thinking that Paul repeatedly offers.

The accusatory mirror Paul holds up to the Galatians is not framed by the new age, but Christ. Paul closes his letter to the Galatians with his claim that he boasts in nothing except Christ's cross through whom the world has been crucified to him, and he to the world (Gal 6:14).[38] Paul admonishes his Galatian converts not for failing to live in the new age but for failing to live in the freedom for which Christ has set them free (Gal 5:1).

Furthermore, if Paul thinks that his converts are liberated from the present evil age into an overlap of the ages—this he does not say. Galatians 1:4 does not support the idea that Paul thought in terms of two-age dualism. Rather, this verse claims that believers are liberated out of the present evil age and, in light of Paul's general thinking, that he conceives they have landed in the freedom of Christ.

In Rom 12:2, Paul proclaims that for those in Christ there is no necessity to be shaped by this age. Eon and cosmos are synonymous in Paul's thought,[39] which is why many English translations of Rom 12:2 will use world to translate αἰών. The apostle speaks of this age so as to speak of the world and its value, priorities, and ways of life.[40] Paul neither explains the reason for the possibility of obeying his command not to be conformed to this age as the result of their currently living in the new age, nor as a result of their living in the overlap of the ages. Paul does not credit the possibility of living in sync with God's will (Rom 12:2) to the replacement of this age with the new age, nor to the overlap of the new over or under the old. Rather, it is by clothing themselves with the Lord Jesus Christ (Rom 13:14) that believers can be free of the flesh and its desires (i.e., this age).

The life and location for believers is not this age (this world) but Christ. The outworking of this recognition produces a transforming way of life, which ceases from the way of life that fits in this age.

Life in union with Christ is the alternative to living in this age. For in Christ there is no condemnation (Rom 8:1) and no separation from the love of God (Rom 8:39).

In 1 Cor Paul makes several claims about this age. In 1 Cor 1:20 (one of the passages where the correctness of the claim that the concept of eon and cosmos are synonymous is obvious),[41] Paul says that God has made foolish the wisdom of this age. The true alternative God offers is Christ the power of God and the wisdom of God (1 Cor 1:24). The opposite of this age is Christ.

---

[38] R. N. Longenecker's comment regarding Gal 1:4 is appropriately applied more generally: "Paul uses κόσμος as a synonym for αἰών." Longenecker, *Galatians* (Dallas, TX: Word Books, 1990), 9.

[39] F. F. Bruce rightly states that for Paul cosmos "denotes a power opposed to God" (*Galatians*, 272). The same can be said of Paul's understanding of this age.

[40] Cf. R. N. Longenecker's observation that these concepts denote not only "the present period of world history but also the way of life that characterizes it" (*Galatians*, 9).

[41] Lincoln writes that in 1 Cor αἰών and κόσμος are "virtually interchangeable": *Paradise Now and Not Yet*, 172.

The wisdom that Paul imparts is not a wisdom of this age (1 Cor 2:6) but the wisdom God decided on before the ages (1 Cor 2:7). The plural αἰών might be taken to refer to two ages, yet, it is noteworthy that Paul does not claim that the wisdom he imparts is that of the new age. Furthermore, it takes an interpretative leap to arrive at the idea that the plural might indicate a two-age framework. If one takes the leap the obvious question arises: if God decided before the two ages, what does that say about the current temporal location of believers? Are they in another third age?

Paul's statement in 1 Cor 10:11 that believers are "those upon whom the ends of the ages has arrived" also calls into question a two-age scenario. Paul says neither that one age has ended and a new age arrived (in either inaugurated or complete form) nor that believers are living in any kind of age whatsoever. He says only that the goals of the ages have come.

In 1 Cor Paul attempts to lift the veil from believers' eyes so that they might recognize the reality in which they live. All things are theirs because they are Christ's and Christ is God's. They do not belong to and are not shaped by this age (1 Cor 3:18–23). This is why they can live as if they are not part of the cosmos that is passing away (1 Cor 7:29–31).

In 2 Cor 4:4 Paul states that unlike those whose minds are blinded by the "god of this age," believers have seen the light of the gospel of the glory of Christ who is the image of God. Believers are not part of this age because God has given them invaluable knowledge (2 Cor 4:4–6)—God's glory in the face of Jesus Christ.

Paul's attempts to help his converts recognize the nature of their existence focus on directing their attention to the fact that their life is lived in union with Christ. In focusing on Christ, Paul neither implies nor indicates that he thinks that this age overlaps their life in Christ or that life in Christ overlaps this age. Rather, Paul's claims and exhortations show that he judges that his converts are tragically not acclimatized to the wonder and freedom of their new reality *apart* from this age.

Paul's burden is to open converts' eyes to the truth of their life in Christ. They are liberated from the present evil age. Paul makes claims about the direct knowledge believers have of God's glory and wisdom, and knowledge also of Christ's glory, the one who is the icon of God. This direct knowledge signals their life in Christ—a way of life in which believers participate in Jesus' death and life while living in mortal bodies (1 Cor 4:11). Paul makes no claims that the alternative to this age is the new age or the inauguration of the new age. The alternative is Christ.

New creation. The phrase "new creation" occurs twice in Paul's letters (Gal 6:15 and 2 Cor 5:17). In Gal 6:14–15 Paul pits "new creation" against cosmos, which Paul claims has been crucified to him and he to it. Whatever cosmos signifies, at the least it denotes an aspect, if not the equivalent, of the "present evil age."[42] Galatians 6:14 echoes 1:4 where Paul claims that Christ's death accomplished deliverance from "the present evil age." For those who are in Christ, Christ's saving death does not destroy the present evil age/the cosmos, but it does liberate them. The evil age/the cosmos remain, but for believers that is of no consequence. Here is not a dualistic presentation

---

[42] See M. V. Hubbard, *New Creation in Paul's Letters and Thought* (Cambridge: Cambridge University Press, 2002), 215–18 for options.

of two overlapping ages. Rather, Paul states that the old does not exist for those who are καινὴ κτίσις.

In Galatians Paul is fighting to have his converts understand that the present evil age should not matter to them; for them the present evil age is not. Paul calls the Galatians to wake up to reality as he sees it. They have been liberated from this age, and presumably he wants them to get to the same awareness that he has: that the world has been crucified to them and they to it. Here is no dualism but a singularity. According to Paul, there is only one location and reality for his converts: καινὴ κτίσις. We will see presently that Paul locates "new creation" in Christ.

In 2 Cor 5:17 Paul writes that being "in Christ" is being "new creation." As wise commentators point out, this likely means both that individuals are new creations in Christ and that in Christ is the new world God desires.[43] As we saw earlier, Paul couples his claim that "if anyone is in Christ, new creation" with the statement, "if anyone is in Christ, new creation, the old things have gone away, behold, new things have come" (2 Cor 5:17; my translation).[44] This remarkable statement contrasts not two ages, but Christ (in whom is new creation and so new things) and the old things.

If τὰ ἀρχαῖα is meant to refer to the old age, Paul says it has passed away and been replaced. When we conflate this claim with Gal 1:4, where Paul asserts not that the old age has ended or been replaced, but rather that Christ has liberated believers out of it, it becomes unlikely that in 2 Cor 5:17 τὰ ἀρχαῖα signifies the old age. That is, since in Gal 1:4, where Paul talks explicitly about the present age (the old age in a dualistic framework), he says nothing about that age ending,[45] and since in 2 Cor 5:17 Paul says nothing to imply that τὰ ἀρχαῖα is synonymous with the old age, 2 Cor 5:17 is not saying anything about the present evil age. Consequently, Paul should not here be understood to be juxtaposing Christ to the old age. Further, this passage certainly does not support the idea that the old age remains but is overlapped by the new. Rather, in 2 Cor 5:17 Paul is describing the state of life in Christ with no nod whatsoever to a two-age temporality.

We do not find here a dualistic temporal framework for believers. For believers there is only the new. Paul is casting light on the sweeping change that exists by virtue of union with Christ. For those in Christ there is only one reality. A. Schweitzer, in

---

[43] David E. Garland, *2 Corinthians* (Waco, TX: B&H Publishing Group, 1999), 286–7. Macaskill writes: "while Paul is speaking here of the personal transformation of the individual, that transformation is located within the bigger eschatological reality of the new creation" (*Union with Christ*, 233).

[44] C. Keener translates the final clause of 2 Cor 5:17: "everything has become new" in *1 and 2 Corinthians* (*The New Cambridge Bible Commentary*; Cambridge: Cambridge University Press, 2005), 182 and determines that Paul is speaking of "realized eschatology, the vanguard of a new world" (185). This is somewhat confusing—either Paul thinks the newness of everything signals that the end *has* been realized or that it is *beginning* to be realized. Keener's other claims indicate that he considers that Paul thinks the latter: Paul was interested in "the hidden, eschatological reality of resurrection life that had begun in Christ's resurrection" (185). Commendably, Keener does not immediately leap to describing what has begun as the new age.

[45] H. D. Betz judiciously notes that "Paul ... speaks of the liberation 'out of' the evil aeon and not of the change of the aeons themselves." Betz, *Galatians* (Philadelphia, PA: Fortress, 1979), 42.

his inimitable way, writes concerning Paul's two references to "new creation": those in Christ "are already creatures of the new world."[46]

Is This Realized Eschatology?

If Paul did not modify an inherited two-age dualism, and if, then, he does not think in terms of already/not yet, does the apostle expect nothing more from God and Christ in the future? *Me genoito!*

Paul clearly anticipates events that will finally defeat what remains of the present evil age. The climax of the coming battle will include the defeat of God's last enemy—Death (1 Cor 15:26). It is critical to note, however, that Paul thinks that those in Christ are *already* freed from God's last enemy by virtue of being in Christ.[47] They eagerly await the redemption of their bodies (Rom 8:23); they know that the Spirit of the one who raised Christ from the dead lives in them and will give their mortal bodies life (Rom 8:11); they know that they will be raised with Christ (2 Cor 4:14) and that there is a house from God waiting for them in the heavens (2 Cor 5:1). Paul personally exhibits the significance of such knowledge in relation to his own death. Writing to the Philippians, Paul faces the strong possibility that he will soon die and finds that possibility to be of no consequence. When he dies, it will in fact be gain (Phil 1:21). The death of his body will allow Paul to depart the flesh and be with Christ (Phil 1:23).

In other words, as Paul exemplifies, believers know and experience and live now apart from this age that is shaped by God's enemy—Death. Those in Christ will physically die, but they live. Put another way, *God's eschatological activity will not change the temporality in which those in Christ now live.* For believers, the eschatological events will not change two overlapping ages into one age. This has already happened by virtue of their being in Christ. The final defeat of death at the eschatological climax will obliterate the age ruled by sin and death, but for those who are in Christ Jesus this has already happened. We will physically die, but we live. The eschaton is of less concern for believers than it should be for the defining actor of this present evil age—Death. At the eschaton those in Christ *will continue* to share Christ's life and time, even to the point of ultimate subjection to God (1 Cor 15:28). For Death, however, Christ's return means its obliteration.

Living in Christ and so in Christ's time is not realized eschatology. That believers do not live in eschatological tension (already/not yet) but in Christ is not the same as there being nothing more to come. There is more to come—more of Christ's God-directed activity in Christ's time. In particular, Paul looks ahead to Christ's return when those who belong to Christ (1 Cor 15:23) will not only experience what he has

---

[46] Schweitzer, *Mysticism*, 119. Schweitzer writes further that those who are united with Christ "are already supernatural beings ... [though] this is not yet manifest" (110).

[47] R. Bultmann famously stated, "For the believer who is 'in Christ' *the decisive event has already happened*" in *History and Eschatology* (Edinburgh: University Press, 1957), 43. Bultmann makes this claim on different grounds than do I. For Bultmann, Paul has reinterpreted apocalyptic on the basis of his anthropology (41) and has "modified the current eschatology" (42). For Paul "the New Aeon is already reality" (42). In this way Paul solved the problem of the delay of Christ's return (47).

already (resurrection), but will be part of him in one of his most important events; for they are in him. As Paul declares in the midst of his most extensive description of the eschaton, "in Christ shall all be made alive."

Conclusion

At the beginning of the last century, A. Deissmann described Paul as conceiving of believers as being "rescued into ... the one sphere of salvation, Christ."[48] My investigation has come to a similar conclusion, though it has been focused on different questions. The apostle's writing is most simply and directly explained as evidence that he thought the ongoing present evil age need have no power over believers. In words from Paul's mature thought, believers have been raised with Christ and their life is with Christ in God (Col 3:1–3).

If Paul came to Christ with an inherited two-age dualism, he did much more than modify it. He transcended it. Believers do not live in the new age or in the overlap of the ages. They live in union with Christ.

Paul gives no evidence of eschatological tension but only of eschatological certainty. Paul calls those in Christ to recognize the truth of their life: they are in Christ alone.

---

[48] Deissmann, *Paul*, 298f. Deissmann diagrammed life in God in Jesus Christ as being entirely separate from that of being without God in the world (299).

5

Remapping Paul within Jewish Ideologies of Inclusion

Matthew Thiessen

In her wonderful book, *The Invention of World Religions*, Tomoko Masuzawa explores the way in which the academic discourse of religious studies developed in Western universities.[1] *The Invention of World Religions* belongs within a steady stream of books that helpfully interrogate the way in which the concept of religion has taken shape, and for this reason is a must-read for biblical scholars who often work with a concept of religion that is undertheorized. One of the most salient points her work makes is that, in the earliest efforts to undertake comparative religious studies in the 1800s, academics repeatedly succumbed to the temptation to use Christianity as the standard for what religion ought to look like. As part of this project, these scholars frequently described Christianity as the one truly universal religion, while describing all other religions as ethnic.[2] Christianity is a world religion, while all others are merely national or regional religions.[3]

Masuzawa's important work provides biblical scholars with a broader social and intellectual context for some of the most influential nineteenth-century work on the apostle Paul. Is it possible that F. C. Baur was influenced by this larger discourse, so that when he wrote about Paul he could not help but read Paul and early Judaism within this line of thinking? After all, the distinction between Christian universalism and Jewish particularism and nationalism is a *leitmotif* running through Baur's writings. For instance, in his *Church History of the First Three Centuries*, Baur argues that Paul "was the first to lay down expressly and distinctly the principle of Christian universalism as a thing essentially opposed to Jewish particularism."[4] Paul, he avers, "broke through

---

I offer this essay out of profound respect and appreciation for Terry, who served as the supervisor for my SSHRC-funded postdoctoral fellowship from 2011 to 2012. Concurrently, I was teaching for the College of Emmanuel and St. Chad in Saskatoon, where Terry began his career and where he and his wife Lois are still held dear by the Anglican community.

[1] Tomoko Masuzawa, *The Invention of World Religions: Or, How European Universalism Was Preserved in the Language of Pluralism* (Chicago, IL: University of Chicago Press, 2005).
[2] Ibid., 78.
[3] Ibid., 111.
[4] F. C. Baur, *The Church History of the First Three Centuries* (trans. Allan Menzies; 3rd ed., 2 vols; London: Williams and Norgate, 1878–9), 1:47.

the barriers of Judaism and rose out of the particularism of Judaism into the universal idea of Christianity."[5] And in his book on Paul he states, "the apostle feels that in his conception of the person of Christ he stands on a platform where he is infinitely above Judaism, where he has passed far beyond all that is merely relative, limited, and finite in the Jewish religion, and has risen to the absolute religion."[6] In fact, he concludes that "Christianity is the absolute religion, the religion of the spirit and of freedom, with regard to which Judaism must be looked at from an inferior standpoint, from which it must be classed with Heathenism."[7]

As Anders Gerdmar shows, Baur's concern for universalism and animus toward particularism arises within a unique historical moment pertaining to Baur's German context: the growing desire to unify over 1,800 distinct German states into one large, universal Germany.[8] In other words, at the very moment that Baur depicts Paul and Christianity as bringing about the triumph of universalism over Jewish particularism, he was involved in a nationalist, ethnocentric, and therefore ultimately particularistic project of unifying Germany along ethnic lines. While transcending the provincialism of pre-unified Germany, this line of thought was only slightly more universalist in its thinking, and in fact contained within it the seeds of a nationalism that would cause unimaginable harm in the twentieth century. Of course, this preference for the universal over the particular was not unique to nineteenth-century Germany. One early English example: in his book *The Church of the Early Fathers*, Alfred Plummer argues, "All religions previous to Christianity were national or state religions. Each tribe, country, and government had its own gods and its own forms of worship."[9]

This universal-particular dichotomy, so prevalent in nineteenth-century scholarship, has enjoyed a resurgence of sorts in the so-called new perspective on Paul, a reading of Paul that stresses the ethnocentric nature of Second Temple Judaism and contrasts it to Paul's anti-ethnocentric gospel. As N. T. Wright pithily puts it, Paul preached "grace, not race,"[10] and railed against the "badges of Jewish privilege."[11] Further, James Dunn compares early Jewish ethnocentrism to modern ethnic conflicts such as apartheid in South Africa, segregation in the United States, and the Rwandan genocide, concluding of early Jewish ethnocentrism:

---

[5] Ibid.
[6] F. C. Baur, *Paul the Apostle of Jesus Christ: His Life and Works, His Epistles and Teachings; A Contribution to a Critical History of Primitive Christianity* (trans. Allan Menzies; 2 vols; London: Williams and Norgate, 1873–85), 2:126. Similarly, Baur states: "The step from Judaism to Christianity could only be made by recognising that Judaism was merely a finite form" (2:131).
[7] Baur, *Paul the Apostle of Jesus Christ*, 1:265.
[8] Anders Gerdmar, "Baur and the Creation of the Judaism-Hellenism Dichotomy," in *Ferdinand Christian Baur and the History of Early Christianity* (ed. Martin Bauspiess et al.; Oxford: Oxford University Press, 2017), 96–115.
[9] Alfred Plummer, *The Church of the Early Fathers*, 4th ed. (London: Longmans, Green, 1890), 2.
[10] N. T. Wright, *The Climax of the Covenant: Christ and the Law in Pauline Theology* (Minneapolis, MN: Fortress, 1992), 194, 247.
[11] Ibid., 247. Although in his more recent work on Paul Wright no longer stresses the purportedly ethnocentric/particularistic nature of the Judaism that Paul rejects, the idea still persists, as seen, for instance, in his claim that Israel's "meta-sin" is believing that its election and vocation are its "exclusive privilege": *Paul and the Faithfulness of God* (2 vols.; Minneapolis,MN: Fortress, 2013), 1:38.

It is a kind of fundamentalism which can only safeguard the correctness of its belief by persecuting those who disagree or by seeking to eliminate (through conversion or otherwise) those who hold divergent views. That sort of exclusivism can produce a complete spectrum of violence, from the most subtle of social pressure to outright force. It was that sort of "attitude to the law" which Paul came to abhor.[12]

Whereas Baur's concern for particularism arose within the context of the nationalistic project of unifying Germany, Wright and Dunn write within the context of concern over and repudiation of British and Western colonialism and racism. Nonetheless, all of these narratives about Paul situate him in relation to Judaism in a fundamentally antagonistic way: Paul opposes Judaism because of some fault within it. These accounts find something wrong or lacking in Judaism, something that Christianity, or at least Pauline Christianity, sets right. According to this reading, Judaism is particularistic and ethnocentric with regard to its treatment and view of non-Jews. As John Gager observes, though, such arguments revert to an "outmoded, unhistorical dichotomy between Jewish particularism and Christian universalism."[13] Of course to make such sweeping comparisons between Judaism and Christianity requires scholars to turn both early Judaism and early Christianity into monolithic entities. And herein lies part of the problem. Paula Fredriksen puts it well: "Judaism ... did not have views of Gentiles; Jews did. Their encounter with other nations, across cultures and centuries, resulted in a jumble of perceptions, prejudices, optative descriptions, social arrangements, and daily accommodations that we can reconstruct from the various literary and epigraphical evidence only with difficulty."[14]

The Diversity of Jewish Thought Regarding Gentiles

Christian theologians and New Testament (NT) scholars alike face the temptation of using Judaism as a foil for Jesus, or Paul, or Christianity.[15] When considering the scholarly output of Terry Donaldson, then, it is remarkable to see the way in which he has continually fought against this temptation, striving to do justice to the diversity of

---

[12] James D. G. Dunn, *The New Perspective on Paul* (rev. ed.; Grand Rapids, MI: Eerdmans, 2008), 417 (cf. 35, 205). Elsewhere Dunn calls the idea that gentiles should Judaize a form of "Jewish ideological and nationalistic imperialism": *The Theology of Paul's Letter to the Galatians* (NTT; Cambridge: Cambridge University Press, 1993), 267.

[13] John G. Gager, *Reinventing Paul* (Oxford: Oxford University Press, 2000). See Dunn's unconvincing response in *New Perspective on Paul*, 32 n.122. Likewise, Barclay rightly notes that "most of the weight in Dunn's argument in fact rests on a set of Enlightenment and 20th-century social values, concerning universalism, inclusion and diversity, retrojected onto Paul": "Paul, the Gift and the Battle over Gentile Circumcision: Revisiting the Logic of Galatians," *ABR* 58 (2010): 35–56 (45). The most trenchant criticisms of this line of interpretation can be found in Denise Kimber Buell, *Why This New Race: Ethnic Reasoning in Early Christianity* (New York, NY: Columbia University Press, 2005).

[14] Fredriksen, "Judaism, the Circumcision of Gentiles, and Apocalyptic Hope: Another Look at Galatians 1–2," *JTS* 42 (1991): 532–64 (533–4).

[15] See here George Foot Moore, "Christian Writers on Judaism," *HTR* 14 (1921): 197–254.

thought within ancient Judaism. Pride of place goes to his 2007 book *Judaism and the Gentiles*.[16] In it, Donaldson outlines four ways in which Jews thought Gentiles could relate to Judaism and its God: sympathizing with Judaism, being ethical monotheists, participating in eschatological salvation, or converting to Judaism. Each of these strategies provides positive ways for Gentiles to relate to Israel and Israel's God.

I will not rehearse here the extensive evidence Donaldson collects and analyzes in order to demonstrate one of his key contentions: long before the rise of Christianity, Jews were already wrestling with questions of if and how Gentiles could relate to Israel's God. As Donaldson puts it: "any proper understanding of the Gentile mission in the early Church needs to recognize that the early Christian movement came to birth in an environment that was already universalistic. Early Christian debates about whether and on what terms Gentiles could be included in the movement are to be seen not as sui generis but as variations of debates that were already well established within Judaism."[17]

Jews, for instance, could envisage Gentiles *sympathizing* with aspects of Jewish customs and beliefs, without needing to become Jews.[18] For example, foreign rulers often provided support for the Jerusalem temple cult (e.g., Cyrus in Ezra 1:1–4; Caesar Augustus in Philo, *Embassy* 309–310) or expressed esteem for Jewish customs, most extensively, the Egyptian king Ptolemy the Second (283–247 BCE) in the *Letter of Aristeas*.[19] Jews could also envisage Gentiles adhering to what Donaldson calls *ethical monotheism*: that is, Gentiles who worshiped one supreme god and who lived a life that from a Jewish perspective was fundamentally moral.[20] For instance, Philo claims that "all Greeks and barbarians unanimously acknowledge" the existence of "the supreme Father of gods and men and the Maker of the whole universe" (*Special Laws* 2.165), while Josephus states that Pythagoras, Anaxagoras, Plato, and the Stoic philosophers held to a conception of God that Moses had taught to the Jews (*Apion* 2.168). Such ancient monotheism often combined with a morally appropriate lifestyle (e.g., Acts 10).[21] Additionally, Jews could also hope for a future time when Israel's God would redeem Israel and include numerous Gentiles in his salvific work. Such Gentiles would *participate in God's eschatological restoration*. Deutero-Isaiah, for instance, depicts God

---

[16] Terence L. Donaldson, *Judaism and the Gentiles: Jewish Patterns of Universalism (to 135 CE)* (Waco, TX: Baylor University Press, 2007).

[17] Donaldson, *Judaism and the Gentiles*, 9.

[18] See Louis H. Feldman, "Jewish 'Sympathizers' in Classical Literature and Inscriptions," *TAPA* 81 (1950): 200–8, and Folker Siegert, "Gottesfürchtige und Sympathisanten," *JSJ* 4 (1973): 109–64.

[19] Cf. Shaye J. D. Cohen, "Respect for Judaism by Gentiles According to Josephus," *HTR* 80 (1987): 409–30.

[20] On non-Jewish and non-Christian monotheism in antiquity, see: Polymnia Athanassiadi and Michael Frede, eds., *Pagan Monotheism in Late Antiquity* (Oxford: Oxford University Press, 1999); Rainer Hirsch-Luipold, ed., *Gott und die Götter bei Plutarch: Götterbilder-Gottesbilder-Weltbilder* (Religionsgeschichtliche Versuche und Vorarbeiten 54; Berlin: de Gruyter, 2005); Stephen Mitchell and Peter van Nuffelen, eds., *One God: Pagan Monotheism in the Roman Empire* (Cambridge: Cambridge University Press, 2010).

[21] See Klaus Müller, *Tora für die Völker: Die noachidischen Gebote und Ansätze zu ihrer Rezeption im Christentum*, 2nd ed. (Studien zu jüdischem Volk und christlicher Gemeinde 15; Berlin: Institut Kirche und Judentum, 1998). More broadly, see David Novak, *The Image of the Non-Jew in Judaism: An Historical and Constructive Study of the Noahide Laws* (Toronto Studies in Theology 14; New York, NY: Edwin Mellen, 1983).

restoring Israel and bringing the Gentiles to Jerusalem, where they will worship Israel's God (Isa 55:5).[22]

None of these three strategies of Gentile inclusion, *sympathization, ethical monotheism,* or *eschatological participation,* requires that Gentiles *become* Jews. In other words, these paradigms undermine the claims of those scholars who posit that Christianity differed from Judaism because the former was universalistic while the latter was particularistic and ethnocentric. Not all, and perhaps not even most, Second Temple Jews, thought that Gentiles ought or needed to (or even could!) convert to "Judaism."[23] Second Temple Jews did not establish missionary organizations or go door to door in Gentile neighborhoods seeking converts to Judaism.[24]

To be sure, though, some Jews did believe that Gentiles could and should become Jews, adopting Jewish customs and beliefs and entering into the Jewish community. We see one first-century CE Jew named Eleazar arguing that Izates, a first-century CE king of Adiabene, needed to undergo circumcision and adopt the entire Jewish law (Josephus, *Ant.* 20.17–47).[25] The strategy of conversion, then, is the only instance where a Gentile presumably ceases to be a Gentile and becomes a Jew. One could perhaps speak of the exclusivism of those Jews who not only thought that Gentiles could convert and become Jews but that they should or must do so. It is this solution to the Gentile question, after all, that new perspective readings of Paul have labeled ethnocentric and exclusivistic. But as Donaldson observes, even the belief that Gentiles should convert to Judaism is inclusivistic. In fact, given ancient thinking about ethnicity and religion, it might be particularly non-particularistic!

> While conversion is not generally seen as a form of universalism in contemporary discourse, our interest here is the world of late antiquity, a world in which proselytism represented a striking step in a universalistic direction. In a world where religion had traditionally been embedded in the constitutive domains of a tribe or a people, the idea that religious identity was something that could be adopted was a significant innovation.[26]

---

[22] Fredriksen rightly notes that this strategy did not generally envisage Gentile conversion: "Judaism, the Circumcision of Gentiles." Cf. Michael E. Fuller, *The Restoration of Israel: Israel's Regathering and the Fate of the Nations in Early Jewish Literature and Luke-Acts* (BZNW 138; Berlin: de Gruyter, 2006).

[23] See Matthew Thiessen, *Contesting Conversion: Genealogy, Circumcision, and Identity in Ancient Judaism and Christianity* (Oxford: Oxford University Press, 2011).

[24] See Edouard Will and Claude Orrieux, *"Prosélytisme juif?" histoire d'une erreur* (Paris: Les Belles Lettres, 1992) and Martin Goodman, *Mission and Conversion: Proselytizing in the Religious History of the Roman Empire* (Oxford: Clarendon, 1994). In contrast, see Louis H. Feldman, *Jew and Gentile in the Ancient World: Attitudes and Interactions from Alexander to Justinian* (Princeton, NJ: Princeton University Press, 1993), 288–341.

[25] See Daniel R. Schwartz, "God, Gentiles, and Jewish Law: On Acts 15 and Josephus' Adiabene Narrative," in *Geschichte—Tradition—Reflexion: Festschrift für Martin Hengel zum 70. Geburtstag* (ed. Peter Schäfer; 3 vols.; Tübingen: Mohr Siebeck, 1996), 1:263–82.

[26] Donaldson, *Judaism and the Gentiles,* 4–5. Similarly, Nils Alstrup Dahl states, "Jewish monotheism at the time of Paul was universalistic in its way and Christian monotheism remained exclusive": *Studies in Paul: Theology for the Early Christian Mission* (Minneapolis, MN: Augsburg, 1977), 191.

Where modern scholars from Baur to Wright and Dunn see ethnocentrism and particularism, ancient actors might very well have seen inclusivism and universalism.

To be sure, some Jews appear to have subscribed to a strategy of straightforward *exclusion*. Perhaps most clearly, the author of the book of *Jubilees* subscribes to an exclusivism that seems to allow for no possibility that Gentiles might positively relate to Israel's God. In relating God's giving of the rite of circumcision to Abraham, the author states: "And anyone who is born whose own flesh is not circumcised on the eighth day is not from the sons of the covenant which the LORD made for Abraham since (he is) from the children of destruction. And there is therefore no sign upon him so that he might belong to the LORD because (he is destined) to be destroyed and annihilated from the earth and to be uprooted from the earth" (*OTP* 15:26 Wintermute). The author connects the rite of circumcision to Deut 32:8-9, concluding, "But he chose Israel that they might be a people for himself. And he sanctified them and gathered them from all of the sons of man because (there are) many nations and many people, and they all belong to him, but over all of them he caused spirits to rule so that they might lead them astray from following him" (15:30-31). In *Jubilees*, Gentiles are destined for destruction and nothing they do can alter this God-ordained fact.[27]

Lest one wrongly conclude that all ancient Jews subscribed to one and only one of the five strategies discussed here, let me stress that there seems to be no reason to conclude that these categories are necessarily mutually exclusive. In fact, Donaldson's *Judaism and the Gentiles* demonstrates this reality: different passages within one work often provide evidence of differing strategies of inclusion. The only incompatible strategies seem to be the belief that Gentiles could convert and become Jews and the belief that Gentiles could never become Jews. But the belief that Gentiles could never become Jews did not necessitate the belief that Gentiles were irrevocably cut off from Israel's God. Perhaps, unlike the author of *Jubilees*, some Jews held that while Gentiles would always remain Gentiles, they could still find ways to honor Israel's God and be pleasing to him. After all, Gentiles could sympathize with Judaism, conform to the pattern of ethical monotheism, or be included in God's eschatological restoration of Israel without needing to become Jews.

Were one to try to plot these various strategies of inclusion (and the various combinations of such strategies!), one might be tempted to argue that one strategy was *more* inclusive than another strategy. For instance, it might seem to be obvious that a strategy that only requires a Gentile to worship one supreme God and to live a moral life is more inclusivistic than a strategy that requires a Gentile to undergo circumcision and adoption of the entire Jewish law. But is it? What if some Jews believed that Gentiles simply could never become Jews, but they could and should be ethical monotheists? Their strategy of inclusion might appear to our eyes to be more inclusivistic than a strategy that requires Gentiles to become Jews, but how would it

---

[27] On genealogical exclusivism, in both *Jubilees* and beyond, see Christine E. Hayes, *Gentile Impurities and Jewish Identities: Intermarriage and Conversion from the Bible to the Talmud* (Oxford: Oxford University Press, 2002).

appear to a Gentile who desires to undergo circumcision, adopt the Jewish law, and become a Jew? Imagine the dismay that Gentiles might experience once they learn that even were they to undergo circumcision and adopt the law, they would remain Gentiles. The message that they do not need to or cannot adopt the entire Jewish law to be acceptable to God might sound very much like they are destined to always being second-class citizens.

Or consider eschatological participation. Again, one might be tempted to conclude that this strategy of inclusion is more inclusive than other strategies because it requires so little of Gentiles: no painful circumcision or abstention from certain foods or need to learn the numerous demands of the Jewish law. But implicit in the belief that God would incorporate Gentiles into the end-time deliverance of Israel is the belief that few (if any) Gentiles would enjoy a positive relationship with Israel or Israel's God now. In other words, an anthropological (or *ethnos*-logical) pessimism appears to drive the inclusivistic hopes of this paradigm. In contrast, as Donaldson argues, conversion might very well be more inclusivistic than the other strategies under consideration.

Paul's Exclusivistic Inclusivism

The preceding discussion demonstrates just how problematic from a historical perspective it is to continue discussing Jewish particularism and ethnocentrism. But what about Paul? Where should we map him in relation to these various strategies of relating to gentiles? In this section we discuss Paul's exclusivistic inclusivism.[28] If Paul does not introduce inclusivism to Second Temple Judaism, is it possible that he introduces an even more inclusive inclusivism? After all, Paul goes so far as to describe uncircumcised gentiles as both sons and seed (*sperma*) of Abraham in Gal 3. This seems to be a rather remarkable claim, which undermines any ethnic particularism. As Donaldson says, "The truly anomalous aspect is Paul's insistence that uncircumcised *ethnē*-in-Christ are at the same time full members of Abraham's 'seed' (*sperma*)."[29]

But consider for a moment what Paul does not say. Paul does not say Abrahamic descent is irrelevant or that it has been superseded by a universalistic gospel. At least in Romans and Galatians, Paul doubles down on the necessity of being related to Abraham in order to receive God's blessing. Abraham's presence in Paul's writings represents a formidable obstacle to any effort to describe Paul's gospel as non-particularistic or nonethnic. As Jon D. Levenson has argued, "Were Paul truly intent on transcending the difference between Jews and Gentiles, would he have so stressed the man known as the father of the Jewish people? And would he have advanced the claim that those

---

[28] I take this term from Christine E. Hayes, *What's Divine about Divine Law? Early Perspectives* (Princeton: Princeton University Press, 2015), 151.

[29] Terence Donaldson, "Paul within Judaism: A Critical Evaluation from a 'New Perspective' Perspective," in *Paul within Judaism: Restoring the First-Century Context to the Apostle* (ed. Mark D. Nanos and Magnus Zetterholm; Minneapolis, MN: Fortress, 2015), 296. I have elsewhere tried to show that even here Paul might not be unique. See Matthew Thiessen, "Paul, the *Animal Apocalypse*, and Abraham's Gentile Seed," in *The Ways that Often Parted: Essays in Honor of Joel Marcus* (ed. Lori Baron et al.; ECL 24; Atlanta, GA: SBL, 2018), 65–78.

who have faith in Jesus had, by that very act, become nothing short of descendants of Abraham?"[30]

Further, Paul's opposition to law observance occurs in letters written to Gentiles who are tempted or being encouraged to adopt the Jewish law. While some may have hesitated to undergo the rite of circumcision, others seem to have positively desired to do so. Paul can speak of at least some of his readers in Galatia as "those who desire to be under the law" (οἱ ὑπὸ νόμον θέλοντες εἶναι, 4:21). For any of his Gentile readers who wanted to adopt the Jewish law in its entirety, Paul's vehement opposition would not have sounded like universalism or inclusivism, but like exclusivism. As Pheme Perkins puts it, "Paul is as intolerant of the Gentile who assimilates to Jewish habits and religious practices as the sharp-tongued Roman satirists who make fun of such Judaizing."[31]

Further, if so many Paul scholars believe that any Jew who thinks that Gentiles need to convert to Judaism is not inclusive, or not inclusive enough, why do so many Paul scholars conclude that Paul or Christianity *is* inclusive. After all, Paul thought that Gentiles needed to abandon their gods and ethics and worship Israel's God, as well as stipulating that they adhere to his gospel about Christ. In other words, why is requiring adherence to a rather difficult-to-believe message about a risen Christ more inclusive than requiring the removal of a piece of skin via the rite of circumcision? Clearly, there is no objective answer to these questions—inclusivity and exclusivity are values that exist only within the eye of the beholder.[32] In other words, we modern scholars are injecting our own ideological, religious, and moral preferences into our purportedly historical work when we choose to narrate early Judaism and Christianity using the categories of exclusivism and inclusivism, respectively.

In *Paul: The Pagans' Apostle*, Paula Fredriksen argues convincingly that the early Jesus movement gave birth to something new within early Judaism: a concerted, systematic outreach to Gentiles.[33] Whereas previously some Jews at least were open to Gentiles becoming Jews, and a few Jews sporadically called Gentiles to do so, it was actually Christ following Jews who first thought to missionize Gentiles in a systematic way. They did so, of course, because they were convinced that the eschaton had arrived—now was the time that God was redeeming the world and dealing with the Gentiles. And he was doing so in Messiah Jesus (*en Christō*). All early Christ followers (or at least all the ones we know much about) believed this. Paul and his opponents agreed that God was now rescuing Gentiles, but they disagreed on the precise implications of this rescue mission

---

[30] Jon D. Levenson, *Inheriting Abraham: The Legacy of the Patriarch in Judaism, Christianity, and Islam* (Library of Jewish Ideas; Princeton: Princeton University Press, 2012), 157.

[31] Pheme Perkins, *Abraham's Divided Children: Galatians and the Politics of Faith* (The New Testament in Context; Harrisburg, PA: Trinity Press International, 2001), 56. So too Albert Schweitzer, *The Mysticism of Paul the Apostle* (trans. William Montgomery; Baltimore, MD: Johns Hopkins University Press, 1953), 196: "[Paul] compels Jews and non-Jews alike to remain in the state in which they first became believers. The champion of the freedom of Gentile Christianity is at the same time its tyrant. If it desired to become partaker in the blessing of the Law and circumcision, he would not suffer it to do so."

[32] See here Anders Runesson, "Particularistic Judaism and Universalistic Christianity? Some Critical Remarks on Terminology and Theology," *JGRChJ* 1 (2000): 120–44.

[33] Paula Fredriksen, *Paul: The Pagan's Apostle* (New Haven, CT: Yale University Press, 2017).

for Gentile behavior in the ever-increasingly awkward period of the now and not quite yet. What exactly was the escape route that God had mapped out for Gentiles? Paul's opponents and perhaps even Paul himself at first, if Gal 5:11 refers to Paul's post-Christ position (as Douglas Campbell has recently argued), thought that Gentiles needed to add law observance and especially circumcision to their gospel faith. Or perhaps it is better to say that they thought gospel faith included circumcision and law observance, Gentiles becoming Jews. As Donaldson's work shows, thinking that Jewish law could be applied to Gentile sinners was not particularly unique, but it also was not some sort of, for lack of a better term, orthodox position, since there simply was no orthodox Jewish position on Gentiles! What was at least relatively anomalous (but it's not Paul alone, rather it's much of the early Christ movement) was the vigor and determination that early Christ followers had in bringing this message about a Jewish messiah to Gentiles. Here Paul and his opponents likely stood out. But at some point, Paul began to rethink the application of the Jewish law to Gentiles. When exactly, I remain unsure.[34] Instead of thinking that Gentile law observance was constitutive of gospel faith, Paul concluded that it signaled its rejection, a cutting oneself off from Christ, a falling away from grace (Gal 5:4). However anomalous or unique Paul purportedly was, it was not with regard to his supposed universalism or inclusiveness—itself a rather odd notion, given the particularistic nature of a gospel that requires one to believe that God has raised Jesus from the dead and initiated the eschaton, even though it is barely visible, if at all.[35] What makes Paul's thinking different from many other Jews of his day was that he was convinced that God was addressing the Gentile condition in the person of Jesus.

Conclusion

Returning to Tomoko Masuzawa's work on nineteenth-century European discourses on religion, I wonder how much progress biblical scholarship has made as a subdiscipline of religious studies. How much of this talk of exclusivity and inclusivity, particularism and universalism, is really just coded theological apologetics? F. C. Baur valued inclusivity and universalism in a Germany that was moving away from provincialism and a fragmented German state, to a unified Germany. Wright and Dunn valued inclusivity and universalism in the United Kingdom at a time when the evils of colonialism were becoming apparent to the Western conscience. Today, we too are influenced by discourses of inclusion and universalism. To my mind, there is

---

[34] On this issue, see Douglas A. Campbell, "Galatians 5.11: Evidence of an Early Law-observant Mission by Paul?" *NTS* 57 (2011): 325–47; Justin K. Hardin, "'If I Still Proclaim Circumcision' (Galatians 5:11a): Paul, the Law, and Gentile Circumcision," *JSPL* 3 (2013): 145–64; and Joshua Garroway, *The Beginning of the Gospel: Paul, Philippi, and the Origins of Christianity* (New York, NY: Palgrave MacMillan, 2018).

[35] As Jonathan Z. Smith puts it, "'Unique' becomes an ontological rather than a taxonomic category; an assertion of a radical difference so absolute that it becomes 'Wholly Other,' and the act of comparison is perceived as both an impossibility and an impiety": *Drudgery Divine: On the Comparison of Early Christianities and the Religions of Late Antiquity* (CSHJ; Chicago, IL: University of Chicago Press, 1990), 38.

much that is praiseworthy in these *modern* discourses. But to allow them to influence our *historical* work on *ancient* Judaism is to give theology, apologetics, or modern ideologies the driver's seat where it is unlicensed to drive. More than that, it is to bear false witness against others who cannot defend themselves. Such discourses of exclusivity and inclusivity are barely masked apologetics for Christianity over Judaism that claim inclusivity for Christianity at the very moment that they are guilty of, in the name of Christianity and via poor historical work, excluding, judging, and condemning the other. When such ideologies masquerade as history, it is our job to unmask them as such. Throughout his scholarship, Terry Donaldson has done just this, and I, for one, am both deeply indebted and grateful to him.

Part Two

Matthew

6

Beyond Universalism and Particularism: Rethinking Paul and Matthew on Gentile Inclusion

Anders Runesson

Introduction

Attitudes to and incorporation of non-Jews in Judaism, including the Jesus movement, is a topic about which there has been considerable disagreement, both in antiquity and among scholars today.[1] The question is closely related to ideas about salvation, so that a certain position on the status of (religio-ethnic) outsiders would have implications for theologies controlling access to the world to come, and vice versa. A third parameter is also frequently involved, that of how to define and understand the role of mission, based on the position taken on matters of inclusion and salvation.[2] Two of the most important texts/collection of texts later included in the New Testament, the Gospel of Matthew and the Pauline writings, have often been referred to in discussions of the status of Gentiles in the church. While for many modern scholars Paul and Matthew may seem to present the reader with divergent positions on several topics involved in this discussion, analyzing and juxtaposing Paul's and Matthew's attitudes to gentile inclusion, traditional scholarship has often favored, as has also the church,

---

This essay is dedicated to Terry Donaldson, friend and colleague. As an undergraduate student at Lund University in the early 1990s, I began reading Terry's work and found it extremely interesting and refreshing. His sharp mind, honesty in interpretation, and consistent refusal to avoid difficult passages and topics made me instantly add him to my list of academic heroes. He is still on that list. It has been an honor and a privilege to get to know Terry, in Canada during my McMaster years and since then after my move to Oslo. I look forward to many more years of discussions of shared interests, not least on Paul and Matthew, who persist in challenging us to always try new ways of understanding their complex and immensely important writings.

[1] For sources and discussion, see the indispensable study by Terence L. Donaldson, *Judaism and the Gentiles: Jewish Patterns of Universalism (to 135 CE)* (Waco, TX: Baylor University Press, 2007). Another important contribution, aiming at understanding Gentiles as they are presented in texts from the Dead Sea Scrolls to the *Didache*, is David C. Sim and James S. McLaren, eds., *Attitudes to Gentiles in Ancient Judaism and Early Christianity* (London: Bloomsbury, 2013).

[2] See Anders Runesson, "Particularistic Judaism and Universalistic Christianity? Some Critical Remarks on Terminology and Theology," *JGRChJ* 1 (2000): 120–44; also published in *ST* 54:1 (2000): 55–75.

a harmonized understanding of the two, not only with regard to the issue of Gentiles, but also on matters concerning Jews, Jewish law, salvation, and mission.

Overall, such readings have tended to downplay the meaning of ethnicity for membership in Christ-groups, understanding the Jewish law as abolished for Jews and Gentiles alike, and institutionalizing an ecclesial setting in which Jews may be saved alongside non-Jews, but not as Jews. The inclusion of Gentiles, in such interpretive trajectories, often results, thus, in the eradication of Jewish identity as a theologically and soteriologically meaningful category. More recent scholarship is moving away from these types of harmonized readings. Debate is still heated, however, over exactly how Matthew and Paul should be understood to differ from one another,[3] and some argue that the two are, after all, compatible, but not along the lines of the traditional interpretation.[4]

The present essay departs from previous conclusions regarding the relationship between Matthew and Paul and argues, based on an analysis of gentile inclusion in the works of these authors, that while Matthew agrees with Paul on the continuing validity of the law for the Jewish people, as they try to solve the Gentile problem the two come to conflicting conclusions about what this would mean for the nations.[5] For Matthew, based on a certain understanding of God's covenant with Israel, it is imperative that there are no distinctions within the people of God, leading to an open-ethnic stance in which Gentiles are accepted as proselytes within the movement. For Paul, on the other hand, the distinction between Jew and Gentile is of key soteriological importance, resulting in an exclusive closed-ethnic position in which Gentiles are included "in Christ" and saved as Gentiles. For both Matthew and Paul, however, Abraham is a strategic figure for their theological constructs, pointing to an understanding of grace and salvation as ethnically oriented categories, so that ethnic identity,[6] far from

---

[3] See David C. Sim, "Matthew's Anti-Paulinism: A Neglected Feature of Matthean Studies," *HTS* 58.2 (2002): 767–83, who argues that Matthew knew of Paul's writings and presented an anti-Pauline view. Ulrich Luz, *The Theology of the Gospel of Matthew* (Cambridge: Cambridge University Press,1993), 146–53, understands Matthew as incompatible with Paul, but cannot see in Matthew that the author would have opposed Pauline writings directly. Similarly, Graham Stanton, *A Gospel for a New People: Studies in Matthew* (Louisville, KY: Westminster John Knox, 1993), 314, cannot see a direct connection between Matthew and Paul, as Sim does, but still understands Matthew as "un-Pauline."

[4] Joel Willitts, "The Friendship of Matthew and Paul: A Response to a Recent Trend in the Interpretation of Matthew's Gospel," *HTS* 65.1 (2009): 150–7.

[5] While it cannot be excluded with certainty, I do not believe that we have enough evidence in Matthew to claim that the author of this text knew Paul's writings first hand. What I do think we can say is that whoever produced the Matthean text (as we have it reconstructed today) was aware of alternative ways of following and proclaiming Jesus and the kingdom, ways that this author did not approve of.

[6] It should be noted that for both Paul and Matthew, the world is divided into these two categories: Jews and Gentiles (i.e., everyone else). Thus, ethnic identity is only relevant in these texts along this line of division. In other words, while being Jewish or not is of paramount importance, other ethnicities, such as Greek or Egyptian, carries no theological meaning at all beyond the fact that they are not Jewish. Such division of the world into two main categories, the in-group and everyone else, was quite common in antiquity; the Judeo-centric worldview of Matthew and Paul is simply a variant on a common theme. It does reveal, however, the primary discursive context from within which these authors write, and, consequently, how they self-identify religio-ethnically.

being neutralized, stands at the hermeneutical center in these authors' efforts to save the world.

The results of the analysis presented here will show that the emerging mainstream church that canonized both Matthew and Paul, chose, in the end, to follow neither, as these authors' Jewish teaching for Gentiles was turned into Gentile teaching for Jews. The reasons for this development are complex and explaining them would involve both theological and sociological analysis that cannot be undertaken within the limited space of a book chapter. The purpose of this essay is only to clarify what may be involved as the question of Gentile inclusion is asked, and to show how different groups in the first century, while maintaining a positive sense of the possibility of the salvation of the nations, chose radically different paths to achieve it.

In the following we shall first discuss how the wider issue of inclusion may be approached. Then, we shall deal, in turn, with three interrelated aspects involved as our authors tackle the issue of Gentile outsiders and the requirements for their salvation: ethnicity, theologies of salvation, and missionary strategies.

Structuring the Question

Twenty years ago, I wrote an article problematizing the use of the terms "universalism" and "particularism" in academic conversations.[7] Somehow, regardless of how scholars applied these words, I found that the end result, mysteriously, always ended up being the same: Christianity was proclaimed, commendably, a "universalistic" religion, while Judaism was caught, lamentably, in "particularism."[8]

A closer look, however, at how these terms move in scholarly discourses reveal at least three very different, although connected, analytical concerns related to the image and status of the "other," when issues of inclusion are highlighted. These three areas of study, I suggest, may provide helpful entry points for discussions of our topic, even though some of the terminology I used originally may benefit from further refinement. They may be summarized as follows[9]:

1. Ethnic Status

    a. Closed-Ethnic Religion: No converts accepted into an ethno-religious group.[10]
    b. Open-Ethnic Religion: Converts accepted into an ethno-religious group).[11]

---

[7] Runesson, "Particularistic Judaism and Universalistic Christianity?"
[8] Cf. Donaldson, *Jewish Patterns of Universalism*, 1.
[9] The examples in the following footnotes are meant only as heuristic guidelines. For a full discussion see Runesson, "Particularistic Judaism and Universalistic Christianity?" One may note that several of the following approaches have been and continue to be endorsed also by groups other than those promoting certain religiously defined identities and practices, such as various political movements and parties.
[10] E.g., the Book of Ezra; *Jubilees*; some strands of rabbinic tradition.
[11] E.g., various other, and more dominant, strands of rabbinic tradition.

c. Non-Ethnic Religion: Rejection of ethnicity as a salvifically significant category.[12]
2. Salvation
   a. Salvation-Inclusive Religion: People outside the group may be considered for salvation under certain circumstances.[13]
   b. Salvation-Exclusive Religion: The boundaries of the group mark the limits of salvation.[14]

3. Mission[15]
   a. Proselytizing Mission: Aim is incorporation of the missionized into the missionary's group.[16]
   b. Ethno-Ethic Mission: Aim is modification of the behavioral patterns of people outside the missionary's group, but not through incorporation.[17]
   c. Inward Mission: Aim is modification of the beliefs and practices of the missionary's own group.[18]

If we approach the question of Gentile inclusion in Paul and Matthew organizing the evidence according to this type of analytical framework, some interesting patterns of thought and practice emerge. These patterns may in turn help clarify the interrelationship of the worldviews exhibited in these texts and uncover, ultimately, their competing understandings of what Christ-oriented Judaism[19] was or, perhaps better, should be.

---

[12] Most (modern) forms of mainstream Christianity; ancient cults such as those of Jupiter Dolichenos and Mithras, which were originally connected to an ethnic-geographic area, also developed to be unbound by ethnic requirements in terms of general membership, even though some priests of Jupiter Dolichenos continued to be exported from Syria. See Anna Collar, *Religious Networks in the Roman Empire: The Spread of New Ideas* (Cambridge: Cambridge University Press, 2013), 123.

[13] Rabbinic tradition, and most modern mainstream forms of Judaism.

[14] The foregrounded perspective of Christianity, even though other more inclusive trajectories have existed throughout its history and continues to do so today.

[15] I have revised the terminology somewhat and discussed at some length the idea of "mission" in Greco-Roman society, Judaism, and among Christ-followers, whether Jews or Gentiles, in: Anders Runesson, "Was There a Christian Mission Before the Fourth Century? Problematizing Common Ideas about Early Christianity and the Beginnings of Modern Mission," in *The Making of Christianity: Conflicts, Contacts, and Constructions* (ed. Magnus Zetterholm and Samuel Byrskog; Winona Lake, IN: Eisenbrauns, 2012), 205–47. On mission, and how mission may be defined, see also the important study by Martin Goodman, *Mission and Conversion: Proselytizing in the Religious History of the Roman Empire* (Oxford: Oxford University Press, 1995).

[16] The traditional Christian form of mission, today questioned in some Christian denominations understanding mission primarily as providing aid and relief during and after natural and political catastrophes, assisting others in need, and sharing knowledge and resources with nations in need of improving their infrastructure, etc. (Matt 25:31–46 is often referred to in such contexts, suggesting that Matt 28:18–20 should be understood as referring back to, and enjoining, the embodied practices outlined there).

[17] E.g., the Book of Jonah.

[18] The most common form of mission in Judaism, Christianity, and a number of other groups.

[19] On Paul as not being a Christian, see Pamela Eisenbaum, *Paul Was Not a Christian: The Original Message of a Misunderstood Apostle* (New York, NY: HarperOne, 2010), and the contributions to Mark Nanos and Magnus Zetterholm, eds., *Paul within Judaism: Restoring the First-Century Context to the Apostle* (Minneapolis, MN: Fortress, 2015). On Matthew as a Jewish, as opposed to a Christian, text, Anders Runesson, *Divine Wrath and Salvation in Matthew: The Narrative World of the First Gospel* (Minneapolis, MN: Fortress, 2016); Anthony J. Saldarini, *Matthew's Christian-Jewish*

In this chapter, I will argue that, while Paul and Matthew agree on the crucial issue of the continuing validity of the law for the Jewish people, including those belonging to the Jesus movement, the two come to conflicting conclusions about what this would mean for the nations, as they try to solve the Gentile problem in the aftermath of Jesus' death and resurrection.[20]

Ethnic Status and Gentile Inclusion

The issue of the relationship between the ethnic status of the worshipper and the nature of the deity worshipped lies at the center of the complex problems facing the Jesus movement as it expanded in the Diaspora. This was not unique to the Jesus movement, though, as Judaism was at home in the Diaspora well before the arrival of the Christ-followers, and other Greco-Roman cults connected with a specific people, like the Egyptian cult of Isis and the Greco-Egyptian cult of Sarapis, had long experienced an increasing interest among nonnative worshippers.[21] De-ethnosizing processes, if we may call them thus, and their opposites, were thus in the air when Paul and Matthew decided to make their voices heard in these debates, providing what they believed were relevant guidelines. Their respective solutions to the Gentile problem should thus be understood as variations on a common socioreligious theme rather than construed as idiosyncratic reactions embedded in a unique process.

Paul's original position on the ethnic aspect of our problem, at least if we are to believe Gal 5:11, was that of an open-ethnic perspective, which allowed for non-Jews to join the Jewish ethnos as they opted to seek the favor of the God of the Jews[22]: "Why am I still being persecuted, if I am still preaching circumcision? In that case, the offense of the cross has been neutralized (NRSV: 'removed'; *katargeō*)." The Paul we know from the letters, however, turned rather violently against those who declined to undergo the same change of mind he himself did, asking them to cut it all off rather than unsettle those whom he counted among his (Gentile) friends (Gal 5:12). In the Pauline world, as it also emerges in 1 Cor 7:17–18, it is of utmost importance that the *ekklēsia* reflects the diversity of the world as he knows it, divided up in two parts: Israel and the Gentiles (cf. Rom 3:29–31). Those who were called as Jews must remain Jews,[23] and the same

---

Community (Chicago, IL: Chicago University press, 1994); David C. Sim, *The Gospel of Matthew and Christian Judaism: The Historical and Social Setting of the Matthean Community* (Edinburgh: T&T Clark, 1998).

[20] On Matthew, see e.g., Matthias Konradt, *Israel, Church and the Gentiles in the Gospel of Matthew* (trans. Kathleen Ess; Waco, TX: Baylor University Press, 2014); John Kampen, *Matthew within Sectarian Judaism* (New Haven, CT: Yale University Press, 2019). On Paul see, e.g., Matthew Thiessen, *Paul and the Gentile Problem* (Oxford: Oxford University Press, 2016); Paula Fredriksen, *Paul: The Pagans' Apostle* (New Haven, CT: Yale University press, 2017).

[21] On this, see Runesson, "Was there a Christian Mission?" and idem, "Judging Gentiles in the Gospel of Matthew: Between Othering and Inclusion," in *Jesus, Matthew's Gospel and Early Christianity: Studies in Memory of Graham Stanton* (ed. Daniel M. Gurtner et al.; London: Bloomsbury, 2011), 133–51.

[22] For our purposes in this essay, I will leave open the question of whether this approach belonged to Paul's previous or current life in Judaism, respectively; the point here is the (major) shift from one position to another.

[23] Circumcision implying full Torah observance; cf. Gal 5:3.

goes for the Gentiles. If people began changing their status as a consequence of their newfound cultic loyalties, it would imply that neither Christ nor God had done a very careful job when the Spirit was poured over new members *regardless* of their ethnic (or other) status.[24] Indeed, a self-imposed obligation to make changes in one's status, post-Spirit, would be tantamount to a rejection of the Christ-event itself; it would place the member outside Christ (cf. Gal 5:4).[25] Paul's change of mind is thus best described as a move toward a closed-ethnic position, refusing, on theo-ethnic grounds, non-Jews entry into the Jewish people. Instead, Paul creates an overarching category, a globalized Christ, as it were, in which a salvific "unity in diversity" may be found.

Interestingly, Matthew's text also describes a radical change of mind on the ethnic issue, but in this story, it is Jesus himself who undergoes a transformation as he receives his resurrection body and the power that comes with it. The pre-resurrection Jesus is staunchly committed to a closed-ethnic approach to Gentiles. We see this in several passages,[26] but perhaps most clearly in Matt 10:5–6,[27] as Jesus instructs his disciples to programmatically avoid not only Gentiles, but even Samaritans. While the blessings of the kingdom, such as healing and exorcism, are not restricted to Israel exclusively (we shall return to this later when dealing with salvation), *the kingdom* is clearly not for the nations. Yet. No Gentile ever becomes a disciple in this gospel, even though some rare individual examples affirm their loyalty to Jesus, as conquered subjects would their sovereign.[28] Indeed, in Matthew's list of rules for the future *ekklēsia*, Gentiles typify the archetypal outsider: the unrepentant sinner (Matt 18:17).

In a somewhat unexpected narrative turn, however, the post-resurrection Jesus, invested with all power not only on earth but also in heaven (Matt 28:18), opens up the ethnically defined gate of discipleship to allow non-Jews to enter (28:19–20). There has been much debate as to what exactly the resurrected Jesus' sudden interest in Gentiles

---

[24] Cf. Acts 15:8–10. As seen here and elsewhere, the basic understanding of the production of theology and the rulings that often follow with it in Acts (and in Paul) is that these are human activities trying to make sense of what the divine (which is ultimately unknowable and uncontrollable; cf. Rom 11:33–36) has already accomplished. In this post-factum sense-making activity—theology—searching biblical texts that illuminate what is presented as God's acting based on certain experiences in the here-and-now plays an important, but not isolated part (Acts 15:14–15). Theology, in these texts, is thus not primarily constructed based on analysis of biblical texts ("biblical theology" represents a phenomenon quite foreign to the authors of the biblical texts), but builds on an understanding of God as a present reality capable of new, surprising, and history-changing interventions in the world.

[25] For further discussion, see Anders Runesson, "Paul's Rule in All the *Ekklēsiai* (1 Cor 7:17–24)," in *Introduction to Messianic Judaism: Its Ecclesial Context and Biblical Foundations* (ed. David Rudolph and Joel Willits; Grand Rapids, MI: Zondervan, 2013), 214–23.

[26] E.g., Matt 15:24: "I was sent only to the lost sheep of the house of Israel."

[27] Matt 10:5–8: "These twelve Jesus sent out with the following instructions: 'Go nowhere among the Gentiles, and enter no town of the Samaritans, but go rather to the lost sheep of the house of Israel. As you go, proclaim the good news, "The kingdom of heaven has come near." Cure the sick, raise the dead, cleanse the lepers, cast out demons. You received without payment; give without payment.'"

[28] So, e.g., the magi from the East (2:1–12), the centurion from the West (8:5–13), and the Canaanite from the North (or past, as Matthew's change of Mark's "Syrophoenician" [Mark 7:26] to "Canaanite" is likely meant to signal, as a generalized description of Israel's enemies; 15:21–28). They all confirm their allegiance to Jesus as if to an emperor, but only as members of "the provinces," or as resident aliens, not as Jews, or "citizens" of "the land of Israel," *gē Israel*, Matt 2:20, 21. For a detailed discussion, see Runesson, *Divine Wrath*, Part II (343–433).

really implies in terms of conversion.²⁹ As for me, I find it very difficult to avoid the following—for some, perhaps controversial—conclusion. In Matthew, discipleship is intertwined with ethnic identity. This is so because Jewish ethnic identity is, in turn, entangled with the Mosaic law (Matt 5:17–19), which itself finds a place only within the Mosaic covenant between the Jewish people and the God of Israel.³⁰ It is in the covenant, too, we find the necessary means of atonement ("grace," if you like). Until chapter 23 atonement was provided by the Jerusalem temple, but after its defilement and predicted destruction in this chapter, it will be offered through a ritual embodying and enacting the benefits of the sacrifice of the messiah (Matt 23:35–24:2; 26:28; cf. 20:28).

For Matthew, then, Jesus' death *restores* the Mosaic covenant with its law, correctly interpreted, and means of atonement,³¹ so that Jesus can save his people from their sins, fulfilling the mission expressed by his own very name (Matt 1:21). As members of the nations³² are invited to become disciples in the last two verses of the gospel, they are to be taught to keep (*tērein*) everything that Jesus has taught his own disciples (28:19), which in Matthew is the Jewish law (e.g., Matt 5–7; 19:17). This makes soteriological sense for the following reasons. (a) The law, in all its detail, will remain in force until the end of the world as we know it, as stated in the Sermon on the Mount (Matt 5:17–19). (b) Jesus reinforces this fundamental requirement for a second time in 23:23, specifying that one must keep both the heavy (such as justice, mercy, and loyalty) and the light (such as tithing) commandments, that is, rules related to both moral and ritual behavior.³³ (c) Jesus tells his own people that whoever wants to gain life in the kingdom (ζωὴν αἰώνιον) must keep the commandments (εἰ δὲ θέλεις εἰς τὴν ζωὴν εἰσελθεῖν, τήρησον τὰς ἐντολάς. 19:16–19).³⁴

It is into this world that non-Jews are invited. Beyond doubt, whatever the method used to get non-Jews to become disciples, they have to keep the Jewish law in full once they join. This, in and of itself, implies circumcision.³⁵ More generally, such a position triggers the question of the location of the law in Matthean Jewish life. We have already noted that the salvific efficacy of the law is only found within the Mosaic covenant, since the covenant provides the necessary means of atonement. Without the covenant,

---

²⁹ See, e.g., Ulrich Luz, *Matthew*, Vol. 3 (Minneapolis, MN: Fortress, 2005) ad loc.; Konradt, *Israel*, 319–20; idem, *Studien zum Matthäusevangelium* (ed. Alida Euler; Tübingen: Mohr Siebeck, 2016), esp. 23–37; Sim, *Christian Judaism*, 251–4.

³⁰ Matthew's gospel, like Mark's, does not contain the notion of a new covenant; the covenant, just as the law, is the same as it has always been, but now restored by Jesus through his sacrifice (Matt 26:28), which was made necessary by the catastrophic events recounted in Matt 23.

³¹ Without atonement, the law, which remains valid no matter what, would lead to the destruction of the people since no one exists who is free of sin, at least not according to the Matthean Jesus' authoritative interpretation of the Mosaic law.

³² On the meaning of *panta ta ethnē* in Matt 28:19, see most recently the comprehensive discussion by Terence L. Donaldson, "'Nations,' 'Non-Jewish Nations' or 'Non-Jewish Individuals': Matt 28:19 Revisited," in *Matthew within Judaism: Israel and the Nations in the First Gospel* (ed. Anders Runesson and Daniel M. Gurtner; SBL Early Christian Literature series; Atlanta: Society of Biblical Literature, forthcoming).

³³ This is also confirmed in narrative sections such as Matt 8:4.

³⁴ On the salvific efficacy of the Jewish law in Matthew, see the recent study by Mothy Varkey, *Salvation in Continuity: Reconsidering Matthew's Soteriology* (Minneapolis, MN: Fortress Press, 2017).

³⁵ Cf. Paul's confirmation of this principle, but from a negative standpoint, in Gal 5:3.

the law can only lead to destruction, and that is not what Israel's God, in Matthew's opinion, has in mind for the Gentiles. Thus, in brief: if disciple, so also law; if law, so also covenant, and with covenant, salvation.

Now, if this is what is expected of converts, what can be said about the method, or ritual, of inclusion? Baptism, or circumcision, or both? While the emphasis in Matthew certainly lies on moral purity as a salvifically meaningful category (e.g., 15:17–20; cf. 7:21–23), ritual commandments are never done away with but, as noted above, explicitly upheld. Given that this, indisputably, is the case in Matthew, I find it extremely awkward, both narratively and halakhically, to assume that a text requiring its readers to "tithe mint, dill, and cummin" (23:23) would understand (male) circumcision as so minor a commandment that it could, or even should, be neglected.[36] This means that, for Matthew, Gentile inclusion in the post-resurrection, pre-Parousia period should be understood as an invitation for non-Jews to join the Jewish ethnos, and there receive access to the two salvifically charged key elements provided by the Messiah: the Mosaic law in its correct interpretation, and a means of atonement valid in a post-temple period (what later becomes known as the Eucharist). Jesus' resurrection thus marks a narrative transition from a closed-ethnic to an open-ethnic position, which coincides with Jesus being invested with uninhibited power in heaven and on earth. Now, at the beginning of the end of the ages, non-Jews may join the Jewish people and there seek protection as the wrath of God is unleashed and the final judgment is approaching.

Paul and Matthew thus describe the exact opposite developments, as a result of their respective understanding of the Christ-event: Paul moves from an open-ethnic stance to a closed-ethnic position, and Matthew leaves behind a closed-ethnic worldview, embracing the open-ethnic option.[37] Both argue that their change of mind is key for

---

[36] Pace Konradt, *Israel*, 319–20. In relation to one of Konradt's arguments in this regard relating to Matt 5:18, it should be noted that Matt 5:18 though speaking of people with less than perfect Torah obedience as also included in the kingdom, is not referring to Gentiles, since this saying is directed to Jewish crowds and Jesus's own disciples; non-Jews are nowhere to be seen. In fact, just a few chapters later, Matthew is explicit about Gentiles not being part of the pre-resurrection Jesus's intended audience: Matt 10:5–6. Indeed, the saying in Matt 5:18 itself is meant to counter any kind of laxity and encourage full Torah obedience.

[37] A comparison of these differences between Paul and Matthew on the one hand and Josephus' story about the conversions related to the royal house of Adiabene (*AJ* 20.34–48) sheds further light on the context within which our authors wrote. One of the "missionaries" in Josephus' story, a certain Ananias, argues that it is quite possible to "worship God without being circumcised, even though he [the king] did resolve to follow the Jewish law entirely" (20.41: δυνάμενον δ' αὐτὸν ἔφη καὶ χωρὶς τῆς περιτομῆς τὸ θεῖον σέβειν, εἴγε πάντως κέκρικε ζηλοῦν τὰ πάτρια τῶν Ἰουδαίων). Even though Ananias' solution is presented as a solution to a difficult political situation (would the king's subjects accept being ruled by a Jew, which the king would become if he went through with his plan of getting circumcised?), following the law in this way without circumcision would require God's forgiveness. Josephus thus does not present Ananias' solution as ideal, but has to invoke God's mercy as a component for his plan to work ("He added, that God would forgive him, though he did not perform the operation, while it was omitted out of necessity, and for fear of his subjects"; 20.42). Ananias's opponent, Eleazer the Galilean, however, was not prepared to suggest to the king to count on such divine lenience, urging the king to undergo the operation, which he also did. For Eleazer, who is presented as "extremely strict" in matters of the law, it is not enough to read the law; one must also practice it in all its parts (20.43–48; cf. Matt 7:21–23). It is of some interest to note, perhaps, that Eleazer is presented as a Galilean, and that an increasing number of scholars now argue that Matthew's gospel was likely composed in the Galilee in the late first century. On this, see the discussion by David C. Sim, "The Gospel of Matthew and Galilee. An Evaluation of an Emerging Hypothesis," *Z Neutestament WISS*, 107.2 (2016): 141–69. Sim himself, however, concludes that

the salvation of the Gentiles. While for Paul the *ekklēsia* requires ethnic diversity, Matthew refuses ethnic distinctions in the kingdom—and the differences between people that come with them[38]—as he welcomes all to consider whether salvation would be something they would be interested in when the divine judge arrives.

The question of the role of ethnic reasoning in relation to Gentile inclusion can hardly be satisfactorily treated without consideration of how ethnicity relates to salvation, since the possibility of salvation for non-Jews is what is at stake in these discourses. Turning now, therefore, to the topic of salvation. As we shall see, while some broader themes are certainly distinguishable, things are not always as simple as they first seem, and Paul and Matthew again part ways.

Salvation and Gentile Inclusion

As noted in the introduction, our source material presents us with two basic attitudes: A salvation-inclusive and a salvation-exclusive position. To repeat, the former refers to the notion that individuals outside of one's own group may attain salvation without conversion, and the latter suggests the opposite: outside the group, there is no salvation.[39] How do Paul and Matthew compare from this perspective? Would it be correct to assume that if Gentiles are asked to join the Jesus movement and they do not, they are condemned? The answer is both yes and no, depending on who we ask.

While it is clear, in my opinion, that Paul takes a salvation-inclusive view with regard to those among his own people who decline the offer of joining the "in-Christ" group (Rom 11:26, 28–29), we do not see Paul fretting too much about the status of those from among the nations who decline his offer. It is true that Paul does mention on one occasion that an unbelieving husband is made holy through his believing wife, and vice versa, and that their children therefore will be holy (1 Cor 7:14). But apart from such specific cases, Paul does not have much to say that is positive about Gentiles outside Christ. This leads us to classify his theology of Gentiles as, in general, salvation-exclusive; if non-Jews want to be saved, they must join in-Christ groups, because these groups embody the Christ. Paul thus combines a closed-ethnic outlook with a salvation-exclusive stance, an intriguing position to take, which can only be explained by his globalized in-Christ theology.

For Matthew, the situation is, equally intriguingly, the opposite. One would have expected that a gospel that uses Gentiles in order to typify the archetypal outsider would also be committing to a salvation-exclusive position. But this is not at all what we find.[40] As in many other forms of Judaism, past and present, the idea of the righteous

---

Antioch is, still, the most likely place of authorship for Matthew. For discussion of the Adiabene story, see Donaldson, *Jewish Patterns of Universalism,* 333–8, and Mark D. Nanos, "Paul's Non-Jews Do Not Become 'Jews,' But Do They Become 'Jewish'?: Reading Romans 2:25–29 within Judaism, Alongside Josephus" *JJMJS* 1 (2014): 26–53, http://www.jjmjs.org/.

[38] Such as the different law-codes for Jews and Gentiles in Acts 15:13–21; cf. Acts 21:20. Such a solution is opposed, we are told, by Christ-following Pharisees more aligned with the views forwarded in Matthew's gospel (Acts 15:5).

[39] Echoing Cyprian's (d. 258) dictum, *extra ecclesiam nulla salus* ("outside the church there is no salvation").

[40] For analysis and discussion, see Runesson, *Divine Wrath,* Part II.

Gentile is an important aspect of Matthew's theology of the Gentile outsider. In the well-known so-called parable of the sheep and the goats in Matt 25:31–46, the heavenly judge (the Son of Man/Jesus) has arrived to pass judgment on *panta ta ethnē* (25:32). I take this phrase as a reference to members of all non-Jewish nations, thus excluding the Jewish people, including the Jesus movement (which is Jewish, since Gentiles who join become Jews in the process).[41] What interests us in this pericope is, primarily, that non-Jewish outsiders, who have responded compassionately to the suffering of (Jewish) Christ-followers, will be saved and allowed entry into the kingdom.[42] What we have here is a programmatic salvation-inclusive position written into Matthew's gospel. With this follows a definition of the righteous Gentile as dependent on those with whom the judge, that is, Jesus, identifies—Jesus-oriented Jews.[43]

In sum, Matthew combines a salvation-inclusive position with an open-ethnic stance, which might seem counterintuitive if you aim at attracting a great number of converts from the nations. It does make both social and theological sense, though, for a minority group suffering persecution and finding unexpected assistance from outsiders. Again, contrary to Paul, Matthew has included in his text, uniquely among the gospels, a carefully outlined theology of righteous Gentiles, a theology more similar to later rabbinic thought on the issue than to any mainstream Christian attempts at making sense of the post-judgment fate of the benevolent other. This leads us, finally, to the issue of mission.

Mission and Gentile Inclusion

Paul's theology (and practice) of mission follows closely from his position on the ethnic issue, and therefore presents us with a complicated, in-between scenario. As we noted earlier when structuring our quest to understand ancient Gentile inclusion in Judaism, any proselytizing mission is based on the conviction that in order to be salvifically effective the effort must be to incorporate the other—in this case the Gentile other—into the group to which the missionary him- or herself belongs. But since Paul has a two-tier system, with two subgroups (Jews and non-Jews) within his overarching group identity (in-Christ), this terminology needs to be modified. Paul does not—emphatically not!—want non-Jews to attain his own status as a *Jewish* member of the *ekklēsia*. But he does want to include them as *non-Jews* in Christ, and he does require them to leave behind their old cultic habits, not only their lamentable ethical behavior, since for Paul cult and ethics are intertwined (cf. Gal 2:15; 4:8–10; 5:16–21, 24).

This results in a position that falls just between proselytizing mission and what we have called ethno-ethic mission, as the latter aims only at correcting the behavior of the other, according to the missionary's own understanding of divinely approved

---

[41] The judgment on the Jewish people, including the Jesus movement, is dealt with elsewhere in the gospel, and will, of course, also occur. On the meaning of *panta ta ethnē*, see the recent study by Donaldson, "Nations."
[42] The pattern here is similar to the pattern of thought surfacing in Gen 12:3.
[43] Cf. the similar pattern of thought applied to Jews, in Matt 10:40–42.

out-group conduct.⁴⁴ Paul's practices related to Gentile inclusion thus changed from the proselytizing mission mentioned in Gal 5:11, which for him led to no persecution, to what we may call an inclusive ethno-ethic missionary strategy, which did cause him suffering (indicating that his was a minority position).

As for Matthew, the approach to mission in this text changes along with the changed understanding of the ethnic issue. While the closed-ethnic stance for Matthew led to an explicit prohibition against mission to the Gentile other (Matt 10:5–6), the post-resurrection Jesus demands of his disciples that they add to their already ongoing inward mission a proselytizing outreach too, in order to extend the offer of salvation to the nations. In the period before Jesus attains all power on earth and in heaven (the narrative until Matt 28:18), we find in this gospel a centripetal movement of non-Jews seeking Jesus' help, wishing to receive a share of the blessings of the kingdom (e.g., Matt 8:5–13; 15:21–28). None of these individuals are taught by Jesus, however; neither are they baptized nor asked to follow him (as for the latter, contrary to Jews who seek his advice: e.g., 19:16–20). There simply is no mission to outsiders taking place during Jesus' lifetime in this story. Indeed, it is only Jesus' disciples after his death and resurrection that are told to device a (messianic-) Jewish mission to non-Jews, designing it based on two fundamental requirements: non-Jews must be baptized,⁴⁵ and they must be taught Jewish law (28:19–20).⁴⁶ This mission is thus best described as a proselytizing mission, aiming to incorporate the "other" in the missionaries' own group, the Jewish people.

Do we see any commonalities here between Paul and Matthew? In practical terms, hardly any. While both of them aim at saving the Gentile other, their strategies, and the convictions that lead to their respective strategies, are diametrically opposed. Indeed, on the issue of Gentile inclusion, Matthew incarnates, one could say, together with the Jesus-believing Pharisees in Acts 15:5, Paul's worst opponents, those he wishes would cut it all off rather than interfere with his own missionary strategies (Gal 5:3, 12).⁴⁷

In light of the path eventually taken by the mainstream churches, the above discussion may seem to foreground convictions and strategies of inclusion quite foreign to Christian sentiments. A few concluding remarks are thus in order to contextualize and be precise about how different the views of Matthew and Paul really were, and how both their views differ from what eventually came to be the standard view of most churches.

---

[44] As noted above, the Book of Jonah would be one of the earliest examples of this type of approach to mission. See also the position of Ananias in the Adiabene case as described by Josephus (note 37, in this chapter). One may, in addition, think of the later rabbinic formulations of the Noahide commandments, which are, today, missionized to non-Jews by some Jewish groups.

[45] One may note here that Jews are never baptized in Matthew's narrative, except for the baptism performed by John the Baptizer in Matt 3.

[46] The content of the teaching to be extended to the nations is clearly the law of Moses, as it was originally intended to be understood. This is what Jesus has been teaching the Jewish crowds and his disciples throughout the narrative; see esp. Matt 5–7; 19:17; 23:23.

[47] One may also point out, of course, that Matthew's position on circumcision of non-Jewish males wanting to join the movement is reflected in Paul's own previous position (Gal 5:11), before he changed his mind on the topic.

Conclusion: A Historical and Canonical Crux

As we put aside the problematic terms "universalism" and "particularism," and focussed on the issues involved rather than risking to be led astray by generalizing expressions more prone to obscuring than to clarifying what is at stake, an interesting pattern has emerged. This pattern reveals significant diversity with regard to how early Christ-groups approached and theologized Gentile inclusion. Applying the three-pronged strategy suggested in this essay to Paul and Matthew, but now also adding comments on the path that the mainstream churches eventually took in order for us to see more clearly the cultural matrix within which we ourselves traditionally operate, a brief summary may take the following form.

Ethnic Status

- Paul: From an open-ethnic stance to a closed-ethnic position.
- Matthew: From a closed-ethnic stance to an open-ethnic position.
- Later Mainstream Churches: Rejecting both of the above; most maintaining until today a nonethnic position.

The Aspect of Salvation

- Paul: Salvation-exclusive (in relation to non-Jews).
- Matthew: Salvation-inclusive.
- Later Mainstream Churches: Predominantly salvation-exclusive regardless of ethnic identity, but with trajectories of salvation-inclusiveness surfacing today more than in previous periods.

Mission (Theology and Practice)

- Paul: From proselytizing to inclusive ethno-ethic mission. Aim is in-Christ, together with, but distinguished from, Christ-oriented Jews.
- Matthew: From non-mission (in relation to Gentiles) to proselytizing mission. Aim is Christ-oriented Jewish identity; Judaism.
- Later Mainstream Churches: Proselytizing mission. Aim is (non-Jewish) Christianity.

Not only do we see here some rather radical disagreements between Paul and Matthew, but we may also note that the mainstream church, which canonized them both, chose a path fundamentally different from either of them.

For the mainstream churches, the move to a nonethnic position turned on its head the very point of departure for Paul's and Matthew's strategizing on Gentile inclusion. What was for Paul and Matthew an ethno-religious matter of course—that Judaism (in its Christ-oriented form) was the gift that would save even the non-Jews—morphed in the hands of Christians into an archetypal heresy. Starting with Ignatius of Antioch, *christianismos* was declared independent of, and contradictory to, *ioudaismos*, changing the core of the interpretive dynamics that explain both Paul's and Matthew's theological behavior. Perhaps this is most clearly evidenced in the fact that whereas the aim of Matthew's proselytism was to invite non-Jews into (his form of) Judaism, the proselytism of the later church aimed at the very opposite: to turn Jews into (Christian) non-Jews. In this process, Paul's letters may have been useful as political tools, but against their intent and, I would argue, beyond their innate hermeneutical span of control. What began as variants of Jewish teachings for Gentiles were thus transformed into Gentile teaching for Jews. And that, as history shows, has made all the difference, even, until very recently, in Academia.

Matthew's Trojan Horse: The Construction of Christian Identity in the Sermon on the Mount through a Stereotype of the Scribes and Pharisees

Stephen Black

The Pharisees and the scribes are cast as the Gospel of Matthew's prime villains. They are hypocritical moral failures and persistent opponents of Jesus. This representation was unquestioned for millennia such that the terms "Pharisee" and "hypocrite" become interchangeable. A 1933 English dictionary defines Pharisee as "a formal sanctimonious hypocritical person." To be pharisaical is "observing the form, but neglecting the spirit of religion."[1] It is not surprising that this definition is not found in some later dictionaries. The ghastly events of World War II with the death of six million Jews has caused many to reconsider how we use the language.[2] As the events of the Holocaust have caused some dictionaries to reconsider what words ought to mean, so too have they prompted many Christians to scrutinize texts, such as Matthew, that gave rise to the stereotype of the Pharisee in the first place.

What did Matthew accomplish through this stereotype? Matthew was involved in a fierce battle with another Jewish group represented by the Pharisees. Matthew was not the only Christian group that had conflicts with the Pharisees, but Matthew's battle may have raged the hottest (with perhaps the fourth gospel being a close rival). The issues behind this battle were multiple, including Matthew's reconfiguration of the prime symbols of the Jewish tradition presenting Jesus as the central, most important religious element within the symbolic universe.

Behind all this, however, is an even deeper issue, and that was the question of identity. Matthew and his community were creating an identity for themselves. In the process of this identity creation they also created an identity for their opponents, and stereotyping is an effective way to do this. Stereotypes, however, are funny things

---

[1] Funk and Wagnalls, *Practical Standard Dictionary of the English Language* (1933), s.v. "Pharisee."
[2] See *Oxford Dictionary of Current English*, 3rd ed. (2001), s.v. "Pharisee." This does not mean that the former meaning portrayed in the earlier dictionaries no longer exists in modern culture. A quick search on the internet for Pharisee or pharisaic will demonstrate that the stereotype is alive and well.

as they usually tell us more about the one doing the labeling than they do about the one being labeled. This means the literary Pharisees in Matthew's gospel may end up telling us very little about the historical Pharisees of either Jesus' or Matthew's time, but will reveal a great deal about Matthew and his community. Stereotypes are a way to draw borders delineating "us" and "them" in such a way that the existence of them is a presupposition to the existence of us. This makes the Pharisees an essential component of Matthew's identity. The Matthean Christ follower would cease being what they are if the Pharisees ceased being the Pharisees.

The Sermon on the Mount has been described as Matthew's "greatest composition," a "harmonious masterpiece of ethical and religious teaching,"[3] and the epitome of Jesus' moral teaching.[4] This Sermon has occupied a central place in Christian thought, such that there is an intimate "connection between the Sermon on the Mount and the church at any given time."[5] The Sermon has been felt to embody the highest possible ethical standards and has thus been given a pride of place in Christian ethical thought.

Matthew 5:20 stands close to the beginning of the Sermon, immediately after the introductory beatitudes and the brief sayings concerning salt and light. It is both the concluding remark for the introductory section (5:17–20), and the introduction for what follows. Matthew 5:20 defines and explains what comes after it, especially 5:21–48. It provides an interpretive key through which the first part of the Sermon is to be understood.

In Matthew 5:18–20 a righteousness that fulfills the law is contrasted with a righteousness that does not fulfill the law. Matthew 5:20 connects the righteousness that does not fulfill the law—a lower "righteousness"—with the Pharisees. This lower righteousness is really no righteousness at all, as possessing it will not gain one entrance into the kingdom of heaven. Matthew 5:20 demands that the righteousness that Matthew's followers of Jesus must attain be better than that of the scribes and Pharisees. The inadequate righteousness of the scribes and Pharisees provides a foil for the higher righteousness.

The Pharisee stereotype provides a negative example against which Jesus' higher righteousness comes to light. The Pharisees represent whatever it is that Jesus' higher righteousness is being contrasted to. Furthermore, because Matt 5:20 is the introduction to the following section (5:21–48), the Pharisees represent what is on the negative pole of the antitheses. Hence, the Pharisee stereotype stands behind each example as the foil for understanding Jesus' new higher fulfilled righteousness. The Pharisee stereotype represents a religious praxis that accepts anger, judgment, lust, revenge, all the while presuming a righteousness that adheres to Torah. It obeys Torah through an external compliance that misses its inner message. In short, the Pharisees are stereotyped as hypocrites.

---

[3] Raymond E. Brown, *An Introduction to the New Testament* (New York, NY: Doubleday, 1996), 178.
[4] F. L. Cross and E. A. Livingstone, eds., *The Oxford Dictionary of the Christian Church* (3rd ed.; Oxford: Oxford University Press), 1997, 1487.
[5] Ulrich Luz, *Matthew 1–7: A Commentary* (Augsburg: Fortress Press, 1989), 218.

Cognition and Stereotypes

But what is a stereotype? The word *stereotype* originally came from the printing industry:

> plate ... [that] is made by setting movable type as for ordinary printing; from these a cast is taken in plaster of Paris, paper pulp, or the like, and upon this cast melted type metal is poured, which, when hardened, makes a solid page or column, from which the impression is taken as from type.[6]

Metaphorically, then, a stereotype came to mean something, "cast into rigid form for the purposes of repetition."[7] In popular thought, using stereotypes is thought to be a pathological activity engaged in by individuals who are "both evil and erroneous, and represent ... flawed thinking (or more correctly, lack of thinking)."[8] However, if stereotyping is indeed the result of misinformation or poor thinking then we might reasonably conclude that all that is needed is more accurate information.[9] While better information might be part of the solution in some cases, researchers have found that one of the most salient features of stereotypes is their "rigidity and resistance to information that contradicts them."[10] This suggests that stereotyping is not merely the result of faulty thinking.

Humans face an enormously complex environment where we are "bombarded with a multitude of stimulation" and to make sense of this, we create categories.[11] Categories serve many functions: they help us to "simplify our environment"; they "enable us to generate expectations" about those objects that have been categorized; they help us to "consider a greater amount of information at any one time."[12] A stereotype is a way that people categorize their social world. Stereotypes give people a means to categorize other people so that they do not need to understand each person individually as discrete entities.[13] It is not individuals by themselves who are stereotyped, but individuals *as members of groups*.[14]

---

[6] *Webster's Revised Unabridged Dictionary* (1998), s.v. "stereotype."
[7] Michael Pickering, *Stereotyping: The Politics of Representation* (Hampshire: Palgrave, 2001), 9.
[8] Stephen Worchel and Hank Rothgerber, "Changing the Stereotype of the Stereotype," in *The Social Psychology of Stereotyping and Group Life* (ed. Russell Spears et al.; Oxford: Blackwell, 1997), 73.
[9] Pickering, *Stereotyping*, 11–12.
[10] Henri Tajfel, *Human Groups and Social Categories: Studies in Social Psychology* (Cambridge: Cambridge University Press, 1981), 133.
[11] David A. Wilder, "Perceiving Persons as a Group: Categorization and Intergroup Relations," in *Cognitive Processes in Stereotyping and Intergroup Behavior* (ed. David L. Hamilton; Mahwah, NJ: Lawrence Erlbaum, 1981), 213.
[12] Ibid., 213.
[13] Victor Ottati and Yueh-Ting Lee, "Accuracy: A Neglected Component of Stereotype Research," in *Stereotype Accuracy: Toward Appreciating Group Differences* (ed. Yueh-Ting Lee et al.; Washington, DC: American Psychological Association, 1995), 40.
[14] Shelley E. Taylor, "A Categorization Approach to Stereotyping," in Hamilton, *Cognitive Processes*, 83. People also regularly stereotype themselves as members of groups. See S. Alexander Haslam, "Stereotyping and Social Influence: Foundations of Stereotype Consensus," in Spears et al., *Social Psychology*, 130–4.

Matthew created cognitive order for himself and his community by forming social categories. These stereotypes are generalizations and simplifications about complex intricate realities, and they assisted him in creating a map of his social world. Like all maps, this one defined boundaries. Stereotypes provided a means to make sense of what was otherwise a very confusing world. How different were the Pharisees of history to the Pharisees of Matthew's gospel? In other words, how accurate might Matthew's stereotype of the Pharisees be? Stereotyping involves naïve essentialist assumptions regarding the nature of groups, which is to say, that social collectives have deep, defining *essences*. The Pharisees were a social creation and not an ontological entity, and even if some Pharisees demonstrated hypocritical tendencies, is it appropriate to understand these tendencies as an essential part of their nature? The essentialist foundation of stereotypes explains their rigidity. It has also caused some to reject a connection between categorization and stereotyping. Categorization, "a necessary way of organizing the world in our minds, creating mental maps for working out how we view the world," is something that "can be used flexibly and their designations can be disputed," whereas stereotyping, also a means of "imposing order on the social world," does so through denying "any flexible thinking."[15] This charge can be responded to by simply affirming that while stereotyping is a form of categorization, it is nevertheless a flawed one.

Bracketing out the question of essentialism, it is helpful to consider what types of error are typically involved in stereotyping. There are three basic types of inaccuracies: (1) *stereotype inaccuracy* where traits are exaggerated; (2) *valence inaccuracy* where a group is "viewed more or less positive than it actually is"; (3) and *dispersion inaccuracy* where the homogeneity of a group, or its "variability," is viewed as more or less distinct than it actually is.[16]

The Pharisee stereotype would suffer from *stereotype inaccuracy* if Pharisees were not found to be any more hypocritical than any other group. It would suffer from *valence inaccuracy* if the trait of being a hypocrite itself was viewed more negatively than it actually is. To get to the "truth" of the matter, one would have to re-narrate the Pharisees so that the same qualities that Matthew presents as negative would be re-represented as positive (or at least neutral). This means taking Matthew's version seriously enough on a surface level, but challenging it on a level of valuation. But can one re-narrate hypocrisy as a positive trait? Finally, the error would have been *dispersion inaccuracy* if Matthew saw a greater homogeneity in the Pharisees than actually existed. Did Matthew unfairly cast all Pharisees as hypocrites despite the fact there were some who were not hypocrites?[17]

A problem with the accuracy question is that demonstrating either the veracity (even if only partial) of a stereotype requires an ability to compare the stereotype against how the group under question *really is in itself*.[18] Even apart from the essentialist

---

[15] Pickering, *Stereotyping*, 2, 3.
[16] Charles Judd and Bernadette Park, "Definition and Assessment of Accuracy in Social Stereotypes," *PsycholRev* 100 (1993): 110–12.
[17] Ibid.
[18] Penelope J. Oakes and Katherine J. Reynolds, "Asking the Accuracy Question: Is Measurement the Answer?" in Spears et al., *Social Psychology*, 51.

presuppositions involved in this, we simply do not have access to the relevant data required to determine what kind of error Matthew might have made. Modern studies that attempt to do this usually use self-questionnaires for the purpose of self-analysis, a process that raises problems for researchers. Obviously, researching the ancient Pharisees cannot include such a self-evaluation, whether problematic or not, and this leaves us only with Matthew's account and perhaps some relevant information from Josephus or the Talmud. All three of these sources have enough ideology in their portrayals of the Pharisees to make them unreliable sources for the purposes of historical reconstruction. Specifically, Matthew's representation of his opponents is so loaded with polemic that one must treat it with extreme caution as a source of historical information.

If Matthew's stereotype of the Pharisees cannot be taken as an accurate representation of the Pharisees of history, it can nevertheless be taken seriously as a narrative creation, reflecting Matthew's social and ideological location. Matthew's Pharisee stereotype reflects reality from his own subjective vantage point and relative to his own values.[19] While stereotypes are not accurate in any objective way, they nevertheless "provide the perceiver with an accurate representation of reality from that perceiver's own vantage point, and relative to that perceiver's own values."[20] Certainly there were real Pharisees "out there" for Matthew, but by taking this relativistic starting point we can sidestep questions relating to Matthew's historical fairness, and simply consider how and what his narrative Pharisee stereotype accomplished for his story and his community. In short, Matthew's stereotype of the Pharisees provides little reliable information concerning the historical Pharisees, but a great deal of information concerning Matthew and his concerns.

Caught in a battle for legitimacy with his Pharisaic opponents, Matthew organized his world by casting them as villains in his grand drama and his own community as heroes (with Jesus as the chief hero), an understandable strategy. He stereotyped his Pharisaic (and scribal) opponents as hypocrites. The Pharisees had to be categorized negatively because to do so in a more neutral (let alone positive) light would be to legitimize the label (of perhaps apostasy?) with which the Pharisees had likely labeled Matthew's community. This is to say that on some level it is likely that Matthew was reacting to a negative stereotype being leveled against him and his community by those represented by the Pharisees. In a predictable gesture of defense, Matthew cast his opponents not just as villains in his story, but as villains with a predictable trait—hypocrisy. This robs them of moral authority. It is not incidental to Matthew's overall story, but serves a vital function in the formation of identity and value.

Social Psychology and Stereotypes

Identity is important to us—people are willing to kill and to die for it. Philosophers, anthropologists, sociologists, psychologists, and theologians define the nature of

---

[19] Ibid., 68.
[20] Ibid.

identity or of the "self" differently. For social psychologists, identity is approached as a social phenomenon—as the social self. Social identity is "that part of an individual's self-concept which derives from his knowledge of his membership of a social group (or groups) together with the value and emotional significance attached to that membership."[21] The social self is an important part of a person's self-understanding and helps to "create and define the individual's place in society."[22]

The social self is the result of a self-categorization process (typically involving stereotypes) based upon what group(s) persons belong to. These groups can be very broad—such as male or female—or narrower—such as pregnant women or plumber. This self-categorization process is a way by which people define themselves.[23] The self-concept is dynamic and fluid with an ever-changing center of gravity. People belong to several groups at any given time and some categories are more important to individuals than other categories, being more "central, valued, and ego involving."[24] It might be relatively incidental to someone that she is a woman but very important that she is a plumber.

A person's social identity can take on such importance that their personal identity is eclipsed. When a woman identifies herself in contrast to men, "she (subjectively *we*) tends to accentuate perceptually her similarities to other women (and reduce her idiosyncratic personal differences from other women) and enhances perceptually her stereotypical differences from men."[25] Inasmuch as her "idiosyncratic personal differences" have been submerged under her stereotypical representation of herself as a group member, she has been *depersonalized*.[26] If a pregnant woman, surrounded by other pregnant women, has "activated" the "pregnant woman" self-concept, she is stereotyping herself (and other pregnant women) by highlighting what is believed to be similarities shared between all pregnant women and has become de-individuated inasmuch as her idiosyncratic personal differences are not the center of gravity for her self-concept, but rather the fact that she is pregnant. Thus, the level and content of the self changes: it changes levels as it either moves "up" or "down" by identifying more or less strongly with a group over against an idiosyncratic personal self; it changes content through identifying with a different group (e.g., married woman vs. pregnant woman).

Relationships between people are in large part determined by the representation (or stereotype) of the self and of the other that people hold at any given time. It has been suggested that there is a continuum in this representation, going from the *interpersonal* to the *intergroup*. At the interpersonal end of the continuum "the interaction ... is determined by the personal relationship between the individuals and by their

---

[21] Henri Tajfel, ed., *Differentiation between Social Groups: Studies in the Social Psychology of Intergroup Relations* (London: Academic Press, 1978), 63.
[22] Ibid.
[23] John C. Turner, "Towards a Cognitive Redefinition of Social Groups," in *Social Identity and Intergroup Relations* (ed. Henri Tajfel; Cambridge: Cambridge University Press, 1982), 17–18.
[24] John C. Turner and Rina S. Onorato, "Social Identity, Personality, and the Self-Concept: A Self-Categorization Perspective," in *The Psychology of the Social Self* (ed. Tom R. Tyler et al.; Mahwah, NJ: Lawrence Erlbaum, 1999), 22.
[25] Italics in original. Turner and Onorato, "Social Identity," 22.
[26] This is not to be confused with *deindividuation*, which denotes a loss of self. To be depersonalized is not to lose the self but to change the "level and content of [the] self" (ibid., 20–1, 24).

respective individual characteristics," while at the intergroup end the relationships are determined exclusively by "membership in different social groups or categories."[27] The extreme interpersonal end of the continuum exists only theoretically as any interaction between people is always conditioned in some fashion by social category and group membership. The extreme intergroup end of the continuum however is imaginable in the real world.[28] As one moves toward the intergroup side the more homogeneous people are seen to be according to the active stereotypes, both within one's group (ingroup) and without (outgroup).[29] One's understanding of one's self is also different on the intergroup side of the continuum as one might cease seeing one's own uniqueness (deindividuation) and one might instead see oneself as a "prototypical representative ... of their ingroup category."[30] A pregnant woman might feel that she is the quintessential pregnant woman and this might prompt different forms of behavior to both ingroup (to other pregnant women as a presumed model and guide) and outgroup (to non-pregnant women or to men).

There are also different levels of commitment that individuals will give to a group. The level of commitment becomes obvious between the "fair-weather" and the "die-hard" group members when the group is threatened. The fair-weather group members, being more concerned with personal identity, are typically inclined to dissociate themselves from the threatened group letting it dissolve. The die-hard group members are likely to fight to protect the group's "distinctiveness, even when that group has a negative image."[31]

The issue of identity was of great significance for Matthew. Being a leader in his community he was certainly a high-identifier group member and his level of commitment may not have been the same as an average group member. However, we cannot be sure from Matthew what the average member's level of commitment was. Given the high level of polemic it is likely that Matthew's community lived as a whole in tension with the community represented by the Pharisees. It could be that some average Matthean believers maintained relations with Pharisaic neighbors by keeping their beliefs hidden, yet Matthew's redaction of Mark 8:34-9:1 speaks against this. In Mark there are severe warnings against being ashamed of Jesus, which would have been appropriate had Matthew wished to combat a trend in his community toward keeping group membership hidden, and these warnings are all excised in Matthew's version. It is possible that given the stakes of being a follower of Jesus (such as losing kinship relations) in Matthew's community that most members were high identifiers. This would mean that for Matthew's community group membership meant a great deal. In other words, they would have typically defined themselves primarily in terms of their membership to the ἐκκλησία.

---

[27] Henri Tajfel, "Interindividual Behaviour and Intergroup Behaviour," in Tajfel, *Differentiation between Social Groups*, 41.
[28] Ibid., 41.
[29] Turner and Onorato, "Social Identity," 19.
[30] Ibid., 21.
[31] Bertjan Doosje and Naomi Ellemers, "Stereotyping under Threat: The Role of Group Identification," in Spears et al., *Social Psychology*, 271.

This means that Matthew's group had power over its members. Because groups retain the right to exclude their own members and to withdraw ingroup status, there is a communal leverage against its individual members to "toe the line." Matthew's community explicitly maintained such power as articulated in 18:17, where the unrepentant follower of Jesus is to be cast out of the community. Stereotypes involve consensus thinking by an ingroup about an outgroup and it can be socially hazardous for a group member to call this consensus into question. A member of a conservative political party who says positive things about radicals will be viewed with suspicion by others in the group and might be expelled from the group if these positive statements that question the accepted stereotype of the other do not cease. This explains, at least in part, why stereotypes can be so widely shared.[32] As concerns Matthew, this meant that there was a collective power to perpetuate the negative representation of the Pharisees. If a group member were to challenge seriously this negative representation this might result in a questioning of ingroup status and might even result in expulsion. If someone started affirming the virtues of the Pharisees, they would likely be seen with suspicion and their commitment to the value of the Matthean community would be questioned, resulting in a loss of ingroup status.

It is probable that Matthew himself was also subject to such pressure as it is unlikely that he manufactured the negative representation in isolation from the rest of his community. This is not to suggest that he was in any way reluctant to perpetuate and develop this theme. Nevertheless, he stood inside the group and thus was subject to the ingroup power dynamics.

The Systemic and Stereotypes

Identity is also relevant systemically. Stereotypes function less obviously at this level. A stereotype that "blacks are lazy" can be an individual way of organizing the world cognitively, and it can be a way of defining the collective other against the collective self. An analysis that stays on these levels might unwittingly obscure the fact that this stereotype may also be a means of rationalizing a system of economic and social injustice.[33]

The systemic world behind Matthew's gospel is the Roman Empire. How did Matthew identify as a member of the empire? It is difficult to know which metaphors were informed by values of the Roman Empire. How much of Matthew's *Kingdom of Heaven* was modeled upon (or against) the Roman kingdom and how much was simply modeled upon Israel's writings and mythic past? It is interesting to note that Matthew seems blissfully unaware of the Roman Empire in Matt 19:28—in the consummation Jesus' followers do not rule over the nations, be they Rome or Greece, but will "sit on twelve thrones, *judging the twelve tribes of Israel*." Matthew's sights are apparently

---

[32] Haslam, "Stereotyping and Social Influence," 119.
[33] Charles Stangor and John T. Jost, "Commentary: Individual, Group and System Levels of Analysis and Their Relevance for Stereotyping and Intergroup Relations," in Spears et al., *Social Psychology*, 339.

not on the nations, but exclusively on Israel, at least in Matt 19:28.[34] Whatever this says about Matthew's identity as a member of the Roman Empire is uncertain, but it does suggest Matthew's contention with the Pharisees had more to do with defining Israel than Christology. Matthew's self-concept as one colonialized by Rome did not explicitly penetrate his eschatological expectations, at least inasmuch as Matt 19:28 is concerned. It is difficult to reconstruct Matthew's view of the Roman Empire, as the subject is not (explicitly) raised in his gospel.

How did Matthew's stereotyping of the Pharisees reinforce or challenge the empire? Minorities that cannot secure "a clear conception of the ingroup" can implode destructively with internal battles.[35] The factional and fragmented nature of Second Temple Judaism was arguably a result of being an occupied people (at least in part)—a result of the Roman Empire. Perhaps one of the hidden factors lying behind the battles between Matthew and the Pharisees was the occupation by Rome of Israel. This is even more central after the events of 70 CE are taken into mind, when Rome destroyed the temple in Jerusalem. A central religious symbol lay in ruins and the people were scattered. Because of this oppressive act of Rome, all Jews, be they non-Christian or Christian, had to reconfigure collective identities (as well as symbolic universes). Matthew writes during the initial cultural rebuilding process. The Pharisees (or perhaps early proto-Rabbis, who may have been represented by the Pharisee) and Matthew had different ideas on how to rebuild.

Matthew highlights the value of interiority in religion. The religion of the Sermon on the Mount is one that while not introspective after the fashion of Luther and the West was nevertheless preoccupied with interiority—that is, in motives or inclinations of the inner person.[36] These inclinations are all related to interpersonal issues and yet are nevertheless a form of interiority. Matthew's stereotyping of the Pharisees in the Sermon on the Mount establishes the Pharisees as the foil for this interiority. They, unlike the Matthean followers of Jesus, have merely an exterior form of religion—a religion that delights in human praise and outward show (see also Matt 23:5-9), but which is essentially hypocritical because, as the illustrations (the antitheses) in the Sermon on the Mount show, it does not come from the heart. Jesus proclaims a faith from the heart (a fulfilled righteousness) and the Pharisee stereotype possess nothing more than empty religion. They do not penetrate to the depths of the matter. Through the Pharisee stereotype Matthew turns away the eyes of the followers of Jesus from the exterior realities toward the interior ones. The Roman Empire existed on the plane of the exterior and thus by directing eyes away from this (through the foil provided by the stereotype of the Pharisees) to the interior, Matthew was doing the Empire a service. By emphasizing piety (interiority) at the expense of politics (exteriority) Matthew made his followers of Jesus more "user-friendly" from the empire's point of view.

---

[34] It should be noted that this is a text from Q, and if it was retained by Matthew merely because it was in a valued source, then it might not represent Matthew's own view. On the other hand, there is no reason to suspect that its usage here does not reflect Matthew's own view.

[35] S. Moscovici and G. Paicheler, "Social Comparison and Social Recognition: Two Complementary Processes of Identification," in Tajfel, *Differentiation between Social Groups*, 266.

[36] Krister Stendahl, "The Apostle Paul and the Introspective Conscience of the West" in *Paul among Jews and Gentiles* (Philadelphia, PA: Fortress Press, 1976), 78–96.

"Borders" and Stereotypes

When one identifies oneself as a plumber or as a pregnant woman, one is defining oneself in categories that have been socially created and are inhabited by others who share them.[37] This shared quality goes hand-in-hand with a non-shared component, so that the "us" is clearly determined in large part by not being "them." Social identity defines people (and the self) "in terms of ... shared similarities with members of certain social categories *in contrast to other categories*."[38] When a pregnant woman stereotypes herself as such, she places herself in a shared location with other pregnant woman as well as differentiating herself from woman who are not pregnant and from men. There is always an implicit "us and them" in self-designations.

Stereotypes, by delineating who is us and who is them, establish, define, and maintain this type of social border. This is important for the construction of identity, as "identity is in fact unthinkable without some sort of imagined or literal boundary."[39] A border demands that some be in and others out. In terms of social identity, this means that without them there would be no us and "this gives symbolic centrality to what has been socially excluded, projected outwards onto the Other."[40] Stereotypes use the Other as a means by which the collective self can be realized.[41] The stereotypic knowledge of the Other is implicated in the knowledge of the collective self.[42]

The specificity and rigidity of the border varies depending upon context, but groups will often seek to achieve a fairly clear delineated distinction between the ingroup and outgroup. This can often be achieved by stereotypes that see the other as a source of contamination or as a social threat.[43]

Matthew's community could only understand itself as such by differentiating itself from other groups. There were various levels of similarity between his group and other groups. For example, Matthew's ἐκκλησία had a great deal more in common with his Pharisaic opponents than it did with a Greek Mystery Religion (although it certainly would have had something in common with this latter social entity as well). It is against that which is the most similar that Matthew most fervently desired to differentiate.[44] Hence, it is the border between and Pharisees and his community that occupies Matthew's attention: this border was important to Matthew. Without borders (geographic or metaphoric) between peoples then it would be impossible to speak of peoples or groups at all. A border is what differentiates in such a way that individuals can be categorized one way or another. Thus, borders are used to construct

---

[37] Turner and Onorato, "Social Identity," 26.
[38] Ibid., 22.
[39] Susan S. Friedman, *Mappings: Feminism and the Cultural Geographies of Encounter* (Princeton, NJ: Princeton University Press, 1998), 3.
[40] Pickering, *Stereotyping*, 49.
[41] Ibid., 74.
[42] Ibid.
[43] Ibid., 76.
[44] This is not to say that Matthew does not also carefully differentiate his community from other non-Pharisaic groups. There are clear examples where Matthew distinguishes his group from the Gentiles (6:7, 6:32, 18:17, 20:25) as well as from some form of Pauline groups (5:17). Nevertheless, neither of these groups receives the attention that Matthew gives to the Pharisees and scribes.

identity. A border tells me where *mine* ends and *yours* starts. Borders "insist ... upon separation" while simultaneously "acknowledg[ing] connection."[45] Thus, the border between Matthew's community and the Pharisees ensured both the connectedness of these two groups as well as their differences. In order for Matthew to maintain his own constructed collective identity, the Pharisees also must maintain their collective identity. These two identities for Matthew are inseparably linked. *His* is what *theirs* is not, and therefore if *theirs* changed so would *his*. This would be true to a lesser degree (although still true) had Matthew not so sharply "othered" the Pharisees through his stereotypes. Borders can be more or less rigid depending upon the context. A less rigid, more porous border might have made Matthean identity less dependent upon the Pharisees. However, Matthew constructed a rigid boundary between his group and the Pharisees. Because of this, in his narrative they served not merely as an *incidental* border but as an *essential* one. In order for Matthew to be Matthew, the Pharisees had to be the Pharisees.

Stereotypes create and strengthen borders by employing specific essentialist assumptions about the nature of the groups being represented: (1) they possess *ontological* status (discussed earlier); (2) membership is *immutable*; (3) knowledge of someone's group membership has a great deal of *inductive potential*; (4) knowledge of someone's membership in the group has a great deal of *interpretive potential*; (5) membership is exclusive.[46]

Groups have an *ontological* status. This means that for Matthew the Pharisees were not merely a constructed communal collective held together by negotiated values and narratives, but that they were a real entity with a defining underlying essence. Hence, the various evils enumerated in the Sermon on the Mount (and elsewhere) were not just incidental features but rather features flowing from an ontologically given and unchangeable inner reality. The Pharisees were believed to be hypocrites not because of poor religious education, a lack of personal reflection, or some other societal cause; they were hypocrites *by nature*—it was an essential component of who they were.

Group members "cannot cease to be a members"—membership is *immutable*. There is nothing in Matthew that indicates he had any hope that his Pharisaic rivals could change or convert, as a group or as individuals. Once a Pharisee, always a Pharisee.[47]

The knowledge of someone's group membership has a great deal of *inductive potential*—"knowing that someone belongs to the category tells us a lot about that person"; the knowledge of someone's membership in the group has a great deal of *interpretive potential* as the already determined underlying essence provides a means by which other features can be understood. For Matthew to know someone was a Pharisee meant that all the descriptions and accusations contained in the Pharisee stereotype could be automatically applied. For Matthew, knowing that someone was

---

[45] Friedman, *Mappings*, 3.
[46] Vincent Yzerbyt et al., "Stereotypes as Explanations: A Subjective Essentialistic View of Group Perception," in Spears et al., *Social Psychology*, 40–1; Nick Haslam, Louis Rothschild, and Donald Ernst, "Essentialist Beliefs about Social Categories," *BJSP* 39 (2000): 117–18.
[47] On the other hand, Matt 18:15–17 demonstrates the possibility that group membership within Matthew's community could be lost. Thus, group membership within Matthew's own community was not immutable, and one could even become a "a Gentile and a tax collector."

a Pharisee included knowledge of the key essential ingredient of their character, namely hypocrisy, which could be used to interpret otherwise ambiguous activities and characteristics.

Members belong *exclusively* to that group and therefore thinking of them in alternative categories can be very difficult for the perceiver. That group membership for Matthew was seen in *exclusive* terms is illustrated by his redaction of Mark's story of the Good Scribe. According to the two-source theory, Matthew altered Mark's version of the story of the good scribe (Mark 12:28–34 | Matt 22:34–40) so that the one who was in Mark commended as not being far from the Kingdom of God is, in Matthew, testing Jesus with ill will. Although this figure is not a Pharisee, it nevertheless indicates an inability on Matthew's part to see Jesus' opponents as anything other than evil. It is, in other words, very difficult for Matthew to think of his opponents in "alternative categories."[48] By extension, it would be impossible for Matthew to think of Pharisees as acting with pure and authentic motives, as this would be a departure from the stereotype established for them. Indeed, to represent the Pharisees positively would be to undermine the symbolic world that was created upon the very foundation of their being hypocrites and villains.

Before moving on, it might be prudent to mention what is at stake in considering the borders created with essentialist stereotypes, both historically and for our current time. Historically, it is important simply because it helps us to evaluate our sources critically and to understand the rhetorical world they inhabited; *contemporarily* it is important as people continue to make all sorts of cognitive connections, and one such connection is between the past and the present. People find connections between disparate pieces of data, even "seeing relationship[s] where these do not exist."[49] Essentialism sees a relationship between surface appearance and a deep underlying structural reality. People can, through naïve essentialist theories, trace a essentialist relationship between the Pharisees and modern Judaism (or simply modern Jews, or perhaps the timeless eternal essence of "Jewishness"). Challenging the "naturalness [and the] immutability" as well as the "uniformity, informativeness, [and] exclusivity" of these social categories is one path to changing them. This is a step toward dismantling racial prejudice. This leads to an analysis of modern culture that is beyond the scope (but not beyond the relevance) of this present work.

Values and Stereotypes

An important function of stereotypes is to establish and protect values.[50] Perhaps more importantly, stereotypes provide justification for the way ingroups *treat* outgroups.[51]

---

[48] Yzerbyt et al., "Stereotypes as Explanations," 41.
[49] Mariëtte Berndsen et al., "Illusory Correlation and Stereotype Formation: Making Sense of Group Differences and Cognitive Biases," in *Stereotypes as Explanations: The Formation of Meaningful Beliefs about Social Groups* (ed. Craig McGarty et al.; Cambridge: Cambridge University Press, 2002), 90.
[50] Tajfel, *Human Groups*, 154. This is not true of every stereotype, as some are more neutral with regard to value than others. For example, a stereotype that "Swedes are tall" does not function in the same way as "blacks are lazy" (152).
[51] Yzerbyt et al., "Stereotypes as Explanations," 38.

Stereotypes explain why things are the way they are, and perpetuates the group's practices and actions.[52] They validate beliefs about the social world,[53] and are believed to provide necessary information upon which to base evaluations to develop strategies.[54] In other words, there is a direct relationship between what groups do and do not do to and for each other and the stereotypes by which they represent each other.

In addition to justifying the group beliefs and behavior, stereotypes establish and protect values by setting up norms. A stereotype acts as a "marker of deviancy" whereby normalcy is reinforced.[55] For example, the stereotype "the poor are lazy" reinforces the value of industry and hard work at the expense of the stereotype's negatively portrayed target. An ethic of "hard work" is encoded within the stereotype and is mirrored back to the ingroup. This means there is a two-fold movement within the value component of stereotypes: (1) There is the negative portrayal of the other and (2) the implicit affirmation of the value that the other is represented as *not* having.[56] This provides another explanation for the rigidity of stereotypes, as calling them into question "threatens or endangers the value system on which is based the differentiation between the groups."[57]

As Donaldson has noted, the Pharisees were likely not the target of the Pharisee Stereotype in the Sermon on the Mount. Are we to imagine that Matthew hoped they would take time to read his gospel? Probably not. Rather, Matthew is using the Pharisees as a warning directed at the disciples to avoid this sort of behavior.[58] However, where Donaldson seems to see this as a move away from an anti-Judaic sensibility, I argue that it is in fact a move toward it. Encoded within Matthew's stereotypes of the Pharisees are implicit value statements about the targets and moral ideals. To call the Pharisees hypocrites is both to call their character into question and to reinforce the negative valuation of hypocrisy and the positive valuation of its opposite, an authentic praxis coming from the heart.[59]

Matthew's Jesus claims that his purpose was not to destroy the law but to fulfill it (5:17–19) and the antitheses demonstrate what fulfilling the law looks like. The antitheses operate by laying out a commandment that is reinterpreted in the way that is consonant with its fulfillment. A deficient interpretation is always implied against which the better interpretation stands out by contrast. If there were no implied deficient interpretation, then the antitheses would not logically "work": they need a foil against which to stand.

Matthew 5:20 stands between the explanation of Jesus' purpose (5:17–19) and examples of this purpose (5:21–48). Thus the righteousness that Matthew's audience is to aspire to must be like the examples given (5:21–48) as well as better than that of the

---

[52] Ibid., 39.
[53] Russell Spears and S. Alexander Haslam, "Stereotyping and the Burden of Cognitive Load," in Spears et al., *Social Psychology*, 204, and Haslam, "Stereotyping and Social Influence," 133.
[54] Gerard Lemaine et al., "Social Differentiation," in Tajfel, *Differentiation between Social Groups*, 270.
[55] Pickering, *Stereotyping*, 5.
[56] Ibid.
[57] Tajfel, *Human Groups*, 152.
[58] Terence L. Donaldson, *Jesus on the Mountain: A Study in Matthean Theology* (Sheffield: JSOT, 1985), 53.
[59] Pickering, *Stereotyping*, 5.

scribes and Pharisees (5:20). The deficient interpretations against which Jesus' higher righteousness becomes visible (5:21–48) as well as the deficient righteousness itself are both attributed to the scribes and Pharisees. Jesus says:

> You have heard that it was said to the men of old, "You shall not kill; and whoever kills shall be liable to judgment." But I say to you that everyone who is angry with his brother shall be liable to judgment; whoever insults his brother shall be liable to the council, and whoever says, "You fool!" shall be liable to the hell of fire.

His audience, however, imagines a defective interpretation of the law that says, "You shall not kill" might prohibit murder, but accepts anger. It says, "don't kill, but by all means be angry with your brother and insult him." This implied interpretation is blatantly unacceptable, so that the superior interpretation eschewing anger and insults is adopted. Matthew intends for his audience to ascribe this deficient interpretation to the scribes and Pharisees. *They* are the ones, Matthew implies through 5:20, who would so teach that anger and insulting a brother or sister is morally acceptable. Furthermore, this presumes that the Pharisees not only taught that anger was acceptable, but that they modelled this by being angry themselves, in violation of Jesus' superior interpretation of this command. Matthew's audience is encouraged not just to avoid doing the blatantly unacceptable acts, but, more importantly, to avoid being like the blatantly unacceptable scribes and Pharisees. In short, the unacceptable righteousness mentioned in 5:20 provides a key for understanding the antitheses that follow. Matthew's message is, in a nutshell, do not be like the scribes and Pharisees!

Matthew's delineation of righteousness was configured around not being like the Pharisees (5:20) and thus if the Pharisees were removed from the equation, or underwent radical change, Matthew's righteousness, at least as it is formulated in 5:21–48,[60] would cease to be meaningful through the terminal loss of a necessary component. This means that Matthew needs the stereotype of the Pharisees in order to achieve the collective self-concept that he has imagined in the Sermon on the Mount. He has configured corporate identity such that the hated other has become written into the DNA (if you will) of Matthean collective identity.

If we were to remove the stereotype of the scribes and Pharisees from their assigned role in Matthew's gospel, what would be left of the Sermon on the Mount? If the "you have heard it said" half of the antitheses were to be excised, Matthew would only have the "I say to you" half and we would simply have a teaching of Jesus that does not stand in comparison to an empty, unfulfilled interpretation. The first thing, therefore, to be lost in such a reconstruction would be any notion of superiority. To state matters tautologically, to be superior 5:21–48 requires something to be superior to. The designation "superior" requires negative comparison, and if this is removed, Jesus' righteousness cannot be considered "superior" any longer.

---

[60] I am primarily focusing on 5:17–48, but this same logic that uses the Pharisees as a foil against which Jesus' higher (fulfilled) righteousness stands in relief occurs often in the Sermon on the Mount. The "hypocrites," obviously meaning the Pharisees, are explicitly mentioned in 6:1–6, 16–18, and might be seen implicitly elsewhere as well. E.g.: Are they the ones who "store up treasures for themselves?" (6:19).

Even if 5:21–48 could survive this deconstruction, its inner logic would be so ruptured that what would remain would be quite different from what we started with. If the distinction between positive inner righteousness and negative outer expression (as found in 5:21–22, 27–28), and between positive original intent and negative later additions (5:31–32, 19:8, and arguably also 5:33–37 and 38–42) were lost, the meaning potential of these statements would also be lost. Such is the danger with binary logic: one cannot have an inner if one has no outer, just as one cannot have original intent if there are no later additions.

The significance of this is simply that Matthew *needs* his literary Pharisee stereotype. The higher righteousness of Jesus requires that the Pharisees maintain their status as empty hypocrites. Any change in this status would challenge the whole value system that is built upon this very distinction. If "they" cease being "them," "we" also cease to be "us."

Conclusion: Is the Sermon on the Mount Ethically Flawed?

Calling just about any New Testament (NT) text "anti-Jewish" is not accurate, if for no other reason than that most of them were written by those who would have identified themselves as being Jewish. This is certainly true for Matthew. Nevertheless, Matthew, while not being anti-Jewish, is explicitly anti-Pharisaic, and it was not too long after its composition when this distinction was lost. There is a connection between the animus that Matthew displayed toward his Pharisaic opponents and the later hostility that existed between Church and Synagogue.

Several passages in the NT are problematic from the perspective of Jewish–Christian relations. John's gospel has "the Jews" (οἱ Ἰουδαῖοι) and the infamous 8:44 ("You are of your father the devil"), and Matthew has chapter 23 and 27:25 ("And all the people answered, 'His blood be on us and on our children!'"). These problematic texts have obvious anti-Jewish implications for many modern readers and it is the obviousness of the problem that in some ways makes them less of a problem (inasmuch as they are at least easier to identity).

The Sermon on the Mount is not usually seen as a text with anti-Jewish implications, and to argue that such implications are present might come as a surprise, especially since it has long been celebrated as the apex of Christian ethics. It is the lack of obviousness that makes it dangerous, as that which is beautiful and harmful is more threatening than that which is ugly and harmful. The Sermon on the Mount is a Trojan horse, which hides that which is dangerous within that which is attractive. When that which is attractive is embraced, that which is dangerous slips in as well without even being recognized.

The Sermon on the Mount is built upon an ethical flaw. It establishes its terms through the negative othering of the Pharisees. Matthew's stereotype of the Pharisee sets the boundary for Christian identity, and despite its demand to love enemies (5:44), this text requires a vilification of the other that can hardly be called love. The fact that Christian identity is built upon and requires this negative representation of the other has troubling implications. If Christians wish to use this text for "spiritual" or "ethical" application, they cannot do so without adopting at least some of the terms of the text. Specifically, the hypocritical Pharisee must be retained if these texts are to have their "meaning-effect." To rehabilitate the Matthean Pharisees by changing the characterization of the Pharisees (if that is even possible) would be to undermine the structure of the Sermon on the Mount and would be for all practical purposes a repudiation of the Sermon.

One reading strategy that attempts to neutralize the effects of this negative othering of the Pharisees sees in the Pharisee the hypocrite that is in us all. Käsemann, writing of Paul, articulates this when he states, "in and with Israel he strikes at the *hidden Jew* in all of us, at the man who validates rights and demands over against God on the basis of God's past dealings with him and to this extent is serving not God but an illusion."[61] This approach, however, does not neutralize the negative othering in Matthew (or elsewhere in the NT), but rather exacerbates the problem by symbolizing Jewishness (or Pharisaism) as that which is evil in everyone. In the words of Daniel Boyarin, it is to "allegorize EveryJew as a condemnable part of Everyman."[62] This is no solution but is the problem itself.

Matthew makes the Pharisees part of Christian identity. Indeed, he makes them essential for Christian identity, at least inasmuch as the Sermon on the Mount is concerned. This evokes the challenge of Rosemary Ruether: "the anti-Judaic myth is neither a superficial nor a secondary element in Christian thought … so it may seem impossible to pull up the weed [of anti-Jewishness] without uprooting the seed of Christian faith as well."[63]

Stereotypes cast large groups of people into value laden categories. This process creates borders placing some "out" and others "in." Is social differentiation inherently a harmful thing? The move toward a unified "one" where there are no social borders can be seen as an imperial move that does not allow for difference. Difference is necessary as an alternative to imperialistic totalities. Furthermore, eliminating social categories is unrealistic and also destructive, if it were even imaginable. Groups exist as a means to assemble disparate people into social configurations so that they may not be alone in their difference.

Matthew insisted upon difference, and established a community of difference. Within his own group it is difficult to determine exactly how much diversity was tolerated. If 5:19 refers to some form of Pauline groups it is interesting to note that these believers are *included* in the kingdom of heaven, albeit with reduced status. This may be some indication of acceptance of difference (if even a rather minimal one), but lacking anything like Paul's celebration of diversity in unity (1 Cor 12:12–31). In any

---

[61] Ernst Käsemann, "Paul and Israel" in *New Testament Questions of Today* (London: S.C.M. Press, 1969), 186, quoted from Daniel Boyarin, *A Radical Jew: Paul and the Politics of Identity* (Berkeley, CA: University of California Press, 1994), 213.
[62] Boyarin, *A Radical Jew,* 210. See also 209–14.
[63] Rosemary Radford Ruether, *Faith and Fratricide: The Theological Roots of Anti-Semitism* (New York, NY: Seabury Press, 1974), 226.

event, Matthew's maintaining of difference could have been an anti-imperialist move, but it is not against Rome that he maintains this difference, but against the Pharisees.

Additionally, Matthew demonstrates a danger of insisting upon difference in the absolute terms of rigid stereotypes. There are historical as well as social psychological reasons why he cast things in this way. These explanations may or may not be helpful for modern readers when it comes to rendering a moral verdict against this ancient writer and his community. How might one determine "guilt" or "innocence" in a case like this?

Perhaps we might do this by using a pragmatic measurement of success? How successful was Matthew in the use of the Pharisees in his gospel? If success is measured by the number of people who profoundly identified with a group so that that group's identity and their own self-concept became fused, at least in part, then Matthew's construction of collective identity was successful. On the other hand, if success is measured by the ethical treatment of the other that this collective identity justified, then Matthew's construction of identity was unsuccessful.

Perhaps Matthew's own standard can be used to evaluate success in this latter sense: did Matthew's constructed collective identity develop a habit of characteristically loving the group's enemies (Matthew 5:38–42)? Matthew's animosity toward the Pharisees suggests that he did not do so personally, and subsequent Christian history suggests that, by and large, the Christian church did not do so either.

8

From Tamar and Mary to Perpetua: Women and the Word in Matthew

Catherine Sider Hamilton

> And Mary said, "My soul magnifies the Lord, and my spirit rejoices in God my Saviour." Luke 1:46–47

In Luke's gospel, famously, Mary speaks—and speaks still, in my own Anglican tradition, every time the Magnificat is sung at Evensong. In Matthew, by contrast, she is silent. "In Matthew," Andries van Aarde and Yolanda Dreyer say, "Mary quickly recedes into the background."[1] As commentators universally note, in Matthew's birth narrative it is Joseph and not Mary who is the main actor.[2] In Dreyer and van Aarde's judgment, the Gospel of Matthew as a whole "relegates women to being supporting characters."[3] Indeed, P. J. J. Botha concludes, in Matthew's gospel "women characters are demeaned … The gender inflection of the Matthean text is implicitly and explicitly male and it reflects a symbolic universe characterised by this androcentric bias."[4]

And yet from the outset Matthew's text places a question-mark against this reading.

In the Matthean genealogy five women appear. In this, Matthew's genealogy contrasts with Luke's, which names no women, and with the genealogy in Gen 5, whose opening words Matthew quotes at the beginning of his gospel (βίβλος γενέσεως, Matt 1:1, Gen 5:1; cf. Gen 2:4a).[5] From Tamar to Mary, in the Matthean genealogy something

---

[1] Andreis G. van Aarde and Yolanda Dreyer, "Matthew Studies Today—A Willingness to Suspect and a Willingness to Listen," *HTS* 66.1 (2010): 1–10, here 6. Cf. P. J. J. Botha, "The Gospel of Matthew and Women," *In die Skriflig* 37.3 (2003): 505–32, here 509: "In Matthew Mary plays an insignificant role … she does not speak nor is she spoken to. She is in a most literal sense just background."

[2] So, for instance, not only Botha, who reads Matthew's gospel as entrenched in androcentric structures ("Matthew and Women"), but also Elaine Wainwright, who argues that the women of Matthew's gospel open up the text to a critique of those structures. At Matt 1:19, she says, "the focus shifts to Joseph … Within this entire story [Matt 1:18–25], Mary is marginalized. She is spoken about by either the narrator or the divine messenger, but she is given no speech herself, no independent action of hers is recorded, nor do we gain any insight into her point of view": *Towards a Feminist Critical Reading of the Gospel according to Matthew* (Berlin: de Gruyter, 1991), 71.

[3] Aarde and Dreyer, "Matthew Studies," 6.

[4] Botha, "Matthew and Women," 517–18.

[5] Davies and Allison, in *A Critical and Exegetical Commentary on the Gospel According to St. Matthew* (ICC, 3 vols.; London: T&T Clark, 2004), 1.170, note that "women are not usually named in Jewish genealogies," though there are exceptions, including several of the genealogies in 1 Chr, on which Matthew draws. Cf. Raymond E. Brown, *The Birth of the Messiah* (Garden City, NY: Doubleday, 1977), 71: the presence of women in Matthew's genealogy is "unusual according to biblical patterns."

unusual is going on. The presence of these women in the genealogy, Janice Capel Anderson argues, stands in tension with its overtly androcentric character and points to the *novum* accomplished in Mary: "God has acted in a radically new way—outside of the patriarchal norm."[6] By this reading, the women in Matthew's genealogy subvert the expectations established by the genealogy's patrilineal character and claim a role for women in the gospel of Jesus Christ.[7] "Their inclusion," Anne Clements writes, "signals that, as a category, women form an important group in the gospel story as told by Matthew."[8]

In what follows I offer a close reading of Matt 1, and especially the women in the genealogy, to argue (with Anderson, Clements, and others) that from the beginning the women of Matthew's gospel are central to its good news. In turning again to the women of the genealogy I propose to argue the point a little differently and, I hope, strengthen it—and this in two ways.

First, I want to ask in particular, in the face of Mary's silence, about voice. Antoinette Wire states that Matthew's gospel reflects a silencing of women's voices as an originally marginal movement of Jesus followers becomes a scribal movement of the "self-sufficient and classically educated."[9] Even Anne Clements, who argues that in the birth narrative Matthew reclaims women's stories and in the gospel generally "subverts and deconstructs the male-centred focus of the gospel,"[10] nevertheless says this of Mary: "she never speaks"; "Mary as a character remains in the background."[11] The question of voice, Mary's voice and Tamar's, the voices of women in the Gospel of Matthew, is compelling for me both personally and historically. Historically: how did we get from the silence of Mary to Perpetua, young mother and convert to Christ, who in the year 203 is hailed as prophet by her small band of catechumens and proclaims Christ in her own voice? Is Perpetua simply a Montanist exception? Does Matthew, alternatively, stand in a tradition of early Christian rhetorical deflection of attention away from ordinary women's voices in the early church, such as Shelly Matthews has drawn attention to in Acts?[12] Or may we find in Matthew's presentation of women in

---

[6] Anderson, "Matthew: Gender and Reading," *Semeia* 28 (1983): 3–27, here 10.
[7] See, to varying degrees, Janice Capel Anderson, "Mary's Difference: Gender and Patriarchy in the Birth Narratives," *J R* 67.2 (1987): 183–202; Anderson, "Matthew: Gender and Reading," 3–27; Wainwright, *Feminist Critical Reading*; Wim J. C. Weren, "The Five Women in Matthew's Genealogy," *CBQ* 59 (1997): 288–305; Dorothy Jean Weaver, "'Wherever This Good News Is Proclaimed': Women and God in the Gospel of Matthew," *Int* 64.4 (2010): 390–401; E. Anne Clements, *Mothers on the Margins: The Significance of the Women in Matthew's Genealogy* (Eugene, OR: Pickwick, 2014). Anderson and Wainwright note that there is a tension in Matthew between androcentric and patriarchal structures reflected in the text, and a treatment of women which at times challenges those structures. Cf. Stuart L. Love, *Jesus and Marginal Women: The Gospel of Matthew in Social-Scientific Perspective* (Matrix: The Bible in Mediterranean Context 5; Eugene, OR: Cascade, 2009), esp. 5, 218.
[8] Clements, *Mothers on the Margins*, 234.
[9] Antoinette Clark Wire, "Gender Roles in a Scribal Community," in Social History of the Matthean Community: Cross-Disciplinary Approaches (ed. David L. Balch; Minneapolis, MN: Fortress, 1991), 87–121, citation 118. Wainwright, in *Feminist Critical Reading*, 323, concurs: women's stories in Matthew have been so "submerged" in the androcentric narrative as almost to be "silenced" by it.
[10] Clements, *Mothers on the Margins*, 234.
[11] Ibid., 169–70.
[12] Shelly Matthews, *First Converts: Rich Pagan Women and the Rhetoric of Mission in Early Judaism and Christianity* (Stanford, CA: Stanford University Press, 2001).

the genealogy and birth narrative a claim for the voices of women in the proclamation of God's word—and not just rich or virgin women, but gentile and prostitute too? The question is compelling to me also personally, because I serve as a priest of the church and have for years (and without any particular angst) sought as a priest to proclaim the gospel. Does my proclamation have roots in Matthew's women?

Second, with respect to the women's "stories": the readings that find in Matthew's genealogy a robust role for women depend on the assumption that Matthew has the biblical stories of the four Old Testament (OT) women in mind.[13] Given the interest in the scriptures of Israel evident throughout the gospel (and manifest in the birth narrative in its fulfilment quotations), this is a fair assumption. Indeed, as Richard Hays has made clear (and as I have argued at length elsewhere, with respect to the birth narrative and to Judas), Matthew's gospel is often in deliberate and thorough-going conversation with the scriptures of Israel not just as proof-text but as saving story, the history of the people of God.[14] But in the genealogy there are no fulfilment quotations; all we have are the names. Can we say with confidence that Matthew's gospel intends to summon up biblical history in the names? And if we can, how can we control for *what* is important to Matthew in each woman's history?

Anne Clements has gone some way toward demonstrating that the biblical history resounds in the women's names. She has drawn links between key themes in each woman's scriptural story and themes in Matthew's gospel—Tamar's righteousness, for instance, and righteousness in the gospel.[15] The argument may be strengthened, however: first by attention to Matthew's anomaly, "the wife of Uriah," and second by attention to the literature of Second Temple Judaism. In several Second Temple Jewish texts, the stories of biblical women are a matter of keen interest, as, indeed, are their voices; their biblical histories underlie and inform the later text. Not only do these texts, from *Jubilees* to Pseudo-Philo, indicate that women's stories played an important role in the retelling and interpretation of the scriptural history, but in Pseudo-Philo—a text roughly contemporaneous with Matthew—it is Tamar who is named as model

---

[13] Readings of the genealogy's women fall into four broad categories: they are all sinners; they are all gentiles; their sexual unions are in some way unusual or extraordinary; by their agency and initiative they carry forward God's purpose. All of these readings, of course, consider the women against their biblical background. For a summary of positions see, still, Brown, *Birth of the Messiah*, 71–2; Davies and Allison, *Matthew*, 1. 170–4; John Nolland, *The Gospel of Matthew: A Commentary on the Greek Text* (NIGTC; Grand Rapids, MI: Eerdmans, 2005), 74–7; and Clements, *Mothers on the Margins*, 28–38. It is worth noting that all of the readings (with the partial exception of the last) wrench the women out of their context in the genealogy and reduce them to a single common denominator. Cf. Clements, *Mothers on the Margins*, 37: "why does the assumption need to be made that all four are named for the same reason? ... The scholarly need to force these four/five varied individuals into one mold to provide a neat theory for their inclusion does not do justice to their individuality as women or the variety of their narrated histories." John Paul Heil, in "The Narrative Roles of the Women in Matthew's Genealogy," *Biblica* 72.4 (1991): 538–45, notes that it is helpful to consider the women in their narrative location in the genealogy. On both these points see further, later in this chapter.

[14] Richard B. Hays, *Echoes of Scripture in the Gospels* (Waco, TX: Baylor University Press, 2016). See also my articles: "The Death of Judas in Matthew: Matt 27:9 Reconsidered," *JBL* 137.2 (2018): 419–37; "Quartet for the End of Time: The Fourfold Gospel, History and Matthew's Birth Narrative," in *Writing the Gospels: A Dialogue with Francis Watson* (ed. Catherine Sider Hamilton and Joel Willitts; LNTS 606; London: Bloomsbury/T&T Clark, 2019), 145–65.

[15] Clements, *Mothers on the Margins*, esp. 63–7, 91–5, 116–20, 179–93.

in that other story of a savior, Moses and the exodus. In this reading of Matthew against a Second Temple Jewish textual background I hope to pay some small tribute to Professor Terry Donaldson, who opened up the world of Second Temple Jewish literature to me, and whose work has been, from the beginning to the present moment in his long and fruitful scholarly career, so important in just this regard to the study of Matthew and Paul.

Women of the Genealogy: Soundings in Scripture and Second Temple Texts.

The Wife of Uriah

In order to see what Matthew is doing, it is helpful to begin with Matthew's anomaly, "the wife of Uriah" (1:6). In this phrase we catch a glimpse of the genealogy's intertextual depth, the extent to which the biblical story underlies and informs it precisely, here, in Matthew's reference to a woman. Though Matthew names all the other women of the genealogy, in this one case he omits the name. Yet 1 Chr, which Matthew here follows, lists Bathsheba, like Tamar, by name (Bathshua, 1 Chr 3:5). Matthew names Tamar, in keeping with 1 Chr 2:4, but does not name Bathsheba. "Wife of Uriah" is a Matthean insertion. The phrase "wife of Uriah" appears not in 1 Chr but in the story of David and Bathsheba in 2 Sam 11–12. In that story of David's adultery and murder, Bathsheba is called "the wife of Uriah" four times. When David first sees her she is called Bathsheba (2 Sam 11:3), but from the time David "takes" her (2 Sam 11:4; cf. 2 Sam 12:9, 10), through his killing of Uriah (2 Sam 12:9), and the death of the child David has conceived with Uriah's wife (2 Sam 12:15) she is always, pointedly, "the wife of Uriah." By substituting "the wife of Uriah" for Bathsheba in 1 Chr, Matthew gains an echo of 2 Samuel's story.[16] It is an echo that raises here, in the genealogy of the son of David (Matt 1:1), the question of David's sin.[17] Indeed (as I have shown elsewhere), the echo offers a logic for the genealogy's decline in the wake of David's sin and subsequent exile.[18] In "the wife of Uriah" Matthew thus deliberately uses a phrase

---

[16] Cf. Robert H. Gundry, *Matthew: A Commentary on His Handbook for a Mixed Church under Persecution*, 2nd ed. (Grand Rapids, MI: Eerdmans, 1994), 15: Bathsheba comes from 1 Chr 3:5 ("Bathshua") but Matthew "switches from the Chronicler's descriptive phrase … to 'the [wife of] Uriah' (so 2 Sam 11:26; 12:10, 15)."

[17] Cf. Francis Watson, *The Fourfold Gospel: A Theological Reading of the New Testament Portraits of Jesus* (Grand Rapids, MI: Baker Academic, 2016), 37: "For the evangelist, Solomon's birth takes place under the dark shadow of adultery and murder." Watson, however, sees "the same shadow hanging over the three earlier women." I do not, as we will see. And I would suggest that Matthew's phrasing ("the wife of Uriah"), echoing as it does Nathan's condemnation of David's actions, puts the onus for the "improper union" squarely on David.

[18] See in more detail my discussion of "the wife of Uriah" in *The Death of Jesus in Matthew: Innocent Blood and the End of Exile* (SNTS 167; Cambridge: Cambridge University Press, 2017), 196–202. Cf. Nolland, *Matthew*, 75; Watson, *Fourfold Gospel*, 37–8; Heil, "Narrative Roles," 545: "the reference to the wife of Uriah (1, 6) … recalls her improper union with an adulterous and murderous king David. As a direct reversal of the Abrahamic ideal of drawing Gentiles to faith, David's egregious sinfulness dooms the people of Israel to a disastrous deportation to the foreign land of Babylon (1,11)."

that calls up in the woman's name a particular scriptural history. It seems likely, then, that each woman's name works in this genealogy intertextually: in it the biblical history is present.[19] In what follows I propose to read the women of the genealogy against their scriptural histories, and then to measure this reading against treatments of women in Pseudo-Philo and *Jubilees*.

Tamar

Tamar, strikingly, and not Sarah is the first woman to appear in the history of God's people that begins with Abraham. Why Tamar? In part, Matthew here follows 1 Chr 2:4, which also names Tamar. But Matthew omits Keturah, whom Chronicles names (1 Chr 2:11–12), and names Ruth, whom Chronicles omits. Why, then, Tamar?

As in the case of "the wife of Uriah," Tamar's scriptural history is instructive. She comes into the genealogy at the time of Judah. Judah is the Lion of Israel (Gen 49:9), "pre-eminent ancestor of the Davidic dynasty."[20] At the least, then, to name Tamar is to draw attention to Judah and the Davidic and messianic focus of the genealogy already here at its beginning.[21] But to read Genesis is to see that Tamar is important to Judah's role as "Lion of Israel" in her own right. Judah, in Gen 38, has no heir; the sons of Judah have not produced a son. Two of them die childless and Judah refuses to fulfil his levirate obligations and give his third son to Tamar their widow. Jacob's prophecy, the Davidic dynasty, is threatened. Enter Tamar. Sent away from Judah's home, childless and a widow in her father's house, Tamar disguises herself and conceives a child—twins—by Judah. In this way she, and not Judah, makes possible the continuation of the Davidic line and the fulfilment of Jacob/Israel's prophecy to Judah ("the sceptre shall not depart from Judah," Gen 49:10).[22] She, and not Judah, fulfils the levirate law.[23] Condemned by Judah to be burnt at the stake for prostitution, she reveals to Judah that she is the daughter-in-law he has abandoned childless, contrary to the law. "She is more righteous than I," Judah says (38:26).

Who is Tamar? She is, in Genesis, both widow and seeming prostitute, and the righteous one who insists on the fulfilment of the law of Israel, when Judah, Lion of

---

[19] On intertextuality in Matthew see especially Ulrich Luz, "Intertexts in the Gospel of Matthew," *HTR* 97.2 (2004): 119–37, esp. 121–2 (citations 122, 121). I use "intertext" here in Luz's first sense: intertexts as the product of the text (as opposed to the reader), belonging to the rhetorical strategy of the text, "consciously invoked by an author." "Intertextuality on the level of the text is primarily *descriptive*; it facilitates the precise description of the strategies of a text."
[20] Heil, "Narrative Roles," 539. Cf. Richard Bauckham, "Tamar's Ancestry and Rahab's Marriage: Two Problems in the Matthean Genealogy," *NT* 37.4 (1995): 313–29, esp. 326.
[21] Heil, "Narrative Roles," 539.
[22] Cf. Weren, "Five Women," 297.
[23] Cf. Clements, *Mothers on the Margins*, 64; Wainwright, *Feminist Critical Reading*, 162. Tikva Frymer-Kensky, "Tamar 1," in *Women in Scripture: A Dictionary of Named and Unnamed Women in the Hebrew Bible, the Apocryphal, Deuterocanonical Books, and the New Testament* (ed. Carol Meyers et al.; Grand Rapids, MI: Eerdmans, 2000), 161–2, here 161, notes: "in-law incest rules are suspended for the purpose of the levirate"; when a son is not available, the father-in-law is permitted, even required, to take the place of the widow's husband in providing a son. Hence there is no "sin" in Tamar; the problem is with Judah, as he himself admits (Gen 38:26).

Israel, does not.[24] She is faithful when Judah is not. By her faithfulness to the law, Jacob's prophecy to Judah is fulfilled.[25] Tamar does not speak, anymore than does Judah or anyone else in the genealogy. But by her faithful action the word of God to Judah is "uttered," brought to fruition in the history of Israel.

Does Matthew intend all this in the mere mention of her name? It is worth noting that elements of her story find a complement later in the birth narrative in the episode of Mary's pregnancy and Joseph's righteousness; indeed, Clements notes, righteousness is "a key discipleship virtue" in Matthew's gospel.[26] Thus there are thematic parallels between Tamar's story and Matthew's gospel that lend credence to the supposition that Matthew has Tamar's scriptural story in mind. External corroboration, however, is also at hand. In Pseudo-Philo, a first-century Jewish text, Tamar (like several other biblical women) plays a starring role.[27] In Pseudo-Philo's story of the exodus, Tamar serves as crucial scriptural reference point, model of faithfulness to God's covenant people and purpose.

When Pharaoh commands the Egyptians to throw the sons of the Hebrews into the river and make their daughters slaves, the Israelites despair. In their despair, they propose to cease having children altogether.[28] Amram protests: this is, he suggests, an act of unfaithfulness to the God who has both commanded and covenanted with Israel that they "be made many on the earth" (*L.A.B.* 9:2; cf. Gen 1:28, 12:2, 15:5, 17:4–7; Exod 1:8, etc.). Precisely here, Amram appeals to Tamar: Tamar who hid her dangerous pregnancy until the third month; Tamar who was willing to die in order that her son might be a son of Israel (*L.A.B.* 9:5); Tamar who believed that it is with Israel that the Lord God has made a covenant. Tamar's pregnancy serves as an example of righteous faith over and against the Israelites' failure of faith—a righteous faith that allows the necessary begetting to continue, so that God's promises to Israel might be fulfilled. Pseudo-Philo's appeal to Tamar in the context of the genealogical fulfilment of God's covenant promises—an appeal to which her scriptural story is essential background—provides a parallel to Matthew's appeal to Tamar in the same context. Thanks to Amram's appeal to faithful Tamar, in Pseudo-Philo, the Israelite line continues and

---

[24] Cf. A. J. Levine, "Rahab in the New Testament," in Meyers et al., *Women in Scripture*, 141–2, here 141: Rahab and the women of the genealogy were seen in contemporary Jewish and Christian literature "not as sinners but as manifesting righteousness." Indeed, they "may also indicate the higher righteousness that Matthew frequently endorses" (142).

[25] Cf. A. J. Levine, *Social and Ethnic Dimensions of Matthean Social History* (Studies in the Bible and Early Christianity 14; Lewiston, NY: Edwin Mellen, 1988), 85: Tamar shows greater faith than Judah through her "fidelity to the tradition of Levirate marriage."

[26] Clements (*Mothers on the Margins*, 63–7, citation 63) draws a parallel between Joseph in his righteousness and Tamar in hers. She is right to see a parallel between the two stories—but the birth narrative, I suggest, draws that parallel a little differently. See further, later in this chapter.

[27] Daniel J. Harrington, in "Pseudo-Philo: A New Translation and Introduction," in *The Old Testament Pseudepigrapha* (ed. James H. Charlesworth; 2 vols.; Garden City, NJ: Doubleday, 1983), 297–377, esp. 299, dates *L.A.B.* to "around the time of Jesus"; parallels with *2 Baruch* and *4 Ezra*, however, may suggest a date between 70 and 100 AD. Translations of Pseudo-Philo follow Harrington. Wainwright, in *Feminist Critical Reading*, 163, notes that the Palestinian Targums "emphasize the role of God" in Tamar's story; "it seems that by the first century, God is explicitly linked to the Tamar story and hence to its double-edged power."

[28] The elders of the people decree that "a man should not approach his wife lest the fruit of their wombs be defiled and our offspring serve idols. For it is better to die without sons" (*L.A.B.* 9:2).

Moses is born. Thanks to Tamar in Matthew, the Davidic line continues and Jesus is born. Literary dependence between Matthew and Pseudo-Philo "is doubtful," Harrington notes.[29] The commonalities thus suggest a Jewish tradition of reflection on Tamar's biblical story as a story of righteous faithfulness—in both cases in the context of the genealogical fulfilment of God's covenant promises.[30]

Rahab

Rahab, too, plays a crucial role in the realization—the "utterance"—of the promises of God. In Josh 2, it is she who shelters the Israelite spies so that the promise of Genesis that Abraham's descendants should take possession of the land might be fulfilled (Gen 28:3–4).[31] Yet Rahab appears as the wife of Salmon nowhere in the Bible or in Second Temple Jewish or rabbinic literature: she is Matthew's insertion.[32] Why? Again, attention to her scriptural story yields interesting fruit. To the Israelite spies Rahab says, "The Lord your God is indeed God in heaven above and on earth below" (Josh 2:11). This is a confession of faith. By Rahab's faith, the spies are saved and Israel wins the promised land. As Tamar is faithful to the law of Israel's God, so Rahab believes the promises of Israel's God: "I know that the Lord has given you the land" (Josh 2:9). Through her, as through Tamar, God's covenant promises to Israel are fulfilled.

There is resonance not only between her faithfulness to the God of Israel and Tamar's, but between her scriptural story and Matthew's larger birth narrative. The Book of Joshua draws a parallel between Rahab's actions and words, and the events of the Exodus. "She hid *him*," the text says, when Rahab hides the *two* men on her roof (Josh 2:4 ותפצנו). The "him," singular, is odd. So it is interesting that the same phrase occurs in Exod 2:2, when Moses' mother hides her son: "she hid him," Exodus says, using the same word (והנצפתו).[33] The recollection of Exodus continues. When Rahab

---

[29] Harrington, "Pseudo-Philo," 316, in relation not to Tamar but Moses. He points out "striking parallels" between Moses' birth in *L.A.B.* 9 and Jesus' birth in Matthew 1–2 (316). The parallels are as follows: (1) Dreams (Miriam, *L.A.B.* 9:10; Joseph/the magi, Matt 1:20; 2:13, 19/Matt 2:12). (2) The Spirit of God comes upon Miriam; the Spirit of God comes upon Mary (*L.A.B.* 9:10; Mary, Matt 1:20). (3) King of Egypt sends officers to kill the Hebrew children; Herod sends soldiers to kill the children of Bethlehem (*L.A.B.* 9:12; Matt 2:16–18). (4) Moses is saved; Jesus is saved (*L.A.B.* 9:15–16; Matt 2:13–15). (5) In her dream Miriam is told that Moses will "save my people"; in his dream Joseph is told that Jesus will "save his people" (*L.A.B.* 9:10; Matt 1:21). I have slightly modified and expanded Harrington's list. Harrington concludes that given the lack of contact between the texts "the points in common show a lively interest in the birth of heroes in the NT period." Yes—but it is an interest expressed in the same way in both texts, and this suggests an interpretive tradition. Tamar appears in this context in both texts, and in *L.A.B.*, explicitly, as a model of righteous faithfulness.

[30] Cf. Wainwright, *Feminist Critical Reading*, 163, notes that the Palestinian Targums "emphasize the role of God" in Tamar's story; "it seems that by the first century, God is explicitly linked to the Tamar story and hence to its double-edged power. Also Tamar is clearly pronounced righteous."

[31] Cf. Heil, "Narrative Roles," 540 and J. Gnilka, *Das Matthäusevangelium: Kommentar zu Kap. 1, 1–13,58* (HTKNT 1/1; Freiburg-Basel-Wien, 1986), 9, cited in Heil, "Narrative Roles."

[32] Bauckham, "Tamar's Ancestry," 324–5, and the commentaries. Bauckham (322) notes, however, that it makes perfect sense that Tamar is here married to Salmon (*contra* Davies and Allison, *Matthew*, 1.173, and many others). Salmon's father, Nahshon, is leader of the tribes of Israel in the wilderness. His son therefore lives, by Matthew's reckoning, at the time of the entry into the promised land.

[33] Frymer-Kensky, "Rahab," in Meyers et al., *Women in Scripture*, 140–1, esp. 141. Like the midwives in the time of Pharoah, Frymer-Kensky adds, Rahab courageously refuses to reveal the sons of Israel at the king's command.

confesses her faith in Israel's God, she quotes from Exod 15 and the song of Miriam.[34] Josh 2:10 echoes Exodus explicitly: "For we have heard how the Lord dried up the water of the Red Sea before you" (Josh 2:10). This story echoes the one in the Book of Joshua; Moses and the exodus find their counterpart in Rahab and the entry into the promised land. In Matt 2, Matthew's birth narrative will echo repeatedly the story of Moses and the exodus. In the genealogy, Matthew names the woman whose scriptural story echoes Moses and the exodus.[35]

In Joshua, it is not only Rahab's actions but her voice that matters: her faith is a matter of word as well as of deed. Rahab confesses that Israel's God is Lord; Rahab sings again the song of Miriam at the Red Sea; Rahab speaks ahead of time of Israel's conquest of the land. It is her message, Frymer-Kensky notes, that the spies take back to Joshua; thus Rahab becomes the "oracle" of the conquest.[36] In rabbinic tradition, Rahab is revered as a prophet.[37] "Rahab," Frymer-Kensky says, "who begins as triply marginalized—Canaanite, woman, and prostitute—moves to the center as *bearer of a divine message* and *herald* of Israel in its new land."[38] It is explicitly by her word that the men are saved and Israel enters the promised land. By her word, in Matthew's scriptural intertext, the promises of God are fulfilled.

Ruth

Ruth marries Rahab's son. In naming Ruth, Matthew recalls another confession of faith, the faith of Ruth will not break with Naomi and Naomi's God, though she is herself a Gentile—indeed, a Moabite. "Whither thou goest I will go; …your people shall be my people, and your God my God" (Ruth 2:16). The text likens her faithfulness to the faithfulness of Abraham. Boaz says to Ruth, "you left your father and mother and your native land and came to a people you did not know before" (Ruth 2:11). His language, Phyllis Trible notes, is reminiscent of the call of Abraham in Gen 12.[39]

Like Rahab, Ruth names the God of Israel Lord (2:16–18). Like Tamar, Ruth is righteous. She goes to great lengths on Naomi's behalf to ensure that the obligations of next-of-kin are fulfilled. Indeed, the Book of Ruth draws the connection with Tamar. As Boaz agrees to marry Ruth and fulfil the obligations of next-of-kin, "all the people and the elders" say, "We are witnesses … may your house be like the house of Perez, whom Tamar bore to Judah" (Ruth 4:12). Matthew's genealogy from Perez to David is found in the Book of Ruth (4:18–22) as well as in 1 Chr 2:5, 10–12, 15. Matthew's text

---

[34] "*Dread* of you has *fallen upon us*" (ונילע םכתמיא הלפנ) she tells the Israelites; "*all the inhabitants of the land melt in fear* before you" (Josh 2:9 NRSV; "melt away" RSV:וגמנ ץראה יבשי־לכ). "Trembling seizes them," Miriam/Moses sings at the crossing of the Red Sea; "*all the inhabitants of Canaan have melted away*" (וגמנ לכ יבשי ענכ); "Terror and *dread fell upon* them" (לפת םהילע התמיא) Exod 15:15–16). Frymer-Kensky, "Rahab," in Meyers et al., *Women in Scripture*, 141.

[35] And, of course, Matthew has also named in Tamar the woman whose scriptural story Pseudo-Philo recalls in the context of the exodus.

[36] Frymer-Kensky, "Rahab," in Meyers et al., *Women in Scripture*, 141.

[37] See, e.g., *midr. r.* on Ruth 2.1; she knows the pursuers will return in three days.

[38] Frymer-Kensky, "Rahab," in Meyers et al., *Women in Scripture*, 141 (italics added).

[39] "Go from your country and your kindred and your father's house to the land that I will show you" (Gen 12:1); Phyllis Trible, "Ruth," in Meyers et al., *Women in Scripture*, 146–7, here 146.

in its brevity follows Ruth closely here. But neither Ruth nor 1 Chr names the women. Matthew adds both Rahab and Ruth to the genealogies he inherits, and in so doing, I suggest, he gives their histories voice.

Soares Prabhu has argued for the Christological focus of Matt 1–2.[40] It is noteworthy that the four OT women Matthew names all occur within three verses, between Judah and David the King, between the promise of a scepter to Judah and its first fulfilment in David. In every case, I have argued, their actions are necessary to the fulfilment of the promise. By their faithful and righteous actions, they fulfil the promise to Judah; they bring David to the throne. To read them against the scriptural history is to see their central role in it: if Jesus is the "Son of David," it is in large part because of the faithful words and righteous actions of these women. In them, the genealogy comes to its first climax in "David the king" (Matt 1:6). After David's sin in the matter of "the wife of Uriah," in the long decline into exile, and the time after exile, no woman is named in twenty-five generations until we come to Mary, from whom is born Jesus called Christ. Here again and finally, at the birth again of the son of David, a woman appears.

Mary

Mary's appearance in Matthew is striking. "Jacob was the father of Joseph the husband of Mary, from whom was born Jesus called the Christ" (Matt 1:16). Mary, *from whom was born*: ἐξ ἧς ἐγεννήθη. In the ἐξ ἧς, Mary falls into the pattern of the other four women of the genealogy (ἐκ τῆς Θαμάρ ...): Μαρίας ἐξ ἧς. But Mary has a verb: ἐξ ἧς ἐγεννήθη. And in the verb, she breaks the pattern, not only of the other women but of the genealogy as a whole. As Dorothy Jean Weaver and others have noted, the long string of males and "begats," ἐγέννησεν, comes to a point here in the woman.[41] The verb goes over to Mary; the genealogy of Jesus, Son of David, son of Abraham ends unexpectedly in the woman and Jesus *her* son. In the end the begetting of the Son of David who is called Christ is not by a man but from a woman by an act of God.

This reading of Mary in the genealogy is now well-known. I want to strengthen it, however. Janice Capel Anderson concludes that Mary's extraordinary role is, nevertheless, "contained by a patrilineal genealogy and birth story."[42] Yet a close reading suggests that Matthew in his treatment of Mary challenges the genealogy more forcefully than we have thought. Already the verb, the final "ἐγεννήθη," problematizes the patrilineal narrative insofar as it belongs not to Joseph but to Mary. Further, Mary's story in Matthew's text does not end at 1:16. Matthew links Mary at the climax of the genealogy to Mary in the birth narrative: Matthew's verbs draw the eye. As the verb ἐγεννήθη in 1:16 traces a break in the patrilineal narrative and places Mary, suddenly, at

---

[40] George M. Soares Prabhu, *The Formula Quotations in the Infancy Narrative of Matthew: An Enquiry into the Tradition History of Mt 1–2* (Rome: Pontifical Biblical Institute, 1976), 17; citing O. da Spinetoli, *Introduzione ai Vangeli dell'Infanzia* (Brescia, 1967), 52, 160, 300.

[41] Weaver, "'Wherever This Good News Is Proclaimed,'" 394–5; Anderson, "Matthew: Gender and Reading," 8, 21; Weren, "Five Women," 292; Wainwright, *Feminist Critical Reading*, 171. Wainwright adds, however, that "this extraordinary verse" has a "counter theme" in the androcentric birth narrative that follows, in which Joseph dominates (171).

[42] Anderson, "Matthew: Gender and Reading," 21. Cf. Anderson, "Mary's Difference," 190.

the center of the genealogy, so the same verb links Mary to the Holy Spirit in 1:20 ("the child conceived [γεννηθέν] in her is from the Holy Spirit"). Mary's story continues in the birth narrative. And the birth narrative is of a piece with the history that was told in the genealogy. Matthew underscores the continuity with repeated verbs: The history that begins with the genealogy (γένεσις) of Jesus in 1:1 continues with the birth (γένεσις) of Jesus in 1:18.[43]

Mary and Joseph

Matthew's story of Joseph in fact underlines the connection between genealogy and birth narrative. It links, as we will see, the last woman of the genealogy to the first, Mary to Tamar ... and Joseph to Judah. It is usually said that in the birth narrative Mary is marginalized; Joseph becomes the main actor.[44] But to read the birth narrative in light of the genealogy is to discover a different portrayal of Joseph. The story of Joseph in Matthew is told as a story of righteousness, and a woman improperly pregnant. This is the question at the center of the story of Judah and Tamar, too. Consider the parallels.

> 1. Judah discovers that the woman belonging to him is pregnant, and not by her lawful husband (for she does not have one anymore). Joseph discovers that the woman belonging to him is pregnant, and not by her lawful husband (for she does not have one yet). **2.** Joseph, being righteous, seeks to fulfil the law; he decides (being also merciful) to put off Mary privately. Judah seeks to fulfil the law; he declares that Tamar shall be burnt. **3.** Tamar sends to Judah the sign that the child is hers by him. The angel gives to Joseph the sign that the child is Mary's by the Holy Spirit. **4.** Judah at the beginning of David's line and Joseph at its end act righteously to put off the woman who bears the child that is not theirs. In their righteousness, unwittingly, they endanger the Davidic line and the whole thrust of the covenant promises/biblical history. **5.** Tamar by her own word, and Mary by the angel's word are saved. **6.** As at the end of Judah's story Judah does not have sexual relations with Tamar because the sons are born, so at the end of the birth narrative Joseph does not have sexual relations with Mary until the son is born.[45]

Mary's pregnancy and Joseph's dangerous righteousness thus bring us full circle, to the first woman named in the genealogy. Mary is linked to Tamar, Judah to Joseph; the last son of David to the ancestor on whom the promise of a royal scepter rests. This is all one story, as Matthew tells it, and it is a story in both instances of the word of God coming to fruition not in the man—not even in his righteousness—but in the woman. "She has been found more righteous than I," Judah says. And Joseph discovers that his righteousness was blind.[46] The word that God is speaking—in which, Matthew's gospel

---

[43] Davies and Allison, *Matthew*, 1.198.
[44] Anderson is representative: "In these episodes Joseph, rather than Mary, is the focus of attention ... Mary is marginalized" ("Mary's Difference," 189–90).
[45] For this last parallel see T. P. Osborne, "Les femmes de la généalogie de Jésus dans l'évangile de Matthieu et l'application de la Torah," *RTL* 41.2 (2010): 243–58, esp. 251 n. 14.
[46] By this reading, Matthew's depiction of Joseph and a righteousness that nevertheless does not see rightly offers a challenge to Wire's reading of the gospel as a scribal community in which the

will go on to say, righteousness is fulfilled—this word is located in Tamar and her child; in Mary and hers. It is not the case that Joseph is the main actor in the Matthean birth narrative. From the perspective of the word of God that Matthew says is here being fulfilled (1:23), Joseph is the supporting character—the problematic supporting character insofar as his righteousness, like Judah's, is blind; the essential supporting character, by whose naming of Mary's son the connection to David is retained. In both cases, he is the supporting character nonetheless. The verb, γεννάω, stays with Mary.

And it is with Mary that the whole story, genealogy and birth narrative together, comes to a climax. The birth narrative and the genealogy come to a point in the quotation from Isaiah at 1:23, which Matthew introduces with these words: "All this took place to fulfil what the Lord had spoken by the prophet" (1:22). "Τοῦτο δὲ ὅλον γέγονεν"—all this, "this whole thing": in these words, Matthew sums up all that has gone before, the birth narrative and the genealogy, Joseph's righteousness and Mary's pregnancy, David the king and the wife of Uriah; Ruth and Rahab and Judah and Tamar. The whole history that Matthew has traced in his first chapter comes to a point here at the chapter's end, in the word of God spoken by the prophet. And it is Mary who stands at its fulfilment:

> Behold, ***a virgin shall conceive*** and bear a son,
> and they shall call his name Emmanuel (1:23) which means God with us.

We tend to put the emphasis in this citation on the son that the virgin bears. But Matthew's shaping of this chapter places the emphasis equally on the woman who bears him. The genealogy's long list of begats comes to its end and climax in Mary, who bears the son called the Christ. The birth story comes to a point in Mary who bears the son called Emmanuel, God with us. At both points, it is Mary who stands at the climax. "This whole thing," the whole history of Israel traced in the genealogy from Abraham to Mary comes to rest in the virgin who conceives, and in her son. Is Mary contained by the patrilineal genealogy? On the contrary, Matthew's text seems to say. As with Tamar, Rahab, and Ruth, she is its essential actor. The word of God spoken through the prophet, in all the generations of Israel's history, is spoken finally in her.

Matthew's genealogy, I have argued, draws attention, in Tamar, Rahab, and Ruth, to women who in the scriptural history carry forward by their righteous faithfulness the covenant promises. The genealogy and birth narrative culminate in Mary, the woman in whom the promises to Abraham and David are fulfilled.[47] This presentation

---

voices of women are increasingly lost. "In this community," Wire says, "responsibility belongs to a designated group of males in the group to identify the right order which tradition requires and to regulate communal life to this end" ("Gender Roles," 106). But Matthew's Joseph, taking on precisely this role with regard to Mary's pregnancy, cannot—any more than can Judah—correctly identify what *is* right order. That right order is now found in Mary, as she conceives outside of the "right order" by the Holy Spirit and bears a son.

[47] The role of "the wife of Uriah" is, I think, rather different, as her lack of a name attests. "The wife of Uriah" calls up as intertext the story of *David*'s sin and its consequences for Israel. Here, too, though, it is the covenant promises that are at issue, and it is the woman whose name signals the issue. Through the righteous faithfulness of Tamar, Rahab, and Ruth, in part, the promise of a scepter for Israel has come to fruition in David. What will happen to the scepter in the wake of David's sin, a sin

of women as central players in the fulfilment of the covenant promises finds a parallel in *Jubilees* and in Pseudo-Philo.

Second Temple Context: *Jubilees*, Pseudo-Philo, and the Voices of Women

As Rahab in Joshua sees God's purpose and speaks God's blessing on the Israelites, so too does Rebekah in *Jubilees*. In *Jubilees,* it is Rebekah and not Isaac who repeatedly—and unexpectedly, for *Jubilees* is not known for its positive depictions of women—is the voice of God's purpose. It is Rebekah and not Isaac who knows that Jacob bears God's blessing (*Jub.* 19:30–31) and tells him so (25:1–3). It is Rebekah and not Isaac (in contrast to Gen 28) who tells Jacob to marry a wife from his own kin and not a Canaanite (25:1–3). It is Rebekah and not Isaac who first blesses Jacob, in a formal blessing vividly depicted:

> And then she lifted her face toward heaven and spread out the fingers of her hands and opened her mouth and blessed the Most High God ... and at that time, when a spirit of truth descended upon her mouth, she placed her two hands upon the head of Jacob and said, "Blessed are you, O Lord ..., and may he bless you more than all the generations of man ... The womb of the one who bore you blesses you. My affection and my breasts are blessing you."[48]

And it is Rebekah whose voice Jacob heeds: "And now my son, heed my voice and do the will of your mother" (25:2). "Do not fear, O mother," Jacob replies, "Trust that I will do your will" (25:10). Betsy Halpern-Amaru notes that in *Jubilees* it is the women who see the promises of God. Each matriarch "uses that knowledge to guide and nurture not only the men in her life, but the covenantal future as well."[49] Just so, I have suggested, for Tamar, Rahab, and Ruth in Matthew's genealogy.

In Pseudo-Philo, whose interest in Tamar and her scriptural story we have already noted, this attention to Rebekah's voice and knowledge of God's purpose expands into a virtually programmatic depiction of strong-voiced women. In the same passage in which Tamar appears as model of righteous faithfulness, the child Miriam speaks of God's saving purpose.

> "Go and say to your parents," the spirit of God says to her in a dream, "Behold, he who will be born from you will be cast forth into the water; likewise through him

---

signaled by the ominous statement, "David had a son by the wife of Uriah"? For more on the wife of Uriah, see my discussion in *Death of Jesus in Matthew*.

[48] *Jub.* 25:11, 14, 19. Translations of *Jubilees* are from O. S. Wintermute, "Jubilees: A New Translation and Introduction," in *OTP*, 35–142.

[49] Halpern-Amaru, *The Empowerment of Women in Jubilees* (Leiden: Brill, 1999), 147, cited in David J. Zucker's excellent recent study: "Rebekah Redux: The View from *Jubilees*," *BTB* 49.2 (2019): 71–81, here 72.

the water will be dried up. And I will work signs through him and save my people." (*L.A.B.* 9:10)

Deborah has several long speeches; in her words the will of God is made known to the people: "And now from this day on let it be known that whatever God has said to me he will do" (*L.A.B.* 32:13).[50] As she lies dying, she leaves her people with her word: "Listen now, my people. Behold I am warning you as a woman of God … obey me like your mother and heed my words" (*L.A.B.* 33:1).

Jephthah's daughter in turn—now given a name, Seila—at her death sings her own lament. In it she compares herself to Isaac offered to God as a willing sacrifice by Abraham (*L.A.B.* 40:2). By her word, indeed, Seila turns her death—a tragic mishap, in her father's understanding—into a self-offering that will be, God declares, "precious before me always" (*L.A.B.* 40:4). She sees God's true purpose and speaks it. "I have seen," God says when he hears her song, "that the virgin is wise in contrast to her father and perceptive in contrast to all the wise men who are here" (40:4). "She is more righteous than I"—Tamar's story rings in the ear.

That Matthew finds in Mary and Tamar, Rahab and Ruth women who see and bring to fulfilment God's purposes for Israel, sometimes in their own voices, is a claim that finds external support here, in these two widely separated works of Second Temple Judaism.

Mary and the Voices of Women in Matthew's Gospel

It remains the case, however, that Mary does not, in her own voice, speak. A final question, briefly, raised by Mary's silence. Does Matthew's interest in women as bearers of God's purpose indicate also an interest in women as speakers of the word? *Time fails me to tell* of Rachel's weeping and the anointing woman at Bethany, of the Canaanite woman and the mother of the sons of Zebedee.[51] I end with two brief observations.

First, the Canaanite woman. In Matthew, the anointing woman at Bethany stands in contrast to the disciples. In her act of anointing, she proclaims Jesus' death; they (even after three passion predictions) do not. "When they saw this," Matthew says, "the disciples were indignant; they said, 'Why this waste?'" (26:8). "The disciples" is a Matthean insertion. Mark has simply "some people." Matthew creates a deliberate contrast between the woman who sees Jesus' purpose and witnesses to it, and the disciples who do not. In the same way, Matthew's gospel commends the Canaanite woman for her "great faith." In this she stands in contrast to the disciples. When the

---

[50] These words come at the end of Deborah's long resumé of Israel's covenantal history: "Go, earth; go, heavens and lightnings; go, angels of the heavenly host; go and tell the fathers in their chamber of souls and say, 'The Most Powerful has not forgotten the least of the promises that he established with us'" (32:13). She is the seer of the promises of God. When Deborah finishes singing she goes together with the people to Shiloh where they offer sacrifices (*L.A.B.* 32:18); she seems to have a priestly as well as prophetic function, and she judges the people.

[51] I hope to explore further Matthew's treatment of these women, and the whole question of women and the word in the New Testament (NT) and in the early church, in a book provisionally entitled—*Women and the Word*.

Canaanite woman begs Jesus repeatedly to heal her daughter, Jesus says to her finally, "O woman, great is your faith" (15:28; Mark 7:29 has simply "For this saying you may go your way," with no reference to her faith).[52] To the disciples, however, Jesus says repeatedly in Matthew, "ye of little faith" (ὀλιγόπιστοι, 6:30, 8:26, 14:31, 16:8, 17:20)

The Canaanite woman, moreover, speaks her faith in her own voice. Whereas Mark merely reports that she speaks, Matthew gives us direct discourse. Twice she cries out to Jesus: "Have mercy on me, Lord, Son of David"; "Lord, help me" (Matt 15:22, 25).[53] In Mark, she has none of these words. In Matthew, even before her final winning line—"Yes, Lord, but even the dogs" (15:27)—she has twice called Jesus "Lord," and she has called him "Son of David." In her own voice, therefore, in Matthew's gospel, the Canaanite woman proclaims Jesus Lord and King. "O woman, great is your faith," Jesus says to her at last; in this address—O woman (ὦ γύναι, a Matthean addition)—Dermience says he uses a title of utmost respect.[54]

Second and finally, the women at the tomb. It is perhaps not surprising, in light of the anointing woman and the Canaanite woman, that at the gospel's end it is women who first see the risen Lord, and women who first proclaim the good news. "Go quickly and tell his disciples that he has been raised from the dead," the angel says to the women (Matt 28:7). And in Matthew, though not in Mark, the women do go and tell. In light of the earlier contrasts between the anointing woman who announces Jesus' death and the disciples who do not see it, and the Canaanite woman who has great faith and the disciples who have little faith, the angels' words are pointed. "Behold, I have told *you*" (ἰδοὺ εἶπον ὑμῖν, 28:7); you go and tell his disciples. The women see; the women hear the angel's voice. The disciples are nowhere to be found. And this time, the women speak. The women are bearers of the word now at the tomb as the Canaanite woman was in the presence of Jesus earlier in the gospel. The women are bearers of the word "with fear and great joy" (28:8) *to the disciples*—the disciples who now again, as before in Matthew's gospel, find themselves doubting (οἱ δὲ ἐδίστασαν, 28:17).

At the gospel's end as at its beginning, then, women carry the word of the Lord; it is through their faithfulness that God's word is heard. The word of God that Mary bears in her body in the gospel's first chapter, "the other Mary" is given to speak, in the last chapter, in her own voice. In the gospel's ending we come full circle, back to its beginning. And we find there not only the constancy of God's word, but Mary. "Behold, I am with you always," the risen Jesus says in the gospel's last verse. So Mary's son speaks in the last verse of the gospel the promise spoken at the gospel's beginning in Mary herself: God is with us. The women in Matthew's gospel are few, but they have

---

[52] Clements compares the Canaanite woman in her faith to Rahab, another Canaanite: "Like Rahab, this woman has believed and acted on her faith and in so doing finds a place inside under the master's table" (*Mothers on the Margins*, 224). I am not sure there is enough evidence to establish (as Clements seeks to do) a deliberate correspondence between the Canaanite woman and Rahab; however, the theme of the faithfulness of the woman resonates with the name of Rahab, and Tamar and Ruth, too.

[53] Wainwright suggests that Matthew's tradition places here on the lips of a Gentile woman the liturgical confession of the emerging Christian communities (*Feminist Critical Reading*, 228).

[54] Alice Dermience, "La péricope de la Cananéenne (Mt 15,21-28): Rédaction et théologie," *EThL* 58 (1982), 25–49, here 43 n. 127, cited in Wainwright, *Feminist Critical Reading*, 242.

starring roles. This gospel, too, in its own way, places women at the center from the beginning; and in the end this gospel gives women voice.

It is no surprise, then, to find in some women of the early church—in Tertullian's unnamed prophet; in Perpetua, in Egeria—a confident appropriation of the gospel proclamation.[55] Perpetua ca. 203 constructs her imprisonment and approaching death in Paul's own terms, as a Pauline *agōn*. Egeria, writing to her sisters back home of her journey through the Holy Land ca. 384 CE, claims for herself Paul's mantle as she makes his words her own.[56] Their proclamation of God's word has its roots here, I propose, in the women of Matthew's gospel.

---

[55] Perpetua's Passion is available in Jacqueline Amat, *Passion de Perpétue et de Félicité suivi des Actes: Introduction, texte critique, tradition, commentaire et index* (SC 417; Paris: Cerfs, 1996) and in English in Thomas J. Heffernan, *The Passion of Perpetua and Felicity* (Oxford: Oxford University Press, 2012). Egeria's travel letters are translated in John Wilkinson, *Egeria's Travels: Newly Translated with Supporting Documents and Notes*, 3rd ed. (Warminster: Aris and Phillips, 1999). The Latin text is available in P. Maraval and M. C. Diaz y Diaz, eds., *Egérie: Journal de voyage et lettre sur la Base. Egérie* (SC 296; Paris: Cerf, 1982). See also my entry, "Egeria: Christianity," in Hans-Josef Klauck et al., eds., *Encyclopedia of the Bible and Its Reception* (Berlin: de Gruyter, 2009–17), and "Egeria," in Marion Taylor, ed. and Agnes Choi, associate ed., *Handbook of Women Biblical Interpreters: A Historical and Biographical Guide* (Grand Rapids, MI: Baker Academic, 2012). For Tertullian's woman prophet see *De anima* 9.4 (CCL 2.792), translated and discussed in Robert D. Sider, *The Gospel and Its Proclamation* (Message of the Fathers of the Church 10; Wilmington: Michael Glazier, 1983), 200–1. Though Tertullian takes her word with utmost seriousness, it should be noted that she speaks it, by his account, only after the formal liturgy has concluded.

[56] For more on these women as preachers, prophets, and interpreters of the gospel see the forthcoming *Women and the Word*.

The "Parting of the Ways" and the Criterion of Plausibility

Adele Reinhartz

Terry Donaldson's contributions to the field of biblical studies has ranged over the entire New Testament canon, from Mark to Revelation, but some of his most substantial contributions have addressed the fraught issue of early Jewish–Christian relations, and especially the "parting of the ways," the process by which Christianity took on an identity separate from its Jewish matrix. In the present short study, I address a methodological issue relevant to scholarly constructions of this process. I dedicate the study to Terry, in friendship and in gratitude for his fine work, from which I have learned so much over the many years of our shared involvement with this important question.

The process by which the institutions, groups, practices, and beliefs that we now call Christianity came to take on an identity separate from what we now call Judaism has generated numerous metaphors. These metaphors stem from human kinship groups (mothers and daughters, twin brothers or sisters), bodies of water (waves in pools; estuaries), social activities (group dances) and the natural world (trees and bushes). In the present moment, the metaphor that has the most currency is "the parting of the ways," understood as a roadway metaphor or perhaps as a divorce metaphor. The parting of the ways metaphor is a handy way to refer succinctly to a complicated set of issues but it is also an oversimplification: it reduces the diversity of Jewish and nascent Christian identities to two ways, and pushes us to identify a distinct moment of separation despite ample evidence of messiness. In my own work in this area, I point to a third concern: the underlying assumption that the process was mutual, symmetrical, and consequential for Jews and Christ-confessors alike.[1] Scholars may disagree on whether the process of parting was linear or messy, widespread or localized, peaceable or conflictual, theologically motivated or not, but they presume that Jews were invested in the relationship with Christ-followers, and

---

[1] In this discussion I use "Jews" to refer to non-Christ-confessing Jews. I acknowledge of course that Jesus and many adherents to the Jesus movement were ethnically Jewish.

exercised some form of agency in moving the process along, at least in some ways, in some places, and at some points in time.

The assumption of mutuality is a welcome antidote to supersessionism and anti-Judaism. I wonder, however, whether scholars' desire to atone for past sins has also caused them to misconstrue the historical processes that the "parting of the ways" discourse intends to clarify.[2] To begin to probe this issue, I will in these pages consider a few of the sources that are used to construct the Jewish side of the "parting of the ways," from the New Testament (NT), Josephus, Justin Martyr, and rabbinic literature, and the ways in which they are used in the "parting" discourse.

I will argue two interconnected points. First, the available evidence for Jewish response to and concern with Christ-confessors can be read in at least two mutually exclusive ways: as evidence for and against Jews' engagement with Christ-confessors. Second, scholars' judgments about the historical value of this evidence, while often presented as objective and even self-evident, are based on an unstated criterion—the criterion of plausibility—that is intuitive and therefore not objective at all.

The Criterion of Plausibility

The criterion of plausibility is discussed explicitly in the fields of epidemiology and biomedicine when proposing a causal association—a relationship between putative cause and an outcome—that is consistent with existing biological and medical knowledge. It has received little direct attention in the historical study of early Christianity despite the fact that it is employed by virtually all scholars. Among the few to discuss this criterion directly are Gerd Theissen and Dagmar Winter. In their book *The Quest for the Plausible Jesus*, Theissen and Winter point out what we all know but prefer not to acknowledge: we cannot know with any certainty what actually happened in the life of Jesus.[3] The same is true, I suggest, with the development of the movement that came to be called Christianity. We can only construct plausible scenarios that are consistent with existing knowledge. The problem is one of circularity, however. The existing knowledge that we need as a foundation for our plausible scenarios is often itself subject to question, as are the methods that we use for constructing our scenarios in the first place. As scholars, therefore, we are always in a position of assessing the plausibility of the scenarios that others propose, and, in turn, we are subject to the criticism of our peers, to whom our own scenarios may seem less than plausible. The sources that are often used to construct the Jewish role in the "parting" process illustrate this conundrum perfectly.

---

[2] Others too have tried it. See, e.g., Tobias Nicklas, *Jews and Christians? Second-Century "Christian" Perspectives on the "Parting of the Ways" (Annual Deichmann Lectures 2013)* (Tübingen: Mohr Siebeck, 2014), 221–3.

[3] Gerd Theissen and Dagmar Winter, *The Quest for the Plausible Jesus: The Question of Criteria* (Louisville, KY: Westminster John Knox Press, 2002).

New Testament

The NT is our richest source of statements about Jews' responses to Jesus and the Jesus movement. As is now well-recognized, the NT is a Jewish source in the sense that most of its authors were Jewish in an ethnic or genealogical sense. It is by no means a disinterested account, however, and, again, most scholars recognize that theNT's christological focus and commitments have shaped its accounts of Jewish views and responses to Jesus and the Jesus movement. I turn now to two examples.

> For you, brothers and sisters, became imitators of the churches of God in Christ Jesus that are in Judea, for you suffered the same things from your own compatriots as they did from the Jews, [15]who killed both the Lord Jesus and the prophets, and drove us out; they displease God and oppose everyone [16] by hindering us from speaking to the Gentiles so that they may be saved. Thus they have constantly been filling up the measure of their sins; but God's wrath has overtaken them at last.
>
> Ὑμεῖς γὰρ μιμηταὶ ἐγενήθητε, ἀδελφοί, τῶν ἐκκλησιῶν τοῦ θεοῦ τῶν οὐσῶν ἐν τῇ Ἰουδαίᾳ ἐν Χριστῷ Ἰησοῦ, ὅτι τὰ αὐτὰ ἐπάθετε καὶ ὑμεῖς ὑπὸ τῶν ἰδίων συμφυλετῶν καθὼς καὶ αὐτοὶ ὑπὸ τῶν Ἰουδαίων, [15] τῶν καὶ τὸν κύριον ἀποκτεινάντων Ἰησοῦν καὶ τοὺς προφήτας καὶ ἡμᾶς ἐκδιωξάντων καὶ θεῷ μὴ ἀρεσκόντων καὶ πᾶσιν ἀνθρώποις ἐναντίων,[16] κωλυόντων ἡμᾶς τοῖς ἔθνεσιν λαλῆσαι ἵνα σωθῶσιν, εἰς τὸ ἀναπληρῶσαι αὐτῶν τὰς ἁμαρτίας πάντοτε. ἔφθασεν δὲ ἐπ' αὐτοὺς ἡ ὀργὴ εἰς τέλος. (1 Thess 2:14–16)

This passage has generated considerable discussion with regard to two interrelated questions: first, is it Pauline? And second, does it have a concrete historical referent? In an article on "1 Thessalonians 2:14–16 and the Church in Jerusalem," Markus Bockmuehl argues that both style and content point to Pauline authorship.[4] He then considers the evidence for Jewish persecution of Christ-confessors to which Paul might have been referring. Most obvious, he suggests, are the hostile measures against Jewish Christ-believers in ca AD 36 (the martyrdom of Stephen) and again under Agrippa I in 41/42 (Herod Agrippa I's execution of James son of Zebedee), as described in Acts 7 and Acts 12 respectively. At this point Bockmuehl invokes the criterion of plausibility: "It would seem most reasonable to begin from the assumption that memories of both experiences are fresh in his mind."[5]

Nevertheless, chronology is a problem. Is it plausible that Paul would still be reacting to events that happened some 9 years before he wrote his letter? For Bockmuehl, the answer seems to be no. To fill the chronological gap, he looks to the sixth-century CE chronicler Malalas of Antioch, who mentions a Jewish persecution of the Jerusalem church during the procuratorship of Ventidius Cumanusa in the eighth year of Claudius' reign (48/49 CE). Bockmuehl acknowledges that Malalas is neither impartial

---
[4] Markus Bockmuehl, "1 Thessalonians 2:14–16 and the Church in Jerusalem." *TynBull* 52.1 (2001): 1–31.
[5] Bockmuehl, "1 Thessalonians 2," 22.

nor reliable, yet, in his view, "there is no obvious reason why such a specific reference to a persecution in CE 48/49 should have been invented." (24). In other words, Bockmuehl applies the criterion of plausibility to Malalas's account, which he can then use to support the view that 1 Thess 2:14–16 refers accurately to recent historical events. He concludes that these considerations render this passage "remarkably intelligible on the historical level," much as we would wish Paul had not written it.[6]

Sarah Rollens reaches the opposite conclusion. In her article entitled, "Inventing Tradition in Thessalonica," Rollens argues that 1 Thess 2:14–16 is not historical at all, but rather an invented history. This tradition posits a backstory that situates the Thessalonians within a larger history and thereby functions as a strategy for social formation.[7] She states that Paul did not simply found communities "but rather, brings these group identities into being through the process of writing and negotiating their concerns."[8] Rollens draws on the work of Eric Hobsbawm and Terence Ranger who describe invented history as a set of ideas, practices, or symbols that allow groups undergoing dramatic change to claim continuity with the past.[9] Greco-Roman voluntary organizations provide evidence for this practice in antiquity.

From this example, we may extrapolate an implicit methodology that allows one to proceed in the face of absent or ambiguous evidence: an assertion of plausibility supported by invoking other pieces of ambiguous evidence (Bockmuehl) or ancient parallels mediated by contemporary theory (Rollens). Our other examples will show the ubiquity of this approach.

> They will put you out of the synagogues. Indeed, an hour is coming when those who kill you will think that by doing so they are offering worship to God. And they will do this because they have not known the Father or me. But I have said these things to you so that when their hour comes you may remember that I told you about them.
>
> ἀποσυναγώγους ποιήσουσιν ὑμᾶς· ἀλλ᾽ ἔρχεται ὥρα ἵνα πᾶς ὁ ἀποκτείνας ὑμᾶς δόξῃ λατρείαν προσφέρειν τῷ θεῷ. [3] καὶ ταῦτα ποιήσουσιν ὅτι οὐκ ἔγνωσαν τὸν πατέρα οὐδὲ ἐμέ. [4] ἀλλὰ ταῦτα λελάληκα ὑμῖν ἵνα ὅταν ἔλθῃ ἡ ὥρα αὐτῶν μνημονεύητε αὐτῶν ὅτι ἐγὼ εἶπον ὑμῖν. (John 16:2–4)

Along with John 9:22 and 12:42, this passage is used to support the view that Jewish synagogue authorities exercised agency in the parting process by excluding Jewish Christ-confessors from the synagogue. Steve Wilson invokes the criterion of plausibility when he argues that the vividness of John's *aposynagogos* passages suggests their accuracy as an experience of the Johannine community. From this he concludes, "excluding Christians from their synagogues was an effective way for Jews to express their disfavor and stifle recruitment to the churches."[10]

---

[6] Ibid., 30.
[7] Sarah E. Rollens, "Inventing Tradition in Thessalonica: The Appropriation of the Past in 1 Thessalonians 2:14–16," *BTB* 46.3 (2016): 123.
[8] Ibid., 124.
[9] Ibid., 127.
[10] S. G. Wilson, *Related Strangers: Jews and Christians, 70–170 C.E.* (Minneapolis, MN: Fortress Press, 1995), 175.

Wilson, like most Johannine scholars, treats John 16:2-4 as a reference to a historical trauma of expulsion, in accordance with the influential work of J. L. Martyn.[11] But, as Martin de Boer has noted, few have noticed that Martyn himself understood John 16 as a reference to a second trauma: the murder, and martyrdom, of Johannine believers at the hands of Jewish authorities. For Martyn, the gospel's high Christology was not the cause of expulsion but the effect of that expulsion, and the catalyst for this second, life-threatening trauma.[12]

The criterion of plausibility is central to de Boer's defense of Martyn's hypothesis. De Boer argues that "the claim that both expulsion and execution were fabrications of the Johannine community is unlikely given the specificity of the charges (which, if false, could easily have been disconfirmed by the first readers of the Gospel) … It is unlikely that such predictions would have been preserved or attributed to Jesus if they had not been fulfilled in the experience of the Johannine community." He further adds that "the external evidence, such as it is, supports this reading."[13]

Like Bockmuehl, de Boer supports the claim of plausibility by appealing to a number of extracanonical sources: Justin Martyr's Dialogue with Trypho, selected rabbinic, and the Pseudo-Clementine literature. Also relevant are the reported martyrdoms of Stephen (Acts 7:58-60), James the son of Zebedee (Acts 12:2-3), and James the brother of the Lord (Josephus, A.J. 20.200), as well as the persecution of Paul (234-45). De Boer concludes that while these texts cannot all be taken at face value, "the number and diversity of sources and witnesses … cumulatively give a considerable degree of plausibility to the historicity of the second trauma mentioned in John 16:2b," that is, the Jewish persecution and murder of Johannine Christ-confessors.[14]

De Boer frames his argument as a rebuttal of my own analysis of these passages; in his words, I went "on the offensive" against Martyn's hypothesis in 1998.[15] It is therefore not surprising that de Boer's "plausible" argument does not seem plausible to me. I agree with Wilson that the descriptions are vivid and with de Boer that they are detailed. But neither vividness nor detail demonstrate historicity, as the work of excellent novelists and poets, from the ancient period to the present, can attest. My own analysis of the gospel as a rhetorical document suggests that the expulsion passages contribute to John's well-developed rhetoric of fear. I do not see John's reference to persecution in chapter 16 as a historical referent but as an echo of a biblical trope deployed for rhetorical purposes.[16] My argument also relies on the criterion of plausibility, as it is based on a particular perspective on the gospel's genre and purpose. This example in particular suggests two important points: the criterion of plausibility is unavoidable in situations where external evidence is sparse, lacking, or ambiguous; and it is not

---

[11] J. Louis Martyn, *History and Theology in the Fourth Gospel* (Louisville, KY: Westminster John Knox Press, 2003).

[12] Martinus C. de Boer, "The Johannine Community under Attack in Recent Scholarship," in *The Ways That Often Parted* (ed. Lori Baron; Essays in Honor of Joel Marcus; Society of Biblical Literature, 2018), 231, http://www.jstor.org/stable/j.ctv7r424g.15.

[13] Ibid., 236.

[14] Ibid., 235.

[15] Ibid., 215.

[16] Adele Reinhartz, *Cast out of the Covenant: Jews and Anti-Judaism in the Gospel of John* (Lanham, MD: Lexington Books/Fortress Academic, 2018), 79-80.

at all objective. What seems plausible to me does not seem so to de Boer; the reverse is also true. This same dynamic is evident in the differing perspectives of Rollens and Bockmuehl regarding 1 Thess 2:14–16 and in the scholarly assessments of other NT texts relevant to the roles of non-Christ-confessing Jews in the "parting of the ways."

Josephus Flavius

Wherever they stand on the NT's historicity, most scholars agree on the tendentious nature of the statements of hostility attributed to non-Christ-confessing Jews. How helpful it would have been had a contemporary author, Josephus Flavius, written on this subject at length! As it is, he left us with three short passages: AJ 18.117, about John the Baptist; AJ 20.201, about the death of James, "the brother of Jesus who is called the messiah"; and AJ 20.200, the so-called *Testimonium Flavianum*.

On the face of it, these passages display indifference toward Jesus and his followers. In his recent study, "John and Jesus in Josephus: A Prelude to the Parting of the Ways," however, Albert Baumgarten tries to draw a bit more, especially from Josephus's brief remarks about the Baptist and James.[17] On the basis of Josephus's description in AJ 20.201 of Jesus as a so-called Messiah, Baumgarten suggests that the original version of the *Testimonium* also contained an unfavorable description of Jesus that was edited out by Christians as they added Christological elements to a Josephan core.[18] Baumgarten therefore finds it plausible to suggest that "Jesus … may have broken the bounds of legitimate variety for Josephus as Jesus and his followers did for Ananus and his followers or as they later would for Celsus's Jew."[19] For this reason, Josephus may be a witness to the limits to acceptable diversity; Jewish messianic understanding did not include the possibility of a crucified messiah (45). Nevertheless, Baumgarten acknowledges that all we know for certain is that Josephus did not believe that Jesus was the Messiah, but we cannot know why.

Baumgarten fills a chronological gap in our sources based on one short phrase in Josephus's *Jewish Antiquities*. Although he argues for the plausibility of his hypothesis, however, he acknowledges its speculative nature and, with admirable restraint, refuses to reify it as historical fact.

Justin Martyr

We move now to the second century and the writings of Justin Martyr. In a number of places, including in the *First Apology* and the *Dialogue with Trypho*, Justin refers to Jewish persecution of Christians during the Bar Kochba revolt and on other occasions. Steve Wilson suggests that Justin's allegations of occasional Jewish murders

---

[17] Albert I. Baumgarten, "John and Jesus in Josephus: A Prelude to the Parting of the Ways," in *The Ways That Often Parted: Essays in Honor of Joel Marcus* (ed. Matthew Thiessen et al.; Atlanta, GA: SBL Press, 2018), 40–64.
[18] Ibid., 44.
[19] Ibid., 57.

of Christians are essentially correct if somewhat exaggerated.[20] In her article, "'The Parting of the Ways': Theological Construct or Historical Reality?" Judith Lieu challenges the historical plausibility of Justin's accounts of Jewish persecution; in her view, these passages are not evidence that Jews persecuted, but only that some Christians perceived and presented themselves as objects of Jewish persecution. The question is why.[21]

Lieu suggests that Justin's references to persecution may have more to do with the long-standing rhetorical tradition concerning the fate of the prophets than with actual events.[22] This tradition begins in the biblical period, but, as Lieu notes, "in Christian hands it easily became a demonstration of Jewish inveterate rejection of God's message, a rejection which might even have reached the point of no return."[23] Justin's use of the trope may also have depended on its NT use, as in Luke 6:23; Luke 11:49–51, and Matt. 23:29–31.[24] She concludes that "Jewish hostility serves an apologetic function in the appeal to fulfilment of prophecy, which qualifies the necessary recognition of their prior claim to the Scriptures."[25] Such tropes of persecution created a persuasive—rhetorical—world that may or may not have a foundation in the actual experiences of Christ-confessors. The process by which perceived experience might create a "reality" for an audience requires modern interpreters to steer "a path between a simple historicism and a sceptical dismissal of theological fantasy."[26] Nevertheless, she presents a plausible alternative to the view that Justin can be taken at face value as a witness to Jewish persecution of Christians, widespread or otherwise.

Rabbinic Literature

Finally, we turn to rabbinic literature. Thankfully, most NT scholars no longer use rabbinic sources from the third to sixth centuries uncritically to reconstruct the background to Jesus and the Jesus movement two or more centuries earlier. Where rabbinic literature is helpful is in showing that the rabbis were aware of Jesus and the Jesus movement, and in suggesting that some rabbis knew of contacts between Jews and Christians. The rabbinic passage that has received the most attention in the "parting of the ways" discourse concerns the so-called *birkat ha-minim*, the euphemistic blessing on the heretics.

> Our rabbis taught: Simeon ha-Paquli organized the Eighteen Benedictions in order before Rabban Gamaliel in Yavneh. Rabban Gamaliel said to the sages: "Isn't there anyone who knows how to fix the Benediction of the Heretics?" Samuel the Small

---

[20] Wilson, *Related Strangers*, 172.
[21] Judith Lieu, "'The Parting of the Ways': Theological Construct or Historical Reality?" *JSNT* 56 (1994): 281.
[22] Ibid., 282.
[23] Ibid.
[24] Ibid.
[25] Ibid., 285.
[26] Ibid., 292.

stood up and fixed it, but another year he forgot it. And he thought about it for two or three hours, [and he did not recall it], but they did not remove him.—Why then did they not remove him? Did not R. Judah say that Rav said: "If someone makes a mistake in any of the benedictions, they don't remove him, but if [he makes a mistake] in the Benediction of the Heretics, they do remove him, since they suspect that perhaps he is a heretic?" Samuel the Small is different, because he formulated it.

להם אמר. ביבנה הסדר על גמליאל רבן לפני ברכות עשרה שמונה הסדיר הפקולי שמעון רבנן: תנו לשנה, ותקנה הקטן שמואל עמד ?המינים ברכת לתקן שיודע אדם יש כלום :לחכמים גמליאל רבן אמר יהודה רב והאמר ?העלוהו לא אמאי. העלוהו ולא שעות ושלש שתים בה והשקיף. שכחה אחרת ?הוא מין שמא חיישינן, אותו מעלין - המינים בברכת, אותו מעלין אין - כלן הברכות בכל טעה :רב תקנה דאיהו, הקטן שמואל שאני. (B. Berakhot 28b–29a)

This passage assigns *birkat ha-minim* to the late first century at the latest. J. L. Martyn drew on this story to support his theory that *birkat ha-minim* was the mechanism by which Jewish authorities expelled Johannine Christ-confessors from the synagogue. Many scholars who still support his expulsion theory no longer see this aspect of the hypothesis as plausible, having been persuaded by the work of Reuven Kimelman and Steven Katz that *birkat ha-minim* probably was not yet in circulation at the time John was written, and in any case could not have served as a mechanism for exclusion.[27]

In his 2009 article, "Birkat ha-minim revisited," however, Joel Marcus argues for the plausibility of Martyn's argument.[28] The article gives a thorough and even-handed summary of the scholarship on the question and nuances Martyn's points in various ways. He then proceeds with his own argument. He argues that, following Uri Ehrlich, one can use the extant versions of *birkat ha-minim*, all of which postdate John's gospel by several centuries, to reconstruct its first-century form. Marcus draws support from Justin's reference to cursing Christians; in his view it is plausible that these statements refer specifically to *birkat ha-minim*. If so, they provide a bridge backward from the Genizah to the second century. To fill the remaining gap between John in the late first century and Justin in the mid-second century, Marcus suggests that we view patristic citations about the curse as a continuation of the NT hostility toward the Pharisees. Pharisees, in turn, are "plausibly linked" to *birkat ha-minim*, because John portrays the Pharisees as the ones enforcing the expulsion in 9:22 and 12:42, and "it is easy to see the self-curse of Birkat Ha-Minim" as the means to enforce the expulsion edict. He dismisses the view that these Johannine passages are "complete fabrications" intended to instill fear in Christians, on the grounds that they do not take into account the "consonance between the New Testament passages and rabbinic tradition."[29] Similarly, while he acknowledges that the rabbis did not yet have widespread authority in the late first century, the evidence for the curse "emerged from places in which the rabbis were

---

[27] Reuven Kimelman, "Birkat Ha-Minim and the Lack of Evidence for an Anti-Christian Jewish Prayer in Late Antiquity," in *Jewish and Christian Self-Definition, 2* (Philadelphia, PA: Fortress, 1981), 226–44; Steven T. Katz, "Issues in the Separation of Judaism and Christianity after 70 CE : A Reconsideration," *JBL* 103.1 (1984): 43–76.

[28] Joel Marcus, "Birkat Ha-Minim Revisited," *NTS* 55.4 (2009): 523–51.

[29] Ibid., 533.

able to establish substantial control over synagogue and Jewish religious life" and were therefore able to enforce an anti-Christian policy.[30]

For Marcus, then, the hypothesis that *birkat ha-minim* was used in the late first century to exclude Christ-confessors from the synagogue fulfills the criterion of plausibility despite the fact that the earliest extant sources for the blessing are dated some centuries later. The article demonstrates a masterful set of connections between apparently disparate materials. It is undermined, however, by circularity: the argument for the historicity depends upon drawing on the same connections between NT and rabbinic literature that prompted the question in the first place. It is also challenged by the absence of evidence concerning local rabbinic control in the late first century.

The most thorough, and, in my view, most persuasive study of this problem is found in Ruth Langer's book *Cursing the Christians?*[31] Langer's analysis—and her sense of what is plausible—differ significantly from those of Marcus. Where Marcus argues for a Qumranian origin for *birkat ha-minim* perhaps as an anti-Roman imprecation,[32] Langer points out that any hypothesis about the origins and first-century use of *birkat ha-minim* depends "on the preconceptions with which one approaches the few hints that can be gleaned from the texts."[33] There is no evidence that the rabbis spread their liturgical system beyond their own narrow circles for several centuries after 70. Patristic references to the curse allow us to date the curse back to the fourth century but no earlier. It is also not at all clear that the curse was formulated in the first instance against Christians, or that it could or would have been used as a mechanism for expelling Christians from the synagogue.[34] In other words, Langer does not find the sorts of arguments put forward by Marcus and others to be plausible. She prefers not to speculate in the absence of evidence.

Conclusion

These brief examples suggest that the criterion of plausibility is invoked at the point at which scholarly arguments run out of unambiguous evidence. In the study of the "parting of the ways" one reaches this point very quickly. The invocation of this criterion is signaled by the increased use of words such as "likely," "probably," and "plausibly," as well as by the use of the subjunctive mood. In all cases, the claim of plausibility is buttressed by interpretations of ambiguous sources so as to create a coherent theory that fills in the gaps in our evidence. Almost all of us do this at one point or another. But here is the problem. Our theories will be considered coherent only to those who accept our basic premises. To a historical minimalist like myself, for example, the claim that the NT and patristic references to persecution are factual accounts of real events or that the rabbinic story of Samuel the Small reliably dates *birkat ha-minim* to the

---

[30] Ibid., 551.
[31] Ruth Langer, *Cursing the Christians?: A History of the Birkat Haminim* (New York, NY: Oxford University Press, 2011).
[32] Marcus, "Birkat Ha-Minim Revisited," 548.
[33] Langer, *Cursing the Christians?* 7.
[34] Ibid., 22.

late first century are not plausible, whereas hypotheses that foreground the rhetorical nature of our sources are much more persuasive. My own arguments, based on literary genre and rhetorical analysis, will not be appealing to those who see our ancient sources as reasonably accurate reflections of historical reality.

These examples also illustrate the conundrum we face in attempting to discern and describe the messy process of the "parting of the ways." As I mentioned at the outset, I have begun to question the mutuality implied by this metaphor, given the relative paucity of reliable evidence for the non-Christ-confessing Jewish role in the process. Of course I recognize that my emphasis on the silence of our sources is also affected by my own views concerning plausible hypotheses. It could be that those who accept as plausible the various statements of the NT and other ancient sources about Jewish persecution of Christ-confessors, as well as the claims that Jews rejected belief in Jesus on theological grounds, will argue that the parting was indeed a mutual affair, and, perhaps, even instigated by the Jewish opponents to Christianity. I know I will not persuade everyone, or even anyone, to take a more skeptical approach, to this topic and others. But I hope that we can all reach the point of acknowledging that plausibility, like beauty, is in the eye of the beholder, and not the same as objective truth.

10

Mark 14:51–52: A Socio-Rhetorical Reading of the Text and Conclusions Drawn from the History of Its Interpretation

L. Gregory Bloomquist and Michael A. G. Haykin

Introduction

In Mark 14:51–52 we read a seemingly inconsequential story of a young man, found in the garden at the same time as Jesus, who is captured by Temple authorities. The lines are not only unparalleled in the Synoptic tradition, but as Albert Vanhoye noted, it is the only passage that is unique to Mark in the passion account[1]:

καὶ νεανίσκος τις συνηκολούθει αὐτῷ περιβεβλημένος σινδόνα ἐπὶ γυμνοῦ, καὶ κρατοῦσιν αὐτό ὁ δὲ καταλιπὼν τὴν σινδόνα γυμνὸς ἔφυγεν.

Why, one asks, would this simple passage not be found in any of the other gospel accounts of the passion, including the Gospel of Matthew? If, in particular, Matthew was not alien to the language and themes found in Mark 14, why did he not include the story, if we presume that he had Mark?

In what follows we seek to provide an answer to this question and thus to helping better understand both the Gospel of Mark and the other gospels, including that of Matthew, by first providing an overview of some of the representative lines of interpretation on this passage from the earliest, extant comments on the Markan passage, through a more extended look at Protestant and Evangelical exegesis of the passage from Calvin to Spurgeon, and ending with a brief overview of historical-critical interpretations. We then move to a discussion of the text from a socio-rhetorical vantage point, starting with a brief introduction to socio-rhetorical interpretation itself, followed by its application to our passage. We conclude by observing the way in which socio-rhetorical interpretation ideally establishes a connection between the biblical passage

---

[1] Albert Vanhoye, "La fuite du jeune homme nu (Mc 14,51–52)," *Bib* 52.3 (1971): 401.

and its "after-life" in use, including its non-use in the Gospel of Matthew. As such, we conclude by reflecting on the way the text created new possibilities of interpretation, some of which were not followed by the other *Synoptic Gospels* and were only picked up on later.

The Main Lines of Interpretation of the Passage

An in-depth account of the history of the interpretation of Mark 14:51–52, what a significant number of modern commentators regard as a "strange passage,"[2] even "ridicule et indécente,"[3] has yet to be written.[4] In what follows we look briefly at Patristic interpretations of our passage and at the historical critical study of the passage, and in between provide a more lengthy overview of Protestant and Evangelical exegesis since this material is not as well known. Furthermore, an overview of this material is important for the conclusions that we draw at the end of this contribution.

Patristic Interpretation

Most commentators in the ancient and early medieval church saw in this text the memory of an actual historical event and accordingly focused on the young man's identity.[5] Ambrose, followed by Gregory the Great and Bede, related our text to John 18:15–16 and concluded that the "young man" was the Apostle John.[6] Epiphanius of Salamis, however, believed that the "young man" was Jesus' half-brother James, since linen was purportedly James's clothing of choice after his conversion.[7] Concurring with Epiphanius, the eleventh-century commentator Theophylact noted further that

---

[2] The quote is from Francis J. Moloney, *The Gospel of Mark: A Commentary* (Peabody, MA: Hendrickson Publishers, 2002), 299 n. 118. See also Mark L. Strauss, *Mark* (Grand Rapids, MI: Zondervan, 2014), 645 for a similar judgment. Other scholars see it as: a "confusing" story, Robert H Stein, *Mark* (Grand Rapids, MI: Baker Academic, 2008), 674; "this bizarre episode," M. Eugene Boring, *Mark: A Commentary* (Louisville, KY: Westminster John Knox, 2006), 403; a "mysterious story," R. T. France, *The Gospel of Mark* (Grand Rapids, MI: Paternoster Press, 2002), 595; and "unusual," albeit "trivial," James A. Brooks, *Mark* (Nashville, TN: Broadman, 1991), 238–9. For other similar judgments, see Abraham Kuruvilla, "The Naked Runaway and the Enrobed Reporter of Mark 14 and 16: What Is the Author Doing with What He Is Saying?" *JETS* 54.3 (September 2011): 527.

[3] Vanhoye, "La fuite du jeune homme nu (Mc 14,51–52)," 401.

[4] See, though, Frans Neirynck, "La Fuite du jeune homme en Mc 14, 51–52," in *Evangelica: Gospel Studies—Études d'Évangile* (Leuven: Uitgeverij Peeters/Leuven University, 1982), 215–38; Brooks, *Mark*, 238; Robert H Gundry, *Mark: A Commentary on His Apology for the Cross* (Grand Rapids, MI: Eerdmans, 1993), 881–2; Adela Yarbro Collins, *Mark: A Commentary* (ed. Harold W. Attridge; Hermeneia—A Critical and Historical Commentary on the Bible; Minneapolis, MN: Fortress Press, 2007), 688–93; and Kuruvilla, "Naked Runaway," 527–33.

[5] Neirynck, "Fuite," 227. The presentation of Patristic interpretation in Collins, *Mark*, 688–9 is overly brief.

[6] Ambrose, *Enarrati. Ps.* 36.53 (PL 14.1040B–C); Peter Chrysologus, *Sermo* 150, 170 (PL 52.600B); Gregory the Great, *Moral.* 14.48.56 in Gregory the Great, *Morals on the Book of Job. Volume II* (Oxford: John Henry Parker, 1845), 14.48.56; Bede, *Mar. exp.* (PL 92.279A–C). See also Kuruvilla, "Naked Runaway," 530.

[7] Epiphanius, *Pan.* 78.13.3 (PG 42.79A). On James' clothing, see Eusebius, *Hist. eccl.* 2.23.6. See Kuruvilla, "Naked Runaway," 530.

the young man in question may have dwelt in the house where Jesus and the disciples had held the last supper.[8] A very different, typological approach can be found in both Bede and a seventh-century commentary attributed to Jerome that stated that the flight of the young man was "like the case of Joseph, who leaving behind his tunic, fled in the nude from the hands of the shameless mistress of the house. Whoever wants to escape from the hands of wicked people, let them mentally abandon the things of the world, and flee after Jesus."[9]

Protestant Exegesis

By the time of the Reformation, both Catholic and Protestant exegetes were far less certain about, or even interested in, the identity of the young man, and few of them regarded him as one of the apostles.[10] John Calvin, for instance, was critical of the patristic identification of the young man as John and offered his own reason for why Mark included the story:

> How it has happened that some have imagined this to be John, I do not know, nor should we greatly care: it is more to the point to grasp the reason for Mark telling the story. I reckon that this was his intention, that we should know that in disorder, shameless and unrestrained (as is the way with ruined causes) the wicked proceeded to arrest a young man, unknown and suspected of no crime, who only just slipped from their clutches, without his clothes. It is likely that the young man mentioned, being a follower of Christ's, heard the riot in the night; put on no clothes but a linen wrap, and hoped either to reveal the plot or at least to perform some duty of devotion. It is certainly evident, as I have just remarked, that those wicked men acted with savage violence when they did not spare a young man who had leapt from his bed half-dressed at the uproar.[11]

Here, the French Reformer sets the parameters for subsequent English Protestant exegesis: the exact identity of the young man is of no concern to the exegete; it is enough to know that he was a disciple, possibly aiming at "some duty of devotion." But what is critical for Calvin is knowing why the evangelist has included this account. For him the answer is clear: the attempted arrest of the young man drives home the fact that the men who had arrested Christ were men of "shameless and unrestrained ... savage violence."

---

[8] Theophylact, *Enarrati. Mar.* 14 (PG 123.657B–D). The suggestion that the young man was an inhabitant of the house in which the last supper was held survived well into the twentieth century as did the theory that the young man is none other than John Mark (Neirynck, "Fuite," 228 n. 242). See Gundry, *Mark*, 882.
[9] For Bede, see *Mar. exp.* (PL 92.279C). For the seventh-century commentary, see Collins, *Mark*, 688–9.
[10] See Neirynck, "Fuite," 228 nn. 242–3, who cites Thomas Cajetan, Juan Maldonado, Franciscus Lucas Brugensis, Hugo Grotius, and Cornelius Jansen.
[11] John Calvin, *A Harmony of the Gospels: Matthew, Mark and Luke, Volume III and The Epistles of James and Jude*, Calvin's Commentaries 3 (Grand Rapids, MI: Eerdmans, 1972), 162–3 (commentary on Mark 14:51).

Elements of Calvin's interpretation clearly shaped later Protestant exegesis. The note opposite Mark 14:51 in the 1599 edition of *The Geneva Bible*, for example, emphasized that the attempted seizure of the young man was included by Mark that "we may understand with how great licenciousnesse [sic] these villaines [sic] violently set upon him."[12] John Mayer—an early seventh-century graduate of Emmanuel College, Cambridge, that was specifically founded as a Puritan seedbed—included the Markan text and reproduced the various patristic comments on it (those by Theophylact, Gregory the Great, Bede, and Pseudo-Jerome) as well as that of Calvin cited here.[13] *The Geneva Bible* and Mayer's intriguing work thus helped to ensure that the heart of Calvin's comments entered mainstream English Protestant exegesis.

For example, Matthew Poole followed Calvin explicitly by criticizing the identification of the young man of Mark 14:51–52 with the apostle John. The actual author of the comments on Mark was the Norwich Presbyterian John Collinges, who collaborated with a number of other Puritan divines to complete the massive *Annotations* when Poole died before finishing his commentary upon Isaiah. Collinges, though, also disagreed with Calvin's view of the young man's possible devotion to Christ. He pointed out that the Markan text does not actually describe the young man as a disciple: the young man "was not concerned in Christ" but came merely as a spectator of his arrest: "being in bed, and hearing the noise of the multitude, going by his lodging with swords and staves, [he] got up, slipt [sic] on his night-garment, and followed them, to see what the matter was." But Collinges did build upon Calvin's proposal as to why the passage had been included: Collinges strengthened Calvin's remarks about the savagery of Christ's captors by stressing that the verses served to warn Christians what they "must expect from the rage of persecutors"—no mercy, even though they be innocent of a crime, as the young man surely was.[14]

Eighty or so years later, John Gill, the Baptist commentator whose voluminous commentary on the entire Bible was an essential part of the library of most English Baptist ministers in the latter half of the eighteenth century, returned to the various patristic views concerning the identity of the young man in his comments on the Mark 14 passage and then gave his own opinion that he lived "in an house in Gethsemane, or in or near the garden."[15] Awakened by the noise of Christ's arrest, the young man came out as a curious onlooker, clad in but "a piece of linen wrapped about his middle."[16] Gill is well-known for a militant monergistic soteriology and that theological predilection shaped his final comment regarding this passage where he laid bare Mark's design in the inclusion of this incident: the incident was intended to show "the rage and fury" of the arresting soldiers who were "for sparing none that appeared to be, or were thought

---

[12] *The Bible* (London: Christopher Barker, 1599), comment on 14:51. Spelling original.

[13] John Mayer, *A Treasury of Ecclesiastical Expositions, Upon the Difficult and Doubtful Places of the Scriptures* (London: John Bellamie, 1622), 360–1.

[14] Matthew Poole et al., *Annotations upon the Holy Bible* (Edinburgh: Heirs and Successors of Andrew Anderson, 1701), II, commentary on Mark 14:51–52. The definitive edition was published in 1700–01, 20 years or so after Poole's death in 1679. For Collinges, see A. S. Hankinson, "Dr John Collinges of Norwich, 1623–90," *NorArch* 42 (1997): 511–19.

[15] For a contemporary evaluation of this suggestion, see Gundry, *Mark*, 882.

[16] John Gill, *An Exposition of the New Testament, Both Doctrinal and Practical* (London: George Keith, 1774), I, 633–4.

to be the followers of Christ." Following the lead of both Calvin and Collinges, Gill drove home the fact that "the preservation of the disciples, was entirely owing to the wonderful power of Christ."[17] Though an opponent of Gill, the Arminian Methodist preacher John Wesley, like both Collinges and Gill, did not believe the young man was a true disciple of Christ, for he observed that while the soldiers were able to lay their hands on this man, they could not touch those who were really Christ's disciples.[18]

But neither the search for the young man's identity nor the desire to see him as a disciple disappeared entirely in the study and preaching of this period. Particularly noteworthy among eighteenth-century English Protestant comments on this passage are those of the Congregationalist Philip Doddridge, whose evangelical study bible *The Family Expositor* (6 vols., 1739–56) was a bestseller in its day. Like Gill, Doddridge thought that the young man "lodged in a house near the Garden" of Gethsemane but returned to the notion of the young man as a disciple when he suggested that the young man, "having an affection for Christ," followed him and the other disciples. His partial nudity was a result of his "apprehending him [that is, Christ] in danger" and, forgetful of his own appearance, he rushed from bed out of "his concern for Jesus."[19] For Doddridge the young man has become not only a disciple but the very exemplar of a model disciple.[20]

Though some later Anglophone Protestant preachers appear to have ventured to preach on the text, Charles Haddon Spurgeon, the celebrated Victorian preacher, who had an eye for unusual biblical texts, returned to some of the reflections of centuries earlier when he observed:

> This little episode in the narrative of the evangelist is very singular. One wonders why it is introduced; but a moment's reflection will, I think, suggest a plausible reason. It strikes me that this "certain young man" was none other than Mark himself.[21]

Spurgeon went on to admit that his identification of the young man as Mark was "merely a supposition," but he appealed to "the more recondite critics of the modern school" who also identified the young man of Mark 14 as the gospel writer. This was an odd move for Spurgeon to make for he was generally opposed to the critical New

---

[17] Gill, *Exposition*, 634. For Gill's monergistic soteriology, see Curt Daniel, "John Gill and Calvinistic Antinomianism," in *The Life and Thought of John Gill (1697–1771): A Terrcentennial Appreciation* (Leiden: Brill, 1997), 171–90 and Michael A. G. Haykin, "Remembering Baptist Heroes: The Example of John Gill," in *Ministry By His Grace and for His Glory: Essays in Honor of Thomas J. Nettles* (ed. Thomas K. Ascol and Nathan A. Finn; Cape Coral, FL: Founders, 2011), 17–37.

[18] John Wesley, *Explanatory Notes upon the New Testament* (2nd ed.; London, 1757), 133 (comments on Mark 14:51).

[19] Philip Doddridge, *The Family Expositor, or A Paraphrase and Version of the New Testament with Critical Notes and a Practical Improvement of Each Section* (London: John Wilson, 1740), 513. For a discussion of this popular work, see Tessa Whitehouse, "The Family Expositor, the Doddridge Circle and the Booksellers," *The Library* 11.3 (September 2010): 321–44.

[20] See the similar view in the seventh-century commentary attributed to Jerome earlier.

[21] C. H. Spurgeon, "John Mark; or Haste in Religion," in *The Metropolitan Tabernacle Pulpit*, Vol. 53 (Pasadena, TX: Pilgrim, 1978), 37.

Testament (NT) scholarship of his day. But Spurgeon was confident that there was "no hypothesis in favour of any other man that is supported by equal probabilities."[22]

Be that as it may, it also becomes clear why Spurgeon has made the connection with Mark, since the rest of his sermon sought out lessons for the Christian life from the career of John Mark as that life is touched on in the book of Acts and the Pauline corpus.[23] Thus, it is clear that for Spurgeon the primary purpose of the Markan passage was to serve as an autobiographical signature. In doing so, however, Spurgeon clearly turned away from the interpretative tradition of Calvin and his followers that had seen little value in seeking to identify the young man of Mark 14 and brought evangelical interpretations back to their patristic roots.

Historical-Critical Interpretation

Though a summary of historical-critical interpretations of the passage suggests that studies of the passage are inconclusive,[24] or that the best that one can say is that the passage is "a major crux of Mark's Gospel,"[25] there are nevertheless identifiable main lines of interpretation that have been followed by interpreters: the passage reflects an eyewitness account; the passage reflects a literary-theological typology; the passage is connected to Old Testament (OT) Scripture.[26]

Mark 14:51–52 has been viewed as an eyewitness account by, among others, Lohmeyer and Taylor.[27] Zahn, followed by Schmid, concluded specifically, as had medieval and some Protestant interpreters, that the young man was Mark.[28] Theissen, on the other hand, argued that the young man was not Mark but a man whose identity was historical and who was protected by the gospel writer Mark through this anonymous narrative, possibly because the man was a member of the endangered,

---

[22] Spurgeon, "John Mark," 37, 39. The supposition is picked up and supported by Ben Witherington III, *The Gospel of Mark: A Socio-Rhetorical Commentary* (Grand Rapids, MI: Eerdmans, 2001), 382, though Witherington does not mention Spurgeon. The identification of the young man with John Mark by Western commentators started in the 1830s: Rupert Allen, "Mark 14, 51–52 and Coptic Hagiography," *Bib* 89 (2008): 265–7. However, there is an early Coptic manuscript dated to 1208 that also makes this identification (267–8).

[23] Spurgeon, "John Mark," 39–47. Knox wisely notes Papias's concern that Mark "neither heard the Lord nor followed him." John Knox, "A Note on Mark 14:51–52," in *The Joy of Study: Papers on New Testament and Related Subjects Presented to Honor Frederick Clifton Grant* (ed. Sherman Elbridge Johnson; New York, NY: Macmillan, 1951), 28, also noted by Kuruvilla, "Naked Runaway," 529.

[24] '[D]ie noch keine befriedigende Erklärung gefunden hat," Ludger Schenke, *Der gekreuzigte Christus: Versuche einer literarkritischen und traditionsgeschichtlichen Bestimmung der vormarkinischen Passionsgeschichte* (Stuttgarter Bibelstudien 69; Stuttgart: KBW, 1974), 122.

[25] Kuruvilla, "Naked Runaway," 527.

[26] The organization of the history here builds on and hopefully develops the work of Harry Fleddermann, "The Flight of a Naked Young Man (Mark 14:51–52)," in *CBQ* (1979): 689–93; Collins, *Mark*.

[27] Ernst Lohmeyer, *Das Evangelium des Markus* (Göttingen: Vandenhoeck & Ruprecht, 1937), 324; Vincent Taylor, *The Gospel According to St. Mark: The Greek Text with Introduction, Notes, and Indexes* (New York, NY: Macmillan, 1966), 561. Taylor also assumes, however, that the text "is obviously appended" to the gospel.

[28] Theodor Zahn, *Einleitung in das Neue Testament* (Leipzig: Deichert, 1897), 249; Josef Schmid, *The Gospel According to Mark: A Version and Commentary* (The Regensburg New Testament; Cork [Ireland]: Mercier Press, 1968), 273, though in fairness Schmid does leave this as a question. For an overview of others who have concluded similarly, see Kuruvilla, "Naked Runaway," 528–9.

early Christian community.²⁹ While other modern interpreters echoed earlier claims for the identity of the young man, Haren took an unusual tack on the basis of John 11 and 12 (especially 12:10–11) and suggested that the "young man" in question was none other than Lazarus, perhaps still depicted as clothed in his garment from the tomb.³⁰

A second line of interpretation is that Mark 14:51–52 presents a literary-theological typology. Here, too, there are essentially three different approaches. Several scholars understood the young man to be a type of the disciples in their flight away from Jesus: "The pericope is a dramatization and concretization of the universal flight of the disciples."³¹ Second, and in sharp contrast, Knox and Vanhoye understood the young man to be a type of Jesus,³² while Collins and others see him as an anti-type of Jesus: "the young man is best interpreted as one whose flight and abandonment of his linen cloth contrast dramatically with Jesus' obedience in submitting to being arrested, stripped, and crucified."³³ Third and finally Waetjen and others understood the young man to be a precursor not to Jesus but to the resurrection appearance of the young man seen by the women in the empty tomb,³⁴ a view supported by Scroggs and Groff who further determined that this connection had baptismal significance: "the reappearance of the young man in a new garment in 16:5 symbolizes rising with Christ."³⁵ Kuruvilla blends this notion with Collins's view, seeing the young man in the garden as one who abandons Christ and the young man in the tomb as the abandoner now restored to faith.³⁶

A third line of interpretation approaches the text on the basis of its intended or implicit connection to the OT. While Waetjen sees a connection to the Gen 39 Joseph story, Loisy understood Mark 14:51–52 to function as a messianic fulfilment of the prophecy found in Amos 2.³⁷ Along the same line, Klostermann saw that the passage was intended to draw on Amos 2:16 in order to enrich the Markan passion account.³⁸

---

[29] Gerd Theissen, *The Gospels in Context: Social and Political History in the Synoptic Tradition* (trans. Linda M. Maloney; Minneapolis, MN: Fortress Press, 1992), 185–7.

[30] Michael J. Haren, "The Naked Young Man: A Historian's Hypothesis on Mark 14, 51–52," *Biblica* 79 (1998): 525–31. If he is right, Haren adds, and the young man in the garden is Lazarus, then indeed he "was actually dressed for conscious effect" (531).

[31] Fleddermann, "Flight," 417. Kuruvilla first presents an extensive overview of scholars who also hold some version of this view ("Naked Runaway," 539), as does Collins, *Mark*, 691.

[32] Knox, "A Note on Mark 14:51–52," 28–30; Vanhoye, "La fuite." Vanhoye states unequivocally that this episode "constitue, dans la rédaction de Marc, une sorte de préfiguration énigmatique du sort de Jésus" (405). Kuruvilla provides a helpful overview of those who have held to this view in Kuruvilla, "Naked Runaway," 529–30.

[33] Collins, *Mark*, 695.

[34] Herman C. Waetjen, "The Ending of Mark and the Gospel's Shift in Eschatology," *ASTI* 4 (1965): 117–20.

[35] Robin Scroggs and K. Groff, "Baptism in Mark: Dying and Rising with Christ," *JBL* 92 (1973): 540. According to Scroggs and Groff, "in 14:51-52 the believer is symbolically baptized; and in 16:5 he emerges clothed in his baptismal robe, symbolizing the resurrected self" (548). Others who have supported this view are surveyed in Kuruvilla, "Naked Runaway," 532–3, while Collins, *Mark*, 690–1 provides a lengthy dismissal of this interpretation.

[36] Kuruvilla, "Naked Runaway," 545.

[37] Alfred Loisy, *L'Évangile selon Marc* (Paris: Nourry, 1912), 425.

[38] Erich Klostermann, *Das Markusevangelium* (Handbuch zum Neuen Testament; Tübingen: JCB Mohr Paul Siebeck, 1971), 153.

Schneider also links our passage to Amos 2:16 and sees a further connection with the events narrated in Mark 13:14–16,[39] as did Farrer.[40]

In our analysis of the text, we shall see that there is something to be said for each of the above interpretations and the methodology employed. However, our analysis will identify the inadequacies in any of these on their own and without a better understanding of the passage 14:51–52 itself.

Socio-Rhetorical Interpretation and Mark 14:51–52

Born from the legacy of form and neoclassical rhetorical criticism, socio-rhetorical interpretation (SRI) has taken shape over the last 30 years through the writings of Vernon K. Robbins and a team of scholars working with him.[41] SRI was initially crystallized in a limited body of programmatic works.[42] It is now recognized as a robust form of rhetorical analysis, including one that takes seriously advances in the cognitive sciences,[43] that at its fullest undertakes a variety of tasks. In this essay we will focus on two of them. The first is an identification of the "textures" found in Mark 14:51–52, and the second, in the form of a conclusion, will set forth how an analysis of the "textures" leads to an understanding of the ways in which Mark 14:51–52 may have contributed to shaping subsequent Christian understandings or may have not contributed, as in the case of the Gospel of Matthew, and why.

By "textures," SRI understands that texts are multidimensional and have various layers and levels of meaning. It builds on Clifford Geertz's essentially semiotic approach to understand texts as the work of authors, who, like any human, "is an animal suspended in webs of significance he himself has spun."[44] SRI does not prescribe how many textures a text may contain or which textures must be brought into analysis; however, SRI does propose a "programmatic" approach that suggests at least three textures for interpretation: innertexture, intertexture, and ideological texture.[45]

---

[39] Gerhard Schneider, "Die Verhaftung Jesu. Traditionsgeschichte von Mk 14 43–52," *ZNW* 63.3–4 (1972): 205–6.
[40] Austin Farrer, *A Study in St. Mark* (London: Dacre, 1951).
[41] A succinct overview of the origins and primary developments in SRI can be found in the introduction to Vernon K. Robbins et al., , eds., *Foundations for Sociorhetorical Exploration: A Rhetoric of Religious Antiquity Reader* (Rhetoric of Religious Antiquity; Atlanta, GA: SBL Press, 2016), 1–26.
[42] Vernon K. Robbins, *Exploring the Texture of Texts: A Guide to Socio-Rhetorical Interpretation* (Valley Forge, PA: Trinity Press International, 1996); Robbins, *The Tapestry of Early Christian Discourse: Rhetoric, Society and Ideology* (London: Routledge, 1996).
[43] For the latter, see Vernon K. Robbins, "Conceptual Blending and Early Christian Imagination," in *Explaining Christian Origins and Early Judaism: Contributions from Cognitive and Social Science* (ed. Petri Luomanen et al.; Biblical Interpretation Series 89; Leiden: Brill, 2005), 161–95, as well as L. Gregory Bloomquist, "Methodology Underlying the Presentation of Visual Texture in the Gospel of John," in *The Art of Visual Exegesis: Rhetoric, Texts, Images* (ed. Vernon K. Robbins et al.; Emory Studies in Early Christianity 19; Atlanta, GA: Society of Biblical Literature, 2017), 89–120. Seminal studies are brought together in Robbins et al., *Foundations*.
[44] Clifford Geertz, *The Interpretation of Cultures; Selected Essays* (New York, NY: Basic, 1973), 5.
[45] See L. Gregory Bloomquist, "Paul's Inclusive Language: The Ideological Texture of Romans 1," originally published in *Fabrics of Discourse: Essays in Honor of Vernon K. Robbins* (ed. David B. Gowle et al.; Harrisburg, PA: Trinity Press International, 2003). See also *Foundations for Sociorhetorical*

Analysis of innertexture starts with the assumption that the fundamental data for human, and thus rhetorical, communication through texts are words.[46] Their repetition and the progression of their use or not in a text reveals the ways in which authors give voice to rhetorical *topoi*.[47] Tracing these *topoi* through a text enables us to identify the narrational texture by which a text presents a reader with specific patterns of voices, actions, and relationships in the text.[48] As well, attention to innertexture will reveal the ways in which a narrative advances argumentatively, either through logical progression—by which a reader is led, as it were, "by the hand" to the desired conclusion—or in the form of pictures of events that are connected in the way one finds them in a fairy tale or in Jesus' parables.[49] Perhaps surprisingly, according to Aristotle, it is the latter form of argumentation that is the most sophisticated since it is the one that requires the reader to use the imagination to "connect the dots."[50]

But SRI is also clear that no text communicates solely on the basis of its own, inner structure. Analysis of intertexture, then, explores the ways in which texts intersect with the larger world or worlds by drawing on social, cultural and historical, oral–scribal, and sacred features of those worlds.[51] The notion of "intersection" is important since no text incorporates all aspects of, say, human behavior (social) but rather specific functions, like meals, families, transportation, governance, warfare, etc., and for specific reasons. Nor does any text incorporate all aspects of a particular, local culture, or the implicit language ("script") that is common to that culture. For example, NT authors may address the common, cultural practice and language of circumcision as Paul does, but they may also ignore it, as the Synoptics do, even though it still presumably was a cultural feature for those authors.

Exploration: A Rhetoric of Religious Antiquity Reader (ed. Vernon K. Robbins et al.; Atlanta, GA: SBL Press, 2016), 119–48.

[46] SRI draws here on the work of Kenneth Burke, *Counter-Statement* (Berkeley, CA: University of California Press, 1931); Wilhelm H. Wuellner, "Reconceiving a Rhetoric of Religion: A Rhetorics of Power and the Power of the Sublime," in *Rhetorics and Hermeneutics: Essays in Honor of Wilhelm Wuellner* (ed. James Hester and J. David Hester; Emory Studies in Early Christianity 9; Harrisburg: Trinity Press International, 2004), 23–77.

[47] Robbins, *Exploring*, 8–14. Some work that is comparable to the analysis of the repetitive texture in this pericope has been carried out by any number of the scholars surveyed, including Vanhoye, "La fuite," 404.

[48] Robbins, *Exploring*, 15–19 and 29–36. In Mediterranean texts such as ours, these actions are easily summarized as external bodily or purposeful actions of the hands, feet, genitals, etc.; self-expressive actions of the mouth, ears, and writing; and "internal" or emotion-fused actions of the mind, heart, bowels, etc.

[49] Robbins, *Exploring*, 21–9. For an in-depth discussion of the parable of the sower using socio-rhetorical interpretation and highlighting the use there of pictorial logic, see L. Gregory Bloomquist, "Rhetoric, Culture, and Ideology: Socio-Rhetorical Analysis in the Reading of New Testament Texts," in *Rhetorics in the New Millennium: Promise and Fulfillment* (ed. J. Hester and J. David Hester; New York, NY: T&T Clark, 2010), 115–46.

[50] Pictorial or paradigmatic argumentation provides a finely woven narrative that presents a compelling picture and can thus be called "picture logic" as well as "example" (*Rhet*. 1.2 1356b3–5). See W. W. Fortenbaugh, "Aristotle's *Art of Rhetoric*," in *A Companion to Greek Rhetoric* (ed. Ian Worthington et al.; Blackwell Companions to the Ancient World. Literature and Culture; Oxford: Blackwell, 2007), 109.

[51] SRI again does not limit the textures within intertexture but rather suggests that these are at least ones that must be considered in addition to others.

Finally, SRI asks interpreters to consider a natural question that should arise in light of these analyses: why do we have this particular text, and why has the author given us this text in this form, employing the features of the world that we have been able to identify in it? This is not to question the authorial intent but rather to suppose that since no text can ever simply be a window on a world, our text presents a world for some reason, one that will be received by a particular audience.[52] And so even without knowing the author's intent we can explore plausible reasons for particular rhetorical configurations, or the ideological texture of our text. SRI is particularly useful for religious materials in this way since "religious books are generally not written to state what is but what the author thinks should be."[53] Even if we ourselves cannot ultimately be certain what the author thought it should be, we can at least begin to suggest some possibilities.[54]

When some textual reconfigurations of the world are compelling or significantly interesting, they often have an impact on readers. In a sense, texts like these actually create new worlds by presenting a picture that is so interesting or compelling or unique or confusing that it urges and enables humans to think about things that they have never thought of before and to do so in new ways. SRI discusses this creative or inventive power in terms of the "emergent structure" of a text. SRI understands early Christian texts not as simply presenting things as they are in some sort of scientific or encyclopedic way but rather by asking readers to consider things other than as they might appear to be.[55] It is this kind of emergent, counterfactual rhetoric that made early Christian discourse such a motor of creative thinking into the Patristic period and beyond.[56] Our study, then, will conclude with our reflections on Mark 14:51–52 in light of emergent structure. Did this text help to create a new interpretive world in its immediate aftermath, or did it not? And, in the case of texts like Matthew that apparently omit any reference to it, though according to most accepted theories of Synoptic formation today would have known it and also have incorporated so much else of the Markan Passion narrative, why did they omit it?

Innertexture

Analysis of the innertexture of Mark 14:51–52 first reveals some words that are repeated within these verses or elsewhere in Mark. The verb κρατέω is used fifteen times in Mark but only in our text and prior to it, including the five final uses (14:1, 44, 46, 49, 51; cf.

---

[52] Even texts that purport to represent objectively and accurately some aspect of a world (e.g., scientific textbooks) can never be merely re-presentations of the world since that world in its totality is so much more vast than any text could ever hope to express.

[53] Frederik Wisse, "The Use of Early Christian Literature as Evidence for Inner Diversity and Conflict," in *Nag Hammadi, Gnosticism, and Early Christianity* (ed. Charles W. Hendrick and Robert Jr. Hodgson; Peabody, MA: Hendrickson Publishers, 1986), 179–80.

[54] A fuller presentation of *ideological texture* can be found in Bloomquist, "Paul's Inclusive Language."

[55] SRI sees classical texts, like the NT, as presenting "counterfactuals" to its readers. See the work of Neal J. Roese and James M. Olson, *What Might Have Been: The Social Psychology of Counterfactual Thinking* (ed. Neal J. Roese; Mahwah, NJ: Lawrence Erlbaum Associates, 1995) and Neal J. Roese, "Counterfactual Thinking," *PsycholBull* 121.1 (1997): 133–48.

[56] The exploration of the rise of Christian discourse is set forth well in Vernon K. Robbins, *The Invention of Christian Discourse: Volume 1* (Rhetoric of Religious Antiquity; Blandford Forum: Deo, 2009).

also 3:21; 6:17; 12:12) where it refers only to the seizing of someone as in an arrest.[57] The verb καταλείπω is only used in our passage and prior to it (10:7; 12:19 and 21); however, in the earlier uses it only ever expresses familial relationships of abandonment or absence, making the use here unique. The verb φεύγω, used only to express human flight, is used three times prior to our passage—including the immediately prior verse (14:50) in which Peter, James, and John flee (14:50; cf. also 5:14 and 13:14)—and once after in the last verse of canonical Mark—to describe the women's action in fleeing the empty tomb (16:8).[58] In contrast, the verb συνακολουθέω is found elsewhere only at Mark 5:37 to describe the action of Peter, James, and John who follow Jesus on his way to the healing of the daughter of the ruler of the synagogue.[59] Three other words are found here and then again only later in the burial or empty tomb scenes: the noun σινδών, repeated twice here and twice in 15:46 to describe the cloth in which Jesus is wrapped at his burial,[60] and the noun νεανίσκος and the verb περιβάλλω, both of which are used here and in 16:5 where one is a descriptor for the person found in the empty tomb and the other as a descriptor for how that person is clothed.[61] Finally, there is one word that is repeated twice in our passage but has no repetitive texture in Mark outside of our passage, namely γυμνός, and in fact a very sparing use anywhere else in the NT.[62]

But how are these words used to depict narration in our passage? In the Markan sequence of events the narrative in which a young man is seized (κρατοῦσιν 14:51) follows immediately the narrative of the seizing of Jesus (14:43-46). Both texts are surrounded by a series of other narratives, including the rather lengthy three-fold prayer-discovery narrative in the garden before the seizing of Jesus (14:32-42) and the dis-ear-ment of the High Priest's slave (14:47)[63] and Jesus' words (14:48-49) after he is seized. These narratives regarding Jesus' seizing are followed by the flight of "all"

---

[57] Following Hawkins, Fleddermann suggests that the verb is a "Markan word," in spite of the fact that its presence is found as commonly in Matthew and only slightly less so in Luke-Acts. Fleddermann, "Flight," 415, citing J. C. Hawkins, *Horae Synopticae* (Oxford: Clarendon Press, 1899), 13.

[58] See also the other uses in Mark 5:14 and 13:14. Fleddermann ignores 16:8 when he concludes regarding 15:40, 42, "The pericope of the flight of a naked young man is a commentary on 14:50; it is a dramatization of the universal flight of the disciples." Fleddermann, "Flight," 415.

[59] In Luke 23:49, the only other NT use, it describes the action of the women who have "followed" Jesus from Galilee. Kuruvilla, "Naked Runaway," 538-9 intentionally or not forces the verb συνακολουθέω/ἀκολουθέω to refer to "discipleship," concluding that therefore the "young man" of 14:51-52 must also be a "disciple," though as is clear in the cases where the verb is used that it need not mean a following that can be equated with "discipleship.

[60] The only other uses in the NT (Matt 27:59 and Luke 23:53) are parallels to Mark 15:46.

[61] Collins notes that the word is also found in the Clementine fragment following Mark 10:34 (Collins, *Mark*, 692) but also wisely notes that "it does not seem prudent to base an interpretation on the fragmentary letter of Clement, as long as its authenticity is in doubt" (694). In Matthew the word is used only in 19:20 and 22 and in Luke 7:14 but in a different context entirely. The lexical use appears to be unique to each gospel. Though it may raise the somewhat unexpected question whether the disappeared Jesus, too, ended up γυμνός like the νεανίσκος who had been clothed with a garment made of σινδών; in the Markan empty tomb story Jesus is simply not seen. The only figure who is, other than the women, is the νεανίσκος who is described as περιβεβλημένον στολὴν λευκήν.

[62] It is used in Matthew only in the final discourse of Jesus (25; 36, 38, 43, 44) and in the Johannine appendix to describe Peter's unclothed state (John 21:7). It is not used in Luke, even in Luke 8:27.

[63] Though not stated in Mark, the action may have been carried out by Peter, James, or John, the only other followers of Jesus mentioned to this point.

(14.50), by which presumably is meant Peter, James, and John from 14:43–46, and our passage, which itself is then followed by two lengthy narratives: the trial of Jesus before the Sanhedrin and Peter's interrogation and denials (14:53–72). In the darkness of the chaotic, confused, and violent action of the night, Jesus and Peter are the two named figures to appear before and after our passage, the former violently seized and treated, the latter failing Jesus (14:32–42) and denying him (14:53–72), a picture of Peter that is in fact consistent with how he is depicted elsewhere in Mark.

There are also similarities between Jesus and Peter when it comes to kinds of action that are narrated: Jesus comes to the disciples, is seized, and speaks throughout; Peter follows Jesus, sleeps, flees, weeps, and speaks but only in the narrative of his denial when he responds to his interlocutors in the courtyard. A similar, multiple series of actions are also associated with Judas, who speaks but only to Jesus and then kisses him, and the High Priest and the others with him, who speak and revile Jesus, tear his clothes, and hit Jesus. But the young man in our passage joins all the other narrational persons in being characterized by only one kind of action: like James and John who sleep and flee, the arresting party who seize Jesus, the man who wields the sword and the dis-ear-ed High Priest's slave, and eventually Peter's interlocutors in the courtyard who only speak and do nothing, our young man is characterized only by purposeful action (he follows as the disciples do earlier in the gospel, is seized like Jesus, has his garment torn from him, and finally flees as the disciples do immediately before him).[64] As such, the actions by which he is described associate him with Jesus and with the fleeing disciples in terms of specific action, but also with all of the characters who have an active role in the violent and chaotic scene in the garden or in the inquisitorial scene in the courtyard of the High Priest, with the exception of Judas.[65] Further afield, but not unconnected, the narrative presentation of the young man associates him with Jesus in his burial, the young man in the tomb, and the women who flee from the tomb. In sum, there is something about the naked young man that links him lexically and pictorially to almost everyone of the individuals and groups in the adjacent narratives. Such a broad series of associations surely calls into question those interpretations that suggest only a single link between the young man in our passage and one other character or sets of characters in the gospel.

It also suggests that this story is anything but an addition or an afterthought. And in this sense, too, it is important to note that the narration of the events in 14:51–52 contains no logical argumentation, in spite of the fact that commentators have long asked who the young man was, why he was following, why he was wearing linen, why he was seized, where he fled, etc.[66] But, while other commentators have lauded Mark's artistic talent in this passage, they appear to have missed the fact that throughout

---

[64] Mark characterizes no one through emotion-fused action.

[65] Kuruvilla tries to retroject the cultural shame that is implicit in purposeful "nakedness" of the "young man" (whom Kuruvilla deems a "disciple") to the other disciples who flee ("Naked Runaway," 539–40). Strikingly in the adjacent narratives the only one who appears to have no connection to the young man in any way that we have explored thus far (lexically or narrationally) is Judas, who, though a pivotal character, is limited to a brief appearance in 14:43–46.

[66] In fact, the only rationale in any of the adjacent narratives appears in the narrator's earlier comment about Jesus' followers falling asleep when they were needed: ἦσαν γὰρ αὐτῶν οἱ ὀφθαλμοὶ καταβαρυνόμενοι (14:40).

his gospel Mark regularly fails to provide argumentative rationales (enthymemes), preferring instead to provide pictorial argumentation, suggesting that Mark's audience did not need to be "led by the hand" but rather, through the presentation of story after story, would "get" what is happening and why it was happening. This suggests that Mark's gospel, including this passage, was intended for an audience that would understand why this story is here and what all of these associations with the other characters mean as this young man finds himself engulfed in the events of that night. With what world or worlds might this audience have been familiar that they would have gotten Mark's point?

Intertexture

There are at least two features of our text that require information from outside the text and thus suggest an intersection with the larger social and cultural world: the fact that our character is described as "a young man" and that he was wearing a garment of "linen." Of all those present in the garden, he is the only one described in this unique way.

Though the narrative gives us no indication as to who the young man is, the noun νεανίσκος suggests first that he is older than puberty and younger than, say, 40, when he might be described as an "old man" (γερός).[67] More importantly, however, νεανίσκος is rhetorically significant, for Laurence notes that throughout the Greco-Roman world "young adults ... were regarded as unstable" and thought to support conspiracies.[68] In fact, Greco-Roman texts describe νεανίσκοι most often in relation to violent, chaotic, and often conspiratorial activity, precisely the kind of activity we find in Mark 14:51–52.[69] The fact that this same noun is used only one other time by Mark in the description of the young man in the empty tomb is associated with the verb of fleeing as here.[70] This may suggest that, for Mark at least, the empty tomb is also a scene of chaos and violence, empty of a body but now filled with misunderstanding and foreboding.[71]

---

[67] Though it is not impossible that the word νεανίσκος describes a slave of any age (cf. Lucian, *Alex.* 53), it is unlikely that that is the meaning here since the immediately adjacent narrative describes clearly the dis-ear-ment of a slave, i.e., τὸν δοῦλον τοῦ ἀρχιερέως (14:47).

[68] Ray Laurence, "Community," in *A Cultural History of Childhood and Family in Antiquity* (ed. Mary Harlow and Ray Laurence; A Cultural History of Childhood and Family 1; Oxford: Bloomsbury Academic, 2010), 33.

[69] Ibid., 35–8. Plutarch's language concerning an earlier attempt to seize and slay Caesar by "young men" (οἱ νεανίσκοι) associated with a conspiracy hatched by Cato is eerily similar to the language of Mark 14 (*Caes.* 8.2).

[70] Our analysis suggests here and in what follows the impropriety of Hatton's contention that the young man "appears out of nowhere at the wrong place in the story, at the wrong place in the text, like a clown at a funeral," Stephen B. Hatton, "Mark's Naked Disciple: The Semiotics And Comedy Of Following," *Neot* 35.1/2 (2001): 45. More a propos is Lowrie's observation that the entire incident in the garden "reminds us that this was a 'youth movement,'" though Lowrie does not indicate that such a "movement" would be associated in the Greco-Roman mind with violence and chaos. See Walter Lowrie, *Jesus According to Saint Mark: An Interpretation of Saint Mark's Gospel* (London: Longmans, Green, and Co., 1929), 520–1.

[71] Kuruvilla, "Naked Runaway," 544 sees the mention of Peter here as a hopeful sign of his restoration and that a disciple's "failure was not a dead end." However, given Peter's depiction throughout Mark, the mention here may actually raise further questions: will Peter fail yet again? In fact, will

The other word, σινδών (linen), is also rare and associated with the tomb, and therefore unsurprisingly attractive to commentators' attention. Now, given the extraordinary range of quality of "linen" that was produced in antiquity, the numerous locations producing flax for linen, and the variety of uses to which linen was put in the ancient world, as well as its limited appearance in Mark, it is almost impossible to conclude anything concretely regarding the appearance of this fabric in 14:51–52. Nevertheless, given its employment in burial practices (especially in Egypt),[72] and the fact that "linen is used to identify the garment in which the presumably naked Jesus was wrapped after being taken down from the cross and which was left behind in the empty tomb,"[73] there may indeed be a further connection here between our young man and Jesus. There certainly is a garment of σινδών that is abandoned by two men in what is very likely a context that causes both men and women to flee, presumably for fear. Might there be oral–scribal intersections with our text along these lines?

In order to answer this question, we return to our analysis of innertexture since lexical clustering can help to give us a clearer notion not only of the author's own language but the language or languages with which our text overlaps.[74] As we have seen, there is some repetition of words in 14:51–52 elsewhere in Mark; however, there is almost no clustering of the same words in any other text upon which an author like Mark might draw, and the clustering in texts that may have drawn on Mark is minimal. For example, we do not find anyone else in the NT or LXX described by the verb περιβάλλω as specifically being clothed in σινδών, even though the verb itself is used in relation to other named fabrics, garments, or colors.[75] In fact, the substantive σινδών itself is found only twice in the LXX: Jdg 14:12 and Prov 31:24 and four of the six times it is used in the NT are the ones that we have already noted in Mark (14:51–52 2x and 15:46 2x).[76] Even the word νεανίσκος, which is certainly not as rare in the LXX, is found elsewhere in the NT only eight times (Matt 19:20, 22; Acts 2:17; 5:10; 23:18; 23:22; 1 John 2:13, 14).

---

the message to Peter ever be delivered by the women who have fled in fear? To assert a message of "forgiveness and restoration" can only be drawn from the larger biblical witness, not from Mark alone.

[72] Anastasia (Frankfurt/Main) Pekridou-Gorecki et al., "Linen, Flax," in *Brill's New Pauly* (New Pauly Online; Leiden: Brill, 2006).

[73] Robert C. Tannehill, "The Disciples in Mark: The Function of a Narrative Role," *JR* 57.4 (1977): 403 made this connection when he asserted that the young man had come to the garden clothed in the dress of a martyr, only to have it stripped from him and to flee, according to Tannehill, because he "changes his mind when death is a real prospect." However, given the absence of any emotion-fused language in the Markan narrative and given the absence of any argumentative rationales, Tannehill's conclusion can only remain in the realm of conjecture.

[74] An important insight into language and the importance of "lexical priming," the arena within which "lexical clustering" works, see Michael Hoey, *Lexical Priming: A New Theory of Words and Language* (London: Routledge, 2005). According to Glenn Hadikin, "The theory argues that every person has a mental store of all the language we have been exposed to and, on some level, we know what words go together based on the people whose speech and writing we like as well as avoiding speaking and writing like people we do not like." See Glenn Hadikin, "This Theory Is Inspiring a New Way to Think about Language," in *WEF*, https://www.weforum.org/agenda/2019/04/evolution-how-the-theory-is-inspiring-a-new-way-of-understanding-language.

[75] Cf. Mark 16:5 and also Rev 3:5, 18; 4:4; 7:9, 13; 10:1; 11:3; 12:1; 17:4; 18:16; 19:8, 13.

[76] The other two uses (Matt 27:59 and Luke 23:53) are parallels to Mark 15:46.

But, repetition in some delimited, rhetorical unit is not entirely absent outside of Mark. Though there is no likely NT passage on which Mark would have drawn for the language of 14:51–52,[77] there are two passages in which we find some clustering of the lexica that we find in Mark 14:51–52: the Joseph story found in LXX Gen 39 and the one to which Loisy drew attention LXX Amos 2:5–16.

Medieval authors had already seen "some similarity" between LXX Gen 39:12 and our passage, particularly in the use of the verb καταλείπω and the verb φεύγω, words that are in fact lexically significant in the Genesis account since they are repeated in 39:13–18.[78] Austin Farrer saw a further connection to the Joseph story in the subsequent Markan reference to the narrative character of Joseph of Arimathea, the one who wraps the crucified Jesus in a σινδών.[79] Though the visual texture of the scene is at first glance compelling, one is hard pressed to see any other reason that connects the Joseph narrative with Mark 14:51–52 than minimal lexical overlap.[80]

More compelling, however, is the connection to Amos 2 as proposed by Loisy. Amos 2:4–16 is a text that falls within the prophetic "day of the Lord" expectation of judgment against Judah or Israel or both and Jerusalem.[81] In this particular prophetic utterance,[82] the Lord through Amos reminds the people of the good and mighty deeds done by the Lord on their behalf: the Lord had given them the Law, had destroyed the giant Amorites, had delivered the people from Egypt, had led them through the wilderness, had dispossessed the Amorites to give Israel their land, and finally—in words that will be important for an understanding of the possible connection to Mark 14:51–52—had raised up prophets from among the sons of Israel and Nazirites from among the young men (ἐκ τῶν νεανίσκων 2:11). But, the Lord then indicates why judgment will fall upon this same people, because in spite of the Lord's good deeds, the people had sinned by rejecting the Law, being led away by lies, oppressing the poor, engaging in incestuous fornication, idolatry, and corruption, and finally—and again this is crucial for our passage—silencing those whom the Lord had raised up

---

[77] Though the verb φεύγω and the substantive γυμνός are indeed found in Acts 19:16, we assume that this text is later and thus not intertextually connected to our passage in Mark from the Markan side; however, we remain open to the possibility that the author of Luke-Acts made use of Mark for his gospel (Luke) and may well have used the material of 15:41–42 in Acts, rather than in Luke. If so, then Mark 14 should be orally and scribally interesting for the understanding of the Acts passage. In doing so, however, while we may have evidence that Luke omitted the story of the naked young man from his gospel account but included elements of it in Acts, this inclusion only further compounds the mystery of the Matthean omission of any reference to the story.

[78] Kuruvilla, "Naked Runaway," 530.

[79] Austin Farrer, *The Glass of Vision* (London: Dacre, 1966), 144–5. See Kuruvilla, "Naked Runaway," 531.

[80] Kuruvilla is right to note that TJos 8:3 does add that Joseph fled "naked" ("Naked Runaway," 530), which could be significant; however, Kuruvilla fails to acknowledge the very fragmented form of TJos, the lack of narrative continuity, and the extensive Christian interpolations throughout, making it not impossible that the word "naked" has been added in this section to make the narrative of Genesis conform to Mark 15:42, as had already begun to happen by the time of Jerome.

[81] See among others David L. Petersen, *Late Israelite Prophecy: Studies in Deutero-Prophetic Literature and in Chronicles* (SBL Monograph Series 23; Missoula, MT: Scholars, 1977).

[82] Though Harper makes a compelling case for understanding them as addressed to the same people: William Rainey Harper, *A Critical and Exegetical Commentary on Amos and Hosea* (International Critical Commentary on the Holy Scriptures of the Old and New Testaments; New York, NY: Scribner, 1910).

as prophets and making the "young men" (2:12) whom the Lord anointed Nazirites to drink prohibited wine. Consequently, and in words that echo the language of our passage in Mark 14 but also in Mark 13, the Lord promises that there is a day coming on which the Lord will judge the people with fire (2:5) and will "press" the inhabitants of Judah and Jerusalem until the swift and strong have no more speed or strength and will flee (καὶ ἀπολεῖται φυγὴ ἐκ δρομέως 2:14), a day on which even the "stoutest of heart" who have remained to the end will finally "flee away naked" after all of the others have fled (καὶ εὑρήσει τὴν καρδίαν αὐτοῦ ἐν δυναστείαις ὁ γυμνὸς διώξεται ἐν ἐκείνῃ τῇ ἡμέρᾳ λέγει κύριος 2:16).[83]

The constellation of words and narrative sequence of action found in such close juxtaposition in a single prophetic text (Amos 2:5–11) and in our very brief text of Mark 14:51–52 and its immediately adjacent narratives seems unlikely to be coincidental.[84] Loisy had drawn a similar conclusion, as had Klostermann, but the former saw it only as a further sign of messianic fulfilment while the latter saw it as an embellishment of the passion narrative. But there is a more compelling argument to be made, one that suggests that the invocation of a prophetic rhetorical unit is characteristic of Mark's rhetoric.

From the first voice heard in the gospel, namely Isaiah the prophet, to the next voice, namely John the Baptist, and through the subsequent words and deeds of Jesus that culminate in his prophetic announcement of the impending "day of the Lord" as judgment on Jerusalem (Mark 13), Mark has led his reader not by the hand through simple enthymematic argumentation but has provided one sophisticated intertextural clue after another regarding the impending "day of the Lord." These clues are hidden from any but an audience that is rhetorically attuned to the prophetic texts and one for whom it would be clear that the "day of the Lord" is nigh on the horizon, starting on the outer fringes with Galilee but concluding in the heartland, in Jerusalem. In this context, this apparently innocuous rhetorical unit of 14:51–52 is yet one more clue that is intended to conjure up in the readers' mind the notion of the "day of the Lord." It is one small clue, one more small stone placed for stumbling over for those who understand the prophetic enunciation—"let the reader understand"— but who fails to repent.

But, commentators who have cast doubts on a connection with Amos have noted, among other things, the absence of other words found in 14:51–52, for example, σινδών. As noted, the word is found only twice in the LXX at Judg 14:12 and Prov 31:24.[85] Of these two texts the former is especially interesting for us since it places the word σινδών in the mouth of the iconic, some would say paradigmatic, Nazirite Samson, that is, in the mouth of one of those "young men" (ἐκ τῶν νεανίσκων) whom the Lord anointed to be Nazirites (Amos 2:11–16) and whom the people of Israel led astray. In Judg 14 it is one of the primary objects by which Samson's enemies, the Amorites, the very people whom the Lord had vanquished according to Amos 2, shame him. Judges

---

[83] For commentary, see Harper, *A Critical and Exegetical Commentary on Amos and Hosea*, 63.
[84] Kuruvilla points to difficulties in the connection of our passage to Amos 2 ("Naked Runaway," 531), but misses the connections that we highlight.
[85] The Hebrew word that it translates (סָדִין) is found elsewhere only in Isa 3:23. A further study of Isa 3:23 might bear fruit.

14 depicts well the violent wrath of this wild and chaotic "young man" who, inspired by the Lord's spirit, repays his shame by wreaking violence on an Amorite village before he returns, his anger unabated, to his father's house.[86] καὶ ἥλατο ἐπ' αὐτὸν πνεῦμα κυρίου καὶ κατέβη εἰς Ἀσκαλῶνα καὶ ἐπάταξεν ἐξ αὐτῶν τριάκοντα ἄνδρας καὶ ἔλαβεν τὰ ἱμάτια αὐτῶν καὶ ἔδωκεν τὰς στολὰς τοῖς ἀπαγγείλασιν τὸ πρόβλημα καὶ ὠργίσθη θυμῷ Σαμψων καὶ ἀνέβη εἰς τὸν οἶκον τοῦ πατρὸς αὐτοῦ (14:19).[87] The language in fact graphically narrates the very kind of violence used by the Lord in the dispossession of that same land of the Amorites in Amos 2 in order to give it to Israel.[88] It may even echo the violence of Nazirites, like Samson, who played a significant role in that dispossession as recorded by Amos.

Again, we suggest that it is not coincidental that this is the same kind of violent, anger-fueled, and divinely directed chaos that is prophetically announced in Mark 13, that is on display in the garden in Mark 14 including vv. 51–52,[89] and that continues through to the end of Mark's gospel. True, the connection is not made explicit through logical rationales provided to connect the dots for unlearned readers, because the astute reader only needs a few choice intertexturally charged clues to "understand."[90]

---

[86] Josephus's rendering of the account of the birth of Samson also is suggestive in that Samson's mother receives the announcement of Samson's birth from an "angel" who is described in *Ant.* 5.8.2 as a νεανίας and in 5.8.3 as a νεανίσκος. See Collins, *Mark*, 795–6 n. 222.

[87] In Amos 2:9–10 the Amorites are mentioned twice as those who kept the land from Israel and those whom God destroyed to give the land to Israel. It may not be clear from Judges that the peoples described in Amos are the same ones described in Judg 14; however, in Judg 14 the "Philistine" or "alien" woman that Samson proposes to marry hails from the Amorite-held town of Timnath, and the town that Samson massacres is likely not the Philistine fortress of Ashkelon on the Mediterranean coast but rather Khirbet ʿAsqalūn in the same Amorite-held land and a city adjacent to Timnath. It is thus possible that the "young men" whom Samson calls to be his wedding party, the same young men who eventually shame him, are also Amorites. For an understanding of the ethnicities and towns in the Judges narrative, see George F. Moore, *A Critical and Exegetical Commentary on Judges* (The International Critical Commentary; Edinburgh: T&T Clark, 1958; orig. 1895), 338. Further exploration of Mark might reveal whether this connection to the Amorites is significant to the author of the Gospel.

[88] It is likely that Amorites in Amos is intended to be a synecdoche in order to refer to all Canaanites. So Harper, *A Critical and Exegetical Commentary on Amos and Hosea*, 55. It is possible that Judg 14 understands this in the same way.

[89] Though outside the bounds of our passage it may be suggestive that in Mark 14:65, members of the priestly assemble and guards mock and strike Jesus, calling on him to prophesy (Καὶ ἤρξαντό τινες ἐμπτύειν αὐτῷ καὶ περικαλύπτειν αὐτοῦ τὸ πρόσωπον καὶ κολαφίζειν αὐτὸν καὶ λέγειν αὐτῷ· προφήτευσον, καὶ οἱ ὑπηρέται ῥαπίσμασιν αὐτὸν ἔλαβον), a possibly ironic reversal of the sin of Israel as God tells the prophets "not to prophesy" in Amos 2:12. Furthermore, the texts in Judges, Amos, and the two stripping of clothes, of the young man (Mark 14) and Jesus (Mark 15), may be linked through the Markan prophetic scripting in the following way. In Mark 14 the forces of the chief priests are presented as stripping a young man of his linen garment, even as forces at the instigation of the high priests and under the authorities of the Romans strip Jesus of his in Mark 15, the same kinds of garments that were to be gifted to Philistines (from whom Samson in the end strips them) and that are associated with Israel's immorality and idolatry in Amos 2.

[90] It is important to note that the Markan account also leaves completely unclear what will happen after the judgment. As such, it is profoundly contracultural, a rhetoric that also is characteristic of the OT "day of the Lord" prophetic rhetoric (with the clear and noteworthy exception of passages like Ezek 40–48). According to K. A. Roberts a contracultural approach is a "short-lived, counter-dependent cultural deviance: "Toward a Generic Concept of Counter-Culture," *SocFoc* 11 (1978): 124. In the Greco-Roman world, contracultural rhetoric was common to the Cynic rhetoric, which "does not present a network of rationales to support its alternative behavior; it prefers the shock that deliberate abandonment of conventional attitudes, values, mores and dispositions produces": Vernon

One might ask, however, did the author of the Gospel of Matthew fail to understand? Clearly that author is aware of and indeed has sought to make explicit the prophetic scripting that is only implicit in Mark.[91] Additionally, and within the Matthean fulfillment statements, the author of Matthew very clearly and somewhat uniquely emphasizes the connection between the notion of Nazirites and Jesus.[92] Though not part of the explicit fulfillment citations, Matthew also seems to know the Amos 2 passage and use it. According to Dodd, it is present in Matthew's rendering of Jesus' words in 11:27.[93] The absence then in Matthew of something that is as suggestive as we have shown Mark 14:51–52 to be for the fulfillment notion found in Mark is striking, all the more so since, as Donaldson himself notes, the fulfillment notion was perhaps "the central conception" in Matthew's presentation of Christ.[94]

Ideological Texture

The title of Mark's gospel (found in Mark 1:1) tells us that Mark's whole narrative concerns the proclamation of the good news of God's victory associated with a man named Joshua/Jesus. The first verse of the gospel provides us with the primary hermeneutical clue as to how to read this "good news" in the mouth of the first narrative character in the gospel, the prophet Isaiah. In other words, at the very outset Mark informs his reader how to read his proclamation—through the lens of "prophetic scripting."[95] In what follows, chapter after chapter, Mark sets forth how what was promised through Isaiah and the other prophets is now being fulfilled first in John (the Baptist), then in Jesus and the "fishers" that he chooses,[96] which is for one purpose

---

K. Robbins, "Rhetoric and Culture: Exploring Types of Cultural Rhetoric in a Text," in *Rhetoric and the New Testament: Essays from the 1992 Heidelberg Conference* (ed. S. E. Porter and T. H. Olbricht; Sheffield: Sheffield Academic Press, 1993), 452. For the non-contracultural rhetoric in OT prophetic literature, see especially Paul D. Hanson, *The Dawn of Apocalyptic*, 2nd ed. (Philadelphia, PA: Fortress, 1979), 209–79.

[91] On the ten fulfillment citations in Matthew, see most recently Zack C. Phillips, *Filling Up the Word: The Fulfillment Citations in Matthew's Gospel* (Ph.D. diss., Duke University, 2017).

[92] R. T. France, "The Forumla-Quotations of Matthew 2 and the Problem of Communication," *NTS* 27.2 (1981): 246–9. To his credit, France argues that this explicit fulfillment passage in Matthew is very obscure, perhaps, almost as obscure as the implicit reference that we have discovered in Mark 14:51–52! The "gratuitous obstacles" that France identifies in the way of understanding the Matthew passage do nonetheless all point again to the figure of Samson as a narrative prototype for Matthew and in some way also for Mark.

[93] C. H. Dodd, "Jesus as Teacher and Prophet," in *Mysterium Christi: Christological Studies by British and German Theologians* (ed. G. K. A. Bell and G. A. Deissmann; London: Longmans, 1930), 63. For other uses of Amos in Matthew, see Michael P. Knowles, *Jeremiah in Matthew's Gospel: The Rejected Prophet Motif in Matthaean Redaction* (Journal for the Study of the New Testament, Supplement Series 68; Sheffield: JSOT Press, 1993).

[94] Terence L. Donaldson, *Jesus on the Mountain: A Study in Matthean Theology* (Journal for the Study of the New Testament, Supplement Series 8; Sheffield: JSOT Press, 1985), 204.

[95] Max Botner, "Prophetic Script and Dramatic Enactment in Mark's Prologue," *BBR* (2016): 369–80 has correctly discerned the importance of the introduction of Mark for what he calls the "prophetic script." In a work in progress on the hermeneutical framework of the Synoptic Gospels, Bloomquist shows that "prophetic scripting" provides one of the essential clues for a proper understanding of the Gospel of Mark.

[96] Read in terms of "prophetic scripting" and the lexical priming that Mark employs to present it, the work of the "fishers" becomes clear: it is not to gather men and women for salvation but to hunt for and gather Israel for judgment (cf. Jer 16:14–18).

only: to prepare for and bring about the judgment in the coming "day of the Lord." In some cases, "the reader" can "understand" relatively easily, as in Mark 13; however, in other cases we find only that Mark has provided much more subtle clues that can only be recognized through careful attention to what would have been on the reader's part a kind of innate inner- and intertextual analysis.[97] Mark's use of the prophets, perhaps particularly in the form of the LXX,[98] is not midrash but rather the kind of lexical priming that was familiar to the rabbis and that uses catchwords and associated imagery to "cue" a complete rhetorical unit in the prophets.[99] Significantly, almost without exception these prophetic readings are about the catastrophic judgment of "the day of the Lord." As Mark uses them, he does so to present Jesus as a prophet who is focused on a judgment that is coming not on the nations but on the temple (cf. Mark 13). Why? As Bruce Malina and others have shown, it is the temple that is the centrifugal core of Israel, radiating the sacrality that is to make holy all of Israel, and through Israel the world.[100] But in Mark's vision—and that of the Gospel of John as well—that temple actually radiates a sickness that weakens and ultimately defiles Israel. It does so for John primarily through the temple as a visible alternative to the invisible God, but it appears to do so for Mark primarily as a result of its personnel, the priests and perhaps most importantly in the form of the members of the family of Annas.[101] Viewed in this way, Mark could actually be read as the very last book of the Christian OT, ending with a prophetic canon that portends the cleansing of the temple.

If this reading of the Markan prophetic scripting is accurate, what purpose does the brief narrative in 14:51–52 play?[102] To someone who has followed Mark's initial lead and found prophetic scripting like a trail of bread-crumbs leading the way to a destination, this seemingly insignificant and certainly enigmatic incident in Mark 14:51–52 would be understood to be yet one more summons to undertake a search

---

[97] The enigmatic and brief narratives of the cursing of the fig tree in Mark 11:12–14 and the resulting discovery in 11:20–25 can both be read in terms of "prophetic scripting" as lexically and narrationally conjuring up Mic 6:9–7:1 and Hos 9:15–10:2.

[98] This connection to a version or possible versions of the Greek OT supports the growing interest in the targumic-like tradition that seems to have been practiced among Greek-speaking scholars of the period, perhaps rabbis.

[99] Though Birger Gerhardsson, *Memory and Manuscript: Oral Tradition and Written Transmission in Rabbinic Judaism and Early Christianity* (trans. Eric J. Sharpe; Acta Seminarii Neotestamentici Upsaliensis; Uppsala and Lund: Gleerup, 1961) overstates the case by making Jesus into a rabbinic master, Gerhardsson's insight that the technique that we find in Mark is consistent with Rabbinic focus on catchwords and the arrangement of material intended to conjure up echoes in the mind of a hearer or reader seems to us to be accurate. See in particular Gerhardsson, *Memory and Manuscript*, 148–9. On Gerhardsson's contribution, see Kelly R. Iverson, "Orality and the Gospels: A Survey of Recent Research," *CurrBS* (2009): 71–106.

[100] In this way, the temple is a kind of topical synechdoche for all of Israel. For an understanding of the permeating influence of cultic centers, see Bruce J. Malina, *The New Testament World: Insights from Cultural Anthropology*, 3rd rev. exp. ed. (Louisville, KY: Westminster John Knox Press, 2001), 173–7.

[101] The fact that Josephus, and even rabbinic texts, remember the family of Annas as "whisperers," that is, promoters of envy, is probably significant in this regard. For the references and for the role of "envy," see L. Gregory Bloomquist, "Eyes Wide Open, Seeing Nothing: The Challenge of the Gospel of John's Nonvisualizable Texture for Readings Using Visual Texture," in Robbins et al., *Art of Visual Exegesis*, 156 n. 86.

[102] Kuruvilla is right to suggest a "pragmatic" reading of Mark's text, that is, a reading that asks "what is Mark doing?" ("Naked Runaway," 535–6). SRI suggests an answer to Kuruvilla's assertion: Mark is getting his readers to go back and read the prophetic texts.

for the oral–scribal intertextural prophetic unit that portends the impending "day of the Lord." Such a reader, who then digs deep and recalls not only the Amos text, but is from there reminded of the Judges text, and perhaps others, "understands" yet one more clue of what is coming. Such a reader "gets it" in a way that the three disciples on the Mount of Olives (Mark 13)—the same three who flee and abandon Jesus on the same Mount only a day later—did not, such that when the "day" did come (at least appeared) they are entirely unprepared to stand firm in the violent, chaotic, and confusing time.[103] Doubtless they had not realized that the same kind of wild violence that had felled the Amorites, and Babylon (LXX Isa 13:10), was now going to fell Jerusalem. When it begins proleptically in the garden, they fail utterly.[104]

As such, while the Markan narrative of chapter 13 and the later narrative of 14 present the final judgment in such a way that even the High Priest himself understands perfectly well what is being foretold (14:62), Mark 14:51–52, and the narrative immediately on either side of it, presents us with an especially ominous word for those who are associated with Jesus, either as followers or as bystanders. In the chaos and confusion all will flee from Jesus, including the disciples who accompanied him. True, Peter returns to the narrative but only to deny Jesus and then disappear from the pages of the gospel. In the end even the last characters of the gospel, the women who come to the tomb, flee, just as the young man had from the garden, presumably out of fear. The women's one commission—to tell Jesus' disciples that he would meet them in Galilee (Mark 16:7)—remains unfulfilled in the Gospel of Mark, unlike the other gospels. In this light, one may ask whether even the νεανίσκος in the tomb—depicted in Matthew (like an angel) or in Luke (like two men garbed in transfiguration-like clothes)—is, like other νεανίσκοι, rhetorically associated with violence and chaos.[105] Therefore, our analysis of Mark 14:51–52 leaves us with a question rather than an answer: when the "day of the Lord" comes not just with the proleptic chaos, confusion, and violence we find here, but fully when the Son of Man comes in judgment, who will stand firm in the midst of the smoke and flames? Certainly, "watch" (Mark 13:37), he tells the three on the Mount, but in watching "understand" (Mark 13:14) that no one is prepared for the fire of tribulation that is coming. Will anyone?[106]

Given Matthew's extended resurrection appearances, including most significantly the so-called Great Commission of Matt 28:16–20, it is possible that Mark's apocalyptic rhetoric clashed with Matthew's wisdom rhetoric, which was grounded in a longer-term

---

[103] Further study would reveal in fact some lexical parallels between our passage and Mark 13, as was noted by Farrer, *A Study in St. Mark*, 141.

[104] This insight drawn from SRI accords with Gnilka's interpretation that the narrative of 14:51–52 fits an apocalyptic motif in which chaos is present. See Joachim Gnilka, *Das Evangelium nach Markus*, 3rd ed. (EKK; Zurich: Benziger, 1989), 2.271.

[105] This suggestion raises the question of how accurately the νεανίσκος in the tomb has been understood and depicted in Christian proclamation and art. Collins, *Mark*, 795 may be right to connect the seating of the νεανίσκος in the tomb on the right in relation to the earlier mention of "the Lord" seated at the right hand of God (12:35–37), but if so it is important to note that the "enthronement" language of 12:35–37 clearly does not portend a seating in glory but rather a seating in judgment until a time of perhaps glory or peace will begin.

[106] The formulation 'When the Son of Man returns will he find faith?' is explicitly found in the "parable of the unjust judge" in Luke 18:8, which suggests that Luke, and possibly Matthew, do pick up on the cautionary note for would-be followers of Jesus.

slave-based Christian lifestyle to be lived out however long, an end-time expectation extended into the future.[107] True, Matthew may not have understood Mark's implicit fulfillment and the apocalyptic expectation that ground Mark 14:51–52; however, if he did, it seems likely that he had reasons for ignoring the passage, perhaps in order not to present end-time expectation couched in fear but rather in his intentional singleminded, Christic lifestyle.

Emergent Structure: How Mark 14:51–52 Creates New Possibilities of Meaning

It is not surprising that the history of interpretation of the gospels, Mark in particular, and this passage even more particularly, has failed regularly to underscore the dramatic implications unveiled by a socio-rhetorical interpretation approach to the material. The "normal science" that developed in the early church regularly subsumed Mark, and stories like ours, to the emergent structure of the developing apostolic tradition and the canon as a development of that apostolic tradition. Specifically, Mark was subsumed to Matthew, which became what we might call the imperial power of the gospel world. As such, our text has been made to disappear through readings of Mark by Matthew, as well as by Luke and Paul, a disappearance that was enshrined in patristic commentators. The process of the eventual canonical shaping of all material within the canonical sequence starting with Matthew, compounded by the development of post-Constantinian "Christendom," meant that eventually the apocalyptic message of Mark would become anathema and his message would become canonically domesticated.

One can see the process at work regarding our passage from the time of the patristic authors and how the same lines of interpretation are reiterated in a more sophisticated and historical way in the historical-critical interpreters. Naturally, this same domestication occurred in many Protestant and evangelical interpreters who sought to relate our text especially to other texts and to make it congenial to providing lessons on living the Christian life.[108] A striking exception to this domestication is found in Calvin and interpreters like Collinges who used our passage to underscore the chaotic violence that the church would experience at the hands of her enemies. But with few exceptions,[109] once the church is beyond a period that, because of the violence

---

[107] For a presentation of Matthew's understanding of the slave-based life-style that he proposes, see L. Gregory Bloomquist, "An Important Stoic Influence in Matthew's Sermon on the Mount: The Significance of Single-Mindedness," *Theoforum* 46.1 (2015): 165–83.

[108] This catechetical and homiletical goal is clearly in mind in Kuruvilla's concluding comments regarding the young man in the garden and the young man in the tomb ("Naked Runaway," 545): Who, then, is the naked runaway? He is Every Disciple, shamefully feeble and fallible. And the enrobed reporter? That one, too, is Every Disciple, gloriously restored by the grace of God, through Jesus Christ!

[109] Perhaps were one to survey medieval or modern apocalyptic communities, the Markan message of 14:51–52 might be more clearly enunciated. But even if that were so, it would still be the case that these communities themselves, somewhat like the passage of Mark 14:51–52 itself, would in fact be "eccentric" to what Christianity became in an emergent post-Nicene structure that was shaped by a canonical biblical understanding.

and chaos, might appear to be a harbinger of the final judgment, the church and her interpreters—even Calvin's followers—turn their attention away from the chaos and violence that Mark adumbrates.

As such, we might say that the emergent structure of Mark 14:51–52, like much of the rest of Mark's proclamation, was significantly muted in the immediate aftermath of its writing and largely failed to produce a significant dent within what came to be known later as Christianity. Following the lead of Matthew, as well as Luke, who likely did not include the story because they both envisioned a future well beyond the events of AD 70, subsequent generations of Christians up to today understandably balk at any suggestion that Mark presents his story of Jesus couched in the imagery of "holy war."[110] Such imagery would be appalling to those who are unaware of the way God is described in the presentation in Judges and Amos, presentations that are echoed in Mark, including our passage. Of course, in this regard, Christians today reflect as much Marcion's antipathy to the OT and this imagery as they do any Nicene, canonical orthodoxy. But our point is that this is not the result of domestication in the second century or later. Already by the end of the first century CE, Mark had disappeared in part by the reconfigured story of Jesus told by Matthew.

If we accept a canonical approach, however, then Mark, including Mark 14:51–52, can have a salutary influence on Western Christian commentary and proclamation by reminding us that things have not always been as they are, and in many places in the world are not. Mark 14:51–52 functions graphically within the Markan framework of "prophetic scripting" by presenting a vivid scene in which every character, named or unnamed, is caught up in the chaotic violence associated with the "day of the Lord." In this context there is no one who is untouched. And though all respond differently no one responds well, except for Jesus, who is the very vehicle of the prophetic fulfilment. Jesus alone is the one whom Mark shows has received and who continues to receive the full impact of the chaotic violence that is experienced "collaterally" by everyone else in the narrative. While the other gospels resolve the tension in an historical future, Mark does not. Even the empty tomb provides no solace: understood sociorhetorically it, too, functions not as a place of confident and hopeful expectation but as a place of chaotic violence and one that forebodes little good for anyone in the Gospel of Mark.

Mark's, then, is a story that the West may have forgotten but that the persecuted church throughout the world today, like the earliest Christian church, knew and knows only too well. The persecuted churches live daily the kind of chaotic violence depicted in Mark and are sobered by the realization that no one appears to come through this fire well. Because their experience is completely alien to most NT exegetes and Christian preachers in the developed world, the heirs of Christendom, but akin to Mark's, they,

---

[110] The imagery of "holy war" was traced some years ago by Bloomquist and his then-student Priscilla Geisterfer Nyvlt in OT, Qumran, NT, and some Islamic texts. See L. Gregory Bloomquist and Priscilla Geisterfer Nyvlt, "Rhetorical Strategies for 'Holy War' in Some Second Temple Texts: Overview, Analysis, and Implications," Conference presentation, Rhetorics, Violence, and Evil, University of Redlands, Redlands, CA, January 23–24, 2004, in *QJRhePwr* (2004), http://www.ars-rhetorica.net. This article shows how "holy war" rhetoric was actually recontextualized in the Gospel of Luke—perhaps in an attempt to salvage Mark but at the same time alter it—and that recontextualization may have had an influence on the Qu'ran's approach to the OT notion of "holy war."

not we, are the ones who are best suited to "understand" this text. And as such, they can help us understand this text better. Certainly if our analysis is correct, a greater appreciation of the canonical message of judgment remains to be more fully explored, especially among those of us who live in the relative peace acquired by Christendom. Socio-rhetorical interpretation can be of great help in this regard.

But ultimately, thanks be to God that his word is inexhaustible in spite of our attempts at domestication, and thus that the work of interpretation remains incomplete. As such, let us pray that good interpretation will emerge and that it will in fact help our persecuted brothers and sisters to remain firm, unlike Jesus' followers as depicted in Mark.[111] As we undertake the work of interpretation and the work of application, we do so with the sure and certain hope that *verbum domini manet*.

---

[111] Only the most discerning of readers will realize that we have sought to honor our fellow Wycliffe College alumnus, colleague, and friend Terry Donaldson with reflections that, while focused primarily on material other than Matthew or Paul, seek to show ways in which early Christian writers chart significantly different paths within the same world. In doing so, our reflections perhaps may and hopefully do successfully suggest where Matthew in particular may have a very different path before him, one that Mark was not able to envision or perhaps did not even wish to envision. As such our study is intended to honor Terry and to contribute to NT study in the same way that Terry has been ever-creative in seeking to unearth aspects of early Christian discipleship and witness with a view to understanding its significance for Christian study and witness today. His unflinching but always diplomatic and gracious approach to difference of interpretation is one that Matthew would have no doubt commended but also one that might have been viewed with suspicion by Mark. Accordingly, is it not appropriate that we highlight Mark's divergence from Matthew on this point? Do we not thus honor Terry's work, the work of a close colleague and friend, by in fact creating the necessity of real dialogue, in this case one between Mark and Matthew, but not just as a historical possibility but as a contemporary reality? Will not this dialogue help us to understand better competing visions of "the end" and our own behavior as we come to "the end?" Is it not better to be prepared to fail, and to acknowledge our failures than to think that God would never let us fail? We offer Terry our collegial respect and support as he helps others to think through these tough questions and honor him for doing so in so many ways already.

Contributors

Stephen Black, Research Associate, Vancouver School of Theology

L. Gregory Bloomquist, Professor, Faculty of Theology, St. Paul University, Ottawa

Ronald Charles, Assistant Professor of Religious Studies, St. Francis Xavier University, Antigonish, Nova Scotia

Catherine Sider Hamilton, Professor of New Testament and New Testament Greek, Wycliffe College, University of Toronto

Michael A. G. Haykin, Professor of Church History and Biblical Spirituality, The Southern Baptist Seminary

L. Ann Jervis, Professor of New Testament, Wycliffe College, University of Toronto

Steve Mason, Distinguished Professor of Ancient Mediterranean Religions and Cultures, Department of Jewish, Christian, and Islamic Origins, University of Groningen

Adele Reinhartz, Professor, Department of Classics and Religious Studies, University of Ottawa

Anders Runesson, Professor of New Testament, Faculty of Theology, University of Oslo

Matthew Thiessen, Associate Professor, Department of Religious Studies, McMaster University

Leif Vaage, Professor of New Testament, Emmanuel College of Victoria University, University of Toronto

Index

Anderson, Janice C. 132, 139, 140

Bauckham, R. 135, 137
Baur, F. C. 87, 88, 92, 95
Beker, Christiaan J. 32, 66
Bloomquist, Gregory L. 164–6, 174, 175, 177, 178
Bockmuehl, Markus 149–52
Boer, Martinus C. de 76, 77, 79, 151, 152
Boyarin, D. 10, 19, 20, 43, 50–3, 128
Brown, Raymond E. 114, 131, 133
Bruce, F. F. 78, 81
Buell, Denise K. 52, 54, 89

Calvin, John 157, 159–62, 177
Campbell, C. 78, 79
Charlesworth, James H. 60, 61, 63, 136
Clements, Anne E. 132, 133, 135, 136, 144
Cohen, Shaye J. D. 19, 51
Collins, Adela Y. 158, 159, 162, 163, 167, 173, 176

Deissmann, A. 78, 85, 174
Donaldson, T. L. 1–5, 10, 11, 13, 41, 42, 65, 68, 73, 75, 89–91, 93, 96, 99, 101, 105, 107, 108, 125, 134, 174, 179
Dunn, James D. G. 10, 14, 36–8, 69, 76, 88, 89, 92, 95

Eisenbaum, Pamela 10, 102

Fredriksen, Paula 67, 73, 89, 94, 103

Gager, John G. 73, 89
Gaston, L. 10, 73
Gundry, Robert H. 134, 158–60

Hamilton, Catherine S. 133, 134
Hayes, Christine E. 65, 92, 93

Hays, Richard B. 32, 133
Hubbard, Moyer V. 72, 77, 82

Käsemann, Ernst 66, 69, 128
Konradt, Matthias 103, 105, 106
Kuruvilla, Abraham 158, 162, 163, 168–72, 175, 177

Lincoln, A. T. 75, 81

Macaskill, Grant 78, 79, 83
Marcus, Joel 154, 155
Martyn, J. L. 77, 78, 151, 154
Mason, Steve 13, 17, 20, 23, 36, 43, 45
Moore, G. F. 89, 173
Munck, J. 9, 10

Nanos, Mark D. 10, 11, 13, 14, 20, 23, 93, 102, 107
Neusner, J. 10, 20, 21

Robbins, Vernon K. 164–6, 174, 175
Rollens, Sarah E. 29, 150, 152
Ruether, Rosemary R. 12, 128
Runesson, Anders 13, 94, 99, 101–5, 107

Sanders, E. P. 10, 21, 60, 61, 79
Schweitzer, A. 9, 66, 75, 78–80, 83, 84, 94
Sim, David C. 99, 100, 103, 105, 106
Smith, J. Z. 20, 94, 95
Stuckenbruck, Loren T. 72, 76

Tajfel, Henri 115, 118, 119, 121, 124, 125, 135
Tannehil, Robert C. 68, 170
Theissen, Gerd 148, 163
Thiessen, Matthew 91, 93, 103, 152
Turner, John C. 118, 119

VanderKam, James C. 59, 60
Vanhoye, Albert 157, 158, 163, 165

Wainwright, Elaine 131, 137, 144
Watson, Francis 133, 134
Wire, Antoinette C. 132, 141

Wright, N. T. 5, 9, 10, 69, 70, 75, 76, 79, 80, 88, 89, 92, 95

Zetterholm, M. 10, 11, 13, 14, 20, 23, 93, 102

www.ingramcontent.com/pod-product-compliance
Lightning Source LLC
Chambersburg PA
CBHW070637300426
44111CB00013B/2142